# Linda Mullins'
## Teddy Bears & Friends
## Identification & Price Guide

**Hobby House Press, Inc.**
Grantsville, MD 21536
www.hobbyhouse.com

# Dedication

In memory of my dear friend and renowned teddy bear collector, historian and author
Pam Hebbs, who will always be joyfully remembered for her invaluable
contribution to the teddy bear world.

# Acknowledgements

One of the great rewards of being involved with the teddy bear world is the wonderful people I have met. Their willingness to share and their kind cooperation has made each of my book projects very gratifying. I wish to acknowledge a special debt of gratitude to my friends Dottie Ayers, Barbara Baldwin, Barbara Lauver and Lisa Vought for sharing their extensive knowledge of value and identification of the teddy bears and animals included in this book. My sincerest appreciation to my special friend Georgi Bohrod for her continued encouragement, assistance and guidance, to Patricia J. Matthews for her professional computer service, to Brenda Wiseman for her tireless creativity in designing this book, and to my publisher Gary R. Ruddell for believing in this book. Finally, my husband Wally. His understanding and support throughout these past 14 years of authoring 15 books has surpassed all the qualifications for a number one husband.

My gratitude to the following companies for their assistance:
North American Bear Company, Inc., Hermann Spielwaren GmbH, Hermann Teddy Original, Christie's South Kensington (Leyla Maniera), Raikes Review®, Russ Berrie and Company, The Boyd's Collection, Horst Poestgens, Auctioneer, Germany, Puppenhausmuseum, Basel, Switzerland and Margarete Steiff GmbH.

A warm thank you to the following collectors for sharing their knowledge and priceless collections with me:

Micki Beston, Bill Boyd, Cynthia Britnall (Cynthia's Country Store, Inc.), Jim and Eleanor Chipman, Judy and Lee Day, David Douglas, Nancy Drabek, Jayne and Susan Elliott, Dot Gillett, Donna Harrison - West, Martha and Jim Hession, Mimi Hiscox, Kay and Wayne Jensen, Renee Kotch, Phillip J. McGilvra, Shirley Praytor, Deborah and Donald Ratliff, Romey Roder, Helen Sieverling, Sherryl Shirran, Emma Stephans, Karen Strickland, Judy Vinson, Susan Wiley, Mort and Evelyn Wood, Richard Yokley and Jim Van Meter.

Additional copies of this book may be purchased at $19.95 (plus postage and handling) from
**Hobby House Press, Inc.**
1 Corporate Drive, Grantsville, MD 21536
1-800-554-1447
**www.hobbyhouse.com**
or from your favorite bookstore or dealer.
© 2000 Linda Mullins and Hobby House Press, Inc.

Printed in the United States of America.

ISBN: 0-87588-580-2

# Table of Contents

It is captivating faces like these two magnificent early 1900s Steiff bears featured on the cover of author's first *Teddy Bear & Friends Price Guide* that enticed many collectors to collect early Steiff bears.

(Left) Steiff. Bi-color Bear. Circa 1926. 24in (61cm); CONDITION: Excellent. **PRICE:** N.P.A.
(Right) Steiff. Bear. Circa 1907. 24in (61cm). Center seam in head. CONDITION: Excellent. **PRICE:** $12,000-up.

# Introduction

Teddy bears are soon to enter their second century. Since I authored my first *Price Guide* seven years ago, collecting teddy bears (and other soft animals) continues to climb both as a casual hobby and a serious form of investment. The surge of teddy bear collecting which overtook the United States during the 1980s wasted no time infiltrating Europe and making its way to Japan and the Pacific Rim. Today, with thousands of collectors on the hunt for these lovable creatures, the necessity for knowledge in this field is more significant than ever.

This book stems from my undying love of teddy bears and my life-long desire to place this magical fellow in his rightful role as an international ambassador of good will. It is that goal which fuels my thirst for teddy bear information and the passion to share some of that wisdom with you. My goal is to help you become your own best expert by teaching you a few methods for establishing the pedigree of your acquisitions.

In selecting bears and animals to be represented on these pages, the focus is on those with the most predominant and obvious identifying characteristics. This should give you a starting point to determine your bear's origin. The challenges of playing bear sleuth and trying to uncover the mystery of the beginnings of some of my favorite bears only deepens my appreciation for them and their animal pals. The more I learn, the more I love them. Hopefully, this will be the outcome for you as well.

For details on the beginning of teddy bears and some of the early manufacturers, please refer to my books *Teddy Bears Past and Present, Volumes I & II* (Hobby House Press).

## Buying For Investment

If you're purchasing teddy bears as an investment, there are five predominant factors to take into consideration: 1) **CONDITION**. Please note: If price shown in this book is for an item rated as "mint or excellent" condition, then an item in "fair" to "worn" condition would be worth approximately 50%-75% less; 2) manufacturer; 3) size; 4) identification marks and 5) rarity. Additionally, value can be increased for special reasons such as age, past history, a sweet facial expression, color and/or mechanical performance. It is extremely important for you to be well informed on your chosen field of collecting. Along the way you can always check with reputable teddy bear dealers or auction houses which have experts on staff to answer questions.

This little bear carries a lot of history. It appears to have been given to a young man when he stopped to see President Theodore (Teddy) Roosevelt in Easton, New York on August 11, 1905. The bear was sent to the young man's brother along with a postcard picturing the president. The handwritten message read: "Had to come to Easton to see Teddy. He stopped here yesterday". All evidence points to the bear as being one of those given to selected campaign supporters. One of the bear's most important and traceable characteristics is his hand-painted eyes glancing to one side mirroring Clifford Berryman's famous cartoon drawing which became the "icon" for Teddy Roosevelt in *The Washington Post* illustrations during that era. Bears with documented history can command far greater prices.
CONDITION: Excellent.
**PRICE:** Bear 9in (23cm) and memorabilia $3,500-up.

Many an avid antique doll collector began bear collecting by buying a teddy bear for a doll to hold or to complete a vignette. The irresistible appeal of the teddy bear has changed many a doll collector into a full time bear aficionado.
(Left) Steiff. Bear. Circa 1907. 25in (63cm); gold mohair; large shoe-button eyes; f.j.; e.s.
CONDITION: Excellent.
**PRICE:** $10,000-up.
(Right) French Bru Jne Doll. Circa 1889. 36in (91cm).
*Courtesy Helen Sieverling.*

Early 1900s Steiff teddy bears have won recognition among collectors because of their appealing characteristics and excellent quality. They are amongst the most highly sought after collectible bears, commanding the highest prices today.

(Left) Steiff. Bear. Circa 1907. 20in (51cm); beige wavy mohair; shoe-button eyes; f.j.; e.s., FF button.
CONDITION: Excellent.
**PRICE:** $6,500-up.
(Right) Steiff. Bear. Circa 1907. 30in (76cm); beige mohair; shoe-button eyes; f.j.; e.s.; FF button.
CONDITION: Very good.
**PRICE:** $12,000-up.

Bears such as this magnificent Schuco Messenger (Bell Hop) "Yes/No" Bear can command a far greater price than estimated value when condition is mint, has manufacturer's identification and lots of facial and/or overall appeal.
Sold at Christie's South Kensington 1997 auction for approximately $9,500.
*Courtesy Christie's.*

Bears that portray the special appeal that only comes with generations of love will not command the price or be looked upon by the majority of collectors as a good financial investment as will bears in good condition. Ideal Bear. Circa 1907. 20in (51cm); beige mohair (worn); shoe-button eyes; f.j.; e.s.
CONDITION: Worn.
**PRICE:** $500-$700.

Bears with provenance or documentation of their origin can command high prices. Steiff. Bear. Circa 1907. 14in (36cm); white mohair; shoe-button eyes; f.j.; e.s. Photograph of bear with original owner (boy on right) having a tea party with his sister and her doll.
CONDITION: Excellent.
**PRICE:** $4,500-up.

## Where To Buy Bears

Some geographic areas provide many more opportunities to hunt for bears. Some collectors will go to any length to hunt their prey; others prefer to stay closer to home. The most contemporary method of acquisition does not require you to leave the comfort of home. Buying and selling on-line is driving collecting at a breakneck speed into the 21st century. Ebay™ is the prototype for all on-line auctions offering high visibility, volume and high quality listings in the antiques and collectibles market. Other auction web-sites operate in similar fashion. Go to your favorite search engine and surf for auctions. It's simple, reliable and fun.

Still, nothing can replace the hands-on experience of discovering the consummate bear for your collection. Shows and conventions offer the opportunity to visit with bear artists, dealers and stores all under one roof.

You'll find advertising notices for these in specialty magazines. Magazines also run ads for teddy bear shops and dealers. Or, if you're on a more limited budget, garage sales and flea markets are an excellent source for bargains. Sometimes an estate sale of furniture and household items will reveal a well-hidden gem. From time to time, even a classified ad may feature a teddy bear or two. Also, although usually more expensive, the major auction houses frequently have special bear and doll sales.

## Identifying Your Bear: What To Look For

Books like this one are a good way to learn about bears, but nothing can compare with a hands-on education. By studying construction and characteristics, comparing different manufacturers and educating yourself on quality and materials, you will be able to make informed decisions in shopping for bears. There are specific focal points that consistently offer indications for identifying your bear. Look at the body shape, limb length, muzzle, the hump (or lack of it), construction and the materials used for fur, eyes, pads and stuffing. Check the design, the stitching of the nose, mouth and claws and the position of the eyes. Over the years, these particular features have varied. Recognizing the bear's age and roots is essential.

Although the education process is quite complex and there are a number of exceptions to the basic rules, here are some very quick tips to get you started:

**Fabric:** Prior to 1930, wool mohair; 1930-40, silk plush; post WWII, synthetics.

**Eyes:** Shoe-button eyes were used first; c. 1908 glass eyes were introduced; after 1950, plastic.

**Ears:** Compare the position to old ads, photographs or similar bears with identification; have the originals been replaced?

**Nose:** Has the stitching been replaced? Has black wool replaced woven silk thread? Familiarize yourself with particular manufacturer's styles.

**Stuffing:** In early bears, excelsior (wood wool), which crunches to the touch; kapok is light; in later years soft, synthetic stuffing is used.

**Paw Pads:** Felt used on vintage bears; velvet and rexine, late 30s; Ultrasuede after 1970. Have they been replaced?

**Identification:** Labels are easiest method for identification, but many have disappeared. Look for embroidered and printed labels on foot, body and ear seams, metal tags and buttons in ears, arms, chest.

**Overall condition:** Make sure no damage, dry rot, moth damage or loving wear and tear has been shrewdly hidden; restoration is possible, but affects the value of the bear.

Decorating your home with teddy bears can be fun and make enchanting scenes. Unidentified American Bears. Circa 1907. 16in (41cm); mohair; shoe-button eyes; f.j.; e.s.
CONDITION: Good.
PRICE: $1,000-$1,200 each.

## Beware of Fakes

As with any collectible item of value, there are some unscrupulous people who insist on offering merchandise that is not what it seems. You can protect yourself from this unfortunate circumstance by studying your facts and learning as much as you can about bears and soft toys. Always purchase from reputable vendors! Get to know reliable and well-known dealers. Rely on referrals from professionals and friends.

One of the finest and largest representations of teddy bears and bear related memorabilia through the ages can be viewed at the Puppenhausmuseum, BASEL, SWITZERLAND.
*Courtesy Puppenhausmuseum, Basel.*

Right:
Because of Theodore Roosevelt's famous 1902 bear hunt and his relationship with the teddy bear, the popular president was often characterized in one form or another.
(Left) Schoenhut Theodore Roosevelt Doll. 1909. 8-½in (22cm); hand-painted carved wood; f.j.; Safari outfit. The doll was part of Schoenhut's "Teddy's Adventures in Africa" based on Roosevelt's legendary African Safari.
CONDITION: Good.
PRICE: $1,800-up.
Steiff Bears. Circa 1907. 3in (8cm); mohair; black bead eyes; f.j.; e.s.
CONDITION: Excellent.
PRICE: $1,000-up each.
Bull Moose. Circa 1912. 11in (28cm); brown velveteen jointed body; composition head (repainted). Teddy Roosevelt's Bull Moose campaign item.
CONDITION: Fair.
PRICE: $800-up.
*Courtesy Helen Sieverling.*

Left:
The popularity and interest in Teddy Roosevelt's association with the teddy bear in the early 1900s inspired toy makers to manufacture toys depicting Roosevelt's image.
(Left to right) Teddy Roosevelt and The Bears Drum. Circa 1907. 6-½in (17cm); images of Teddy Roosevelt and bears surround drum; leather and twine fittings.
CONDITION: Good.
PRICE: $800-$1,000.
Teddy Roosevelt and The Bears Sand Pail. Circa 1907. 3in (8cm); images of Teddy Roosevelt and bears surround the tin sand pail.
CONDITION: Worn.
PRICE: $300-$400.
Steiff. Bear. Circa 1910. 5in (13cm); honey colored mohair; tiny black button eyes; f.j.; e.s.; no paw pads; FF button.
CONDITION: Good.
PRICE: $600-up.

Right:
Since Steiff's beginning, it has been commended for creating some of the most realistic type animals. Steiff Dachshund Dogs. (Movable Head Mechanism). Circa 1930. 8in (20cm) and 10in (25cm); black and tan mohair; glass eyes; jointed arms and legs; mechanical head (head moves in circular motion when tail is moved). Steiff mohair ball. Circa 1950.
CONDITION: Excellent.
PRICE: (Left) $1,200-$1,300  (Right) $1,600-$1,700 (Center) $200-$250.
*Courtesy David Douglas.*

8

## Using This Book

Please remember that the prices here are only a guide. Each price listed is for the current retail value of the bear. The data for pricing was gathered during 1998-99 from antique shops, shows, auctions, doll and teddy bear specialty shops, conventions, advertisements in periodicals, lists from teddy bear and doll dealers, purchases and sales reported by both collectors and dealers and research on-line via the Internet. They are not absolute and correspond only to the particular bears shown here. There may be fluctuations in market value and geographic region and cycles in other conditions, popularity and demand. Neither the author nor the publisher assumes responsibility for any losses which may occur as a result of following this guide.

Please keep in mind that no price guide, no matter how complete and thorough, can be the last word. It should only be an aid. The final decision is up to you. You alone know the meaning of your decision: perhaps he completes a set or his face is particularly soulful or she carries the name of your first child. You alone can make that price decision while examining the specific piece in question.

Before buying, do a lot of looking and comparison. Don't be afraid to ask questions. There is only one thing bear collectors love more than their bears, and that is talking about them. It is the best way for you to learn and the finest way to get the most value for your purchase.

The excellent workmanship and creativity of teddy bear artists have earned them international recognition. Renowned American pioneer teddy bear artists Joan Woessner and Steve Schutt were commissioned by Japanese theme park Huis Ten Bosch in Nagasaki to create a royal family of studio size teddy bears for the entrance to their new teddy bear museum, "Teddy Bear Kingdom." Pictured are two of these outstanding creations. (Left) *Dutchess*. 1998. 42in (104cm). (Right) *Duke*. 1998. 52in (131cm). German beige mohair; large shoe-button type eyes; f.j. (flex-limb armature in arms); e.s. and s.s. Exquisitely costumed in silks, satins and gold brocade trims.
CONDITION: Mint.
**PRICE:** $5,000-$6,000 each.

Some of the most beautiful and rare English bears, such as this outstanding 1914 Farnell bear, are offered for auction at Christie's auction house in London. Farnell Bear. *Edward*. Circa 1914; 22in (56cm); rich golden mohair; clear glass eyes (replaced); f.j.; e.s.; webbed paw claws; cardboard lined feet. Came with original photograph of Edward's family holding this magnificent bear.
CONDITION: Excellent.
Sold at Christie's South Kensington's 1997 auction for approximately $9,500.
*Courtesy Christie's.*

# Chapter One
# American Bears and Friends

America comes to its love of bears naturally. Native Americans worshiped the great bear for thousands of years. The origin of the name "Teddy Bear" is linked to American President Theodore Roosevelt and the story told by Clifford Berryman's famous cartoon for *The Washington Post*. Since the very first teddy bear was made, the popularity of teddy bears in the United States never waned. The rich heritage of collectible American bears and toys is evident by the many companies represented here.

## MANUFACTURERS:

### Aetna Toy Animal Company
(New York City, NY)
*Important Milestones*: Date Founded: **1906**; Purchased by E.I. Horsmann Co.: **1919.**
Former Name(s): Keystone Bear; Aetna Doll and Toy Co..
*Trademark/Identification:* "Aetna" in oval outline stamped on right foot.
*Characteristics:* Seven sizes; quality mohair; felt footpads lined with heavy cardboard.

### Russ Berrie & Co. Inc.
(Oakland, New Jersey)
*Important Milestones:* Date founded: **1963**; Registered public company: **1984.**
*Founder:* Russ Berrie.
*Trademark/Identification:* Sewn-in cloth labels; hang tags.

### Boyds Bears
(Gettysburg, Pennsylvania)
*Important Milestones:* Date founded: **1979;** began wholesaling: **1982;** first plush bear: **1984.**
*Founders:* G..M. Lowenthal and partner (now wife) Justina Unger.
*Trademark/Identification:* "Bears and Hares...You Can Trust" Plush bears: The Boyds Collection LTD.®; Resin bears: Boyds Bears & Friends™, Bearstone Collection® (1993), Folkstone Collection® (1994); Accouterments and props: The Bear Necessities™; Dolls: Dollstone Collection™ (1996).
*Characteristics:* Plush bears and collectible Resin figurines.

Russ Berrie and Company. *Lady Eleri*™ 1999. From the Vintage Collection™ is a flax colored Vintage Plush floppy beanbag teddy bear with jointed head and hand embroidered features. Limited edition 15,000. Comes with parchment Certificate of Authenticity.
CONDITION: Mint.
**PRICE:** $50.
*Courtesy Russ Berrie and Company.*

Aetna Bear. Circa 1912. 17in (43cm); Beige mohair; glass eyes; f.j.; cardboard lined feet; e.s.;
CONDITION: Excellent.
**PRICE:** $3,300-up.
*Courtesy Puppenhausmuseum, Basel.*

Aetna. Bear. Circa 1910. 20in (51cm); light beige mohair; glass eyes; f.j.; cardboard lined feet; e.s.
CONDITION: Excellent.
**PRICE:** $3,500-up.
*Courtesy Mort and Evelyn Wood.*

Right: The Boyds Collection. *Amanda K. Huntington* and *Devin Fallsbeary*. 1999. 14in/16in (36cm/41cm); synthetic plush with bean and polyester stuffing. Direct from the Hunt Ball, this foxy pair wears the latest Hunt Country Fashions in Harvest tones of earth, spice and goldenrod — finely cut velvets and hand-knit sweater. Designed by Gary M. Lowenthal.
CONDITION: Mint.
**PRICE:** (Left) $39. (Right) $57.
*Courtesy The Boyds Collection.*

**Bruin Manufacturing Company**
(New York City, New York)
*Important Milestones:* First advertised in
*Playthings:* **1907**; Production ends: **1909**;
*Selling Agents:* Strobel & Wilken Co./Frank W.
Owens;
*Trademark/Identification:* "B.M.C".; (cloth
label on sole of foot, woven in gold);
*Characteristics:* Long, silky, quality mohair;
excelsior and Kapok stuffing; eyes placed fairly
close together; endearing smiling expressions.

Left: Bruin Manufacturing Company (B.M.C).
Bears. Circa 1907.
(Left) 18in (46cm); silky white mohair; glass
eyes; tan stitched nose, mouth and claws; f.j.;
e.s. and k.s.
CONDITION: Good.
**PRICE:** $2,500-$3,500.
(Right) 14in (36cm); faded cinnamon silky
mohair; shoe-button eyes; smiling stitched
mouth; f.j.; e.s.
CONDITION: Fair.
**PRICE:** $1,000-$1,200.
*Courtesy Martha and Jim Hession.*

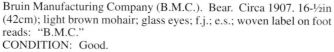

Bruin Manufacturing Company (B.M.C.). Bear. Circa 1907. 16-½in
(42cm); light brown mohair; glass eyes; f.j.; e.s.; woven label on foot
reads: "B.M.C."
CONDITION: Good.
**PRICE:** $4,000-$4,700.
*Courtesy Puppenhausmuseum, Basel.*

Bruin Manufacturing Company (B.M.C). Bear. Circa 1907. 20in (50cm);
white mohair; shoe-button eyes; f.j.; e.s.; woven label on foot reads:
"B.M.C."
CONDITION: Excellent.
**PRICE:** $6,000-up.
*Courtesy Puppenhausmuseum, Basel.*

## Character Novelty Company Inc.
(Norwalk, Connecticut)

*Important Milestones:* Established: **1932**; showroom in New York: **Post-1945**; Co-founder retires and dies: **1960**; Second co-founder dies, business ceases: **1983.**

*Founders:* Ceasar Mangiapani (designer) and Jack Levy (sales).

*Trademark/Identification:* Printed cloth ear tag.

*Characteristics:* Early bears long quality mohair, white felt circles behind black button eyes; large round ears; no claws; some have red felt tongue.

Right: Character Bears. Circa 1940. 7in-17in (18cm-44cm); mohair blends; shoe-button and amber glass eyes; n.j.; and f.j.; s.s. Character cloth tags sewn into seams.
CONDITION: Good to Excellent.
**PRICE:** $45-$150 each.
*Courtesy Micki Beston.*

Character Bears. Circa 1940. (Back) 11in (28cm); (Front) 8in (20cm); tan mohair; glass eyes; n.j.; k.s.; cloth label sewn into seam of ear reads: "Designed by Character." Cardboard tag attached to chest reads: "A Character Toy/Timme/Made in U.S.A./Character Novelty Co., Inc. NYC."
CONDITION: Mint.
**PRICE:** (Back) $150-$175. (Front) $110-$125.
*Courtesy Helen Sieverling.*

Left: Character Bears and Animals. 1950-1960. 10½-21in (27cm-54cm); synthetic plush; plastic safety lock eyes; n.j.; cotton and synthetic foam stuffing. Character cloth tags sewn into ear seam.
CONDITION: Excellent.
**PRICE:** $25-$100 each.
*Courtesy Micki Beston.*

Right: (Left and right) Character Bears. Circa 1945. 14in (36cm); mohair; black button eyes with white felt circles behind; f.j.; (Left) n.j. (Right); k.s.; Character cloth tag sewn into ear seam. (Center) Possibly Gund. Circa 1945. 18in (46cm); gray mohair; top stitched; glass eyes; k.s.; n.j.
CONDITION: Good.
**PRICE:** $50-$100 each.
*Courtesy Martha and Jim Hession.*

Character Riding Monkey. Circa 1950. 11-½in (29cm); cinnamon synthetic fabric head and paws; beige felt face; glass eyes; n.j.; e.s.; cotton and felt clothes an integral part of body; Character cloth tag stitched to ear; seated on a black metal trike with red wooden wheels. Legs go in cycling motion when trike is pulled by cord.
CONDITION: Very good.
PRICE: $125-$150.
*Private collection.*

Left:
Character Bears. (Back) Circa 1950. 22in (56cm); white mohair; glass eyes; red felt tongue; f.j.; k.s.; Character cloth tag sewn into right ear.
CONDITION: Excellent.
PRICE: $195-$225.
(Front) Circa 1940. Boy. 7in (18 cm); Girl. 10in (25cm); brown mohair head and paws; cloth body; black button eyes underlined with white felt circles; red felt tongue; n.j.; k.s.; Character cloth tag sewn into right ear. Dressed as boy and girl.
CONDITION: Excellent.
PRICE: $125-$150 each.
*Courtesy Karen Strickland.*

**Columbia Teddy Bear Manufacturers**
(New York City, New York)
*Important Milestones:* Founded: **1907.**

Columbia Teddy Bear Manufacturers. "Laughing Roosevelt" Bear. Circa 1907. 16in (41cm); gold mohair; glass eyes; wooden open mouth with two milk glass teeth; f.j.; e.s.
CONDITION: Good.
PRICE: $3,000-$3,500.
*Courtesy Barbara Lauver.*

Columbia Teddy Bear Manufacturers. "Laughing Roosevelt". Bear. Circa 1907. 16in (41cm); rust brown mohair; glass eyes; f.j.; e.s.; wooden open mouth with teeth; mouth opens when tummy is squeezed.
CONDITION: Good.
PRICE: $3,000-$3,500.
*Courtesy Puppenhausmuseum, Basel.*

### Commonwealth Toy & Novelty Co. Inc
(New York City, New York)
*Important Milestones:* Founded: **1934-35;**
Produced "Feed Me" teddy: **1937**; still in business today.
*Trademark/Identification:* Hang tag.

### Eden Toys
*Important Milestones:* Bear production commenced: **1970s**; acquired U.S. licensing and manufacturing rights to Paddington Bear: **1980s.**
*Trademark/Identification:* Label sewn in body; hang tag.

### Gund Inc.
(Edison, New Jersey)
*Important Milestones:* Founded: **1898** as Gund Manufacturing Company in Norwalk, Connecticut; moves to New York City ; c. **1900**; adds teddy bears to line: **1906**; Jacob Swedlin joins business as janitor becomes Adolph Gund's assistant: **1919**; Gund retires, business and patents sold to Swedlin; Swedlin's 3 brothers join him, company becomes J. Swedlin Inc., retaining Gund name for trade, makes mechanical jumping animals: **1925**; gains exclusive rights to produce Disney, King Features and Harvey Comics: **1948**; factory moves to Brooklyn, NY: **1956**; firm moves to Edison, NJ (showroom stays in NYC): **1973**; Jacob Swedlin dies: **1976**; Collectors Classics line introduced: **1979**; Bialosky Bears introduced: **1982**; moves to larger facilities in Edison, NJ; **1988**: buys French company, Anima:**1992**; privately owned; still in the hands of Jacob Swedlin's daughter Rita Raiffe (Director of Design) and son Bruce (President).
*Founder:* Adolph Gund.
*Trademark/Identification:* Early tags read: "A Gund Product, A Toy of Quality and Distinction"; From WWII on, the tags show the stylized "G" most often appearing as a rabbit with ears and whiskers. From mid-1960s until 1987, straight block type featured a signature bear's head above the letter "U" and from 1987 the current capital book type "GUND" has been the official logo. "Gee Line" was trademark of colored velveteen jumping animals made in the 20s.

Commonwealth Toy and Novelty Co. Inc. (Left and right) *Feed Me Bears.* Circa 1937. (Left) 16in (14cm); cinnamon-colored mohair; (right) 13in (33cm) gold mohair; glass eyes; n.j. arms and legs; stationary head; when ring located on top of head is pulled, the mouth opens and dry foods and candy are swallowed. The food can be removed by opening a zipper at the back of bear, disclosing a metal compartment where food is stored, without harming the bear.
CONDITION: Good.
PRICE: $450-$500 each.
(Center) Musical Bear. Circa 1960. 15in (38cm); light brown synthetic plush; white synthetic plush inset snout; unjointed body; stationary head. Music is produced by key located at back of torso.
CONDITION: Excellent.
PRICE: $45-$75.

Right:
Eden Toys, Inc. *Paddington Bears.* Circa 1982. 14in (36cm). (Left to right) Golfer, Tuxedo, Santa; beige shades of synthetic plush; plastic eyes; n.j.; s.s. Label reads: "Please look after this bear! Thank you." Square tag reads: "*Paddington Bear* usually wears his duffle coat and brush hat. To purchase a duffle coat, fill reverse side of this tag and mail it with a check or money order for U.S. $4.00 for each set."
CONDITION: Excellent.
PRICE: $75-$95 each.
*Courtesy Emma Stephens.*

Gund. **Teddi Gund**. Bear. Circa 1948. 16in (41cm); gold mohair; inset short pile mohair snout; glass eyes; f.j.; k.s.; top stitched. Remains of manufacturer's label stitched into right arm.
CONDITION: Very Good.
**PRICE:** $500-$600.

Gund Bear. 1947. 15in (38cm); bright gold mohair; glass eyes; f.j.; e.s.; cardboard lined foot pads. Picture of original owner (Susan Elliott at one year old) with bear in 1947.
CONDITION: Mint.
**PRICE:** $300-$400.
*Courtesy Susan Elliott.*

(Left) Gund. *Woolie Lamb*. Circa 1950. 9in (23cm); white wool; plastic eyes; n.j.; e.s. (Right) Gund. *Monkey*. Circa 1950. 12in (31cm); cinnamon rayon plush; molded vinyl face; painted features; n.j.
CONDITION: Good.
**PRICE:** $35-$75 each.
*Courtesy Martha and Jim Hession.*

Gund. **Cubbie Gund**. Bear. Circa 1952. 10in (25cm); brown rayon plush; cream-colored rayon plush paw pads and inside ears; painted features on molded vinyl snout; white plastic eyes with black plastic movable disk under clear plastic covering; n.j.; s.s. Manufacturer's label sewn into side seam.
CONDITION: Excellent.
**PRICE:** $50-$75.

A representation of popular Gund animals and dolls. (Back row) Gund. *Minnie Mouse*. Circa 1950. 8in (20cm).
CONDITION: Good.
**PRICE:** $40-$50.
*Cowboy Bear*. Circa 1940. 12in (31cm).
CONDITION: Good.
**PRICE:** $100-$150.
*Santa*. Circa 1940. 10in (25cm).
CONDITION: Good.
**PRICE:** $40-$50.
*Winnie-the-Pooh*. Circa 1960. 8in (20cm).
CONDITION: Good.
**PRICE:** $150-$200.
*Courtesy Helen Sieverling.*

(Left) Gund. *Lulu-Belle*. 1949. 13in (33cm); pale gold rayon plush; fabric mask face; painted facial features; n.j. body; swivel head. Label reads: "Gund Mfg. Co./ J. Swedlin Inc." Reverse: "Bongo/copyright Walt Disney." CONDITION: Good. PRICE: $300-$400. (Right) Gund. *Bongo*. 1949. 13in (33cm); brown rayon plush; fabric mask face; painted facial features; n.j. body; swivel head. Label reads: "Gund Mfg. Co./ J. Swedlin Inc." Reverse: "Bongo/copyright Walt Disney." CONDITION: Good.
**PRICE:** $350-$450.

Right:
Gund. Bears. (Left to Right) *Abinee Smoothie*. 1983. 15in (38cm); brown synthetic plush; plastic eyes; n.j.; s.s. *Bialosky Bear*. 1982-1984. 11in (28cm); beige synthetic plush; plastic eyes; f.j.; s.s. *Collector's Classics Bear*. 1986. 16in (41cm). Pale beige synthetic plush; inset short synthetic plush snout; plastic eyes; f.j.
CONDITION: Excellent.
**PRICE:** $45-$65 each.
Courtesy: *Emma Stevens*

(Left) Gund. *Pepe*. Dog. Circa 1949. 7in (18cm) tall; gray rayon plush; glass eyes; n.j.; e.s.; original paper manufacturer's tag; cotton outfit. (Right) *Swani* Gund. Circa 1949. 10in (25cm) tall; white cotton plush; black tin eyes; orange felt beak and feet; n.j.; s.s.; original cotton sailor collar and hat.
CONDITION: *Pepe*. Mint; *Swani*. Good.
PRICE: $40-$60 each.
*Courtesy Martha and Jim Hession.*

Gund. Rabbit. Circa 1940. 21in (53cm); white silk plush; pink glass eyes; cotton twill body; n.j.; e.s.; dressed in Scottish outfit. Gund tag.
CONDITION: Mint.
PRICE: $200-$300.
*Courtesy Philip J. McGilvra.*

Left:
(Back) F.W. Woolnough Co. *Winnie-the-Pooh*. Circa 1930. 14in (36cm); gold mohair; button eyes (possibly replaced); f.j.; e.s.
CONDITION: Worn.
PRICE: $600-$800.
(Front left) Gund. *Winnie-the-Pooh*. Circa 1960. 7in (18cm); bright gold velveteen; black felt eyes, nose and eyebrows; n.j.; wood chips stuffing; red knit sweater.
CONDITION: Excellent.
PRICE: $30-$50.
(Front center) Gund. *Winnie-the-Pooh*. Circa 1960. 10in (25cm); gold plush; n.j. (legs sewn in seated position); glass eyes; knitted sweater with matching cap.
CONDITION: Excellent.
PRICE: $150-$200.
(Front right) F.W. Woolnough Co., *Winnie-the-Pooh*. Circa 1930. 9in (23cm); bright gold mohair; fully jointed; glass eyes (replaced). F.W. Woolnough Co. was a division of Gund.
CONDITION: Very good.
PRICE: $2,500-$3,000.

**Harman Manufacturing Company**
(New York City, New York)
*Important Milestones:* Produced teddy bears
and bear-related items: **1907** ; No longer in
business.
*Characteristics:* Short bristle mohair, arms set
low on the body and straight legs.

**Hecla**
*Important Milestones:* Produces teddy bears:
Early **1900s.** No longer in business.
*Characteristics:* Wide-set/ American-style ears,
rust-colored noses, claw stitching, clear glass
eyes with painted backs set close together,
hump on bear's back, Steiff-like large feet and
long limbs, arms set high on body.

Right:
Harman Manufacturing Company. Bear. Circa
1907. 11in (27cm); beige mohair, shoe-button
eyes; f.j.; e.s.
CONDITION: Excellent.
**PRICE:** $1,300-$2,000.
*Courtesy Puppenhausmuseum, Basel.*

Harman. Purse Bear. Circa 1910. 12in (30cm); beige mohair; shoe-but-
ton eyes; f.j.; e.s.; metal purse frame in back of bear.
CONDITION: Excellent.
**PRICE:** $1,700-$2,300.
Courtesy: *Puppenhausmuseum, Basel.*

Hecla. Bear. Circa 1907. 16in (40cm); white mohair; glass eyes; f.j.; e.s.
CONDITION: Excellent.
**PRICE:** $3,000-$3,500.
*Courtesy Puppenhausmuseum, Basel.*

Hecla. Bear. Circa 1907. 14in (36cm); white mohair; glass eyes; brown stitched nose, mouth and claws; f.j.; e.s.
CONDITION: Excellent.
**PRICE:** $2,500-$3,000.
*Courtesy Puppenhausmuseum, Basel.*

Ideal. Bears. Early 1900s. (Top Row) 9in (23cm); (Bottom Row) Left 14in (36cm); Right 13in (33cm); various shades of short gold mohair; black and white "googlie" eyes; black twisted pearl and cotton horizontally stitched nose; f.j.; e.s.; torso seam closes in front; foot pads come to a point. Note the similarity of the eyes glancing to the side of the plush bears to Clifford Berryman's bear depicted in this original Berryman cartoon.
CONDITION: Very Good.
**PRICE:** (Bears) $2,500-$3,500 each. (Cartoon) $600-$800.

Hecla Bears. Circa 1907. (Left) 17in (43cm); (Right) 15in (38cm); blonde mohair; clear glass eyes (eyes fastened at neck); rust stitched nose, mouth and claws; f.j.; (neck joint sewn into place in torso); excelsior, kapok and mohair scraps stuffing.
CONDITION: (Left) Fair, (Right) Good.
**PRICE:** (Left) $700-$900, (Right) $1,500-$1,800.
*Courtesy Martha and Jim Hession.*

### Ideal Novelty and Toy Company
#### (Brooklyn, New York)
*Important Milestones:* Inspired by Clifford Berryman's Washington Post cartoon, Morris and Rose Michtom produce hand made "Teddy's Bears": **1902:** Butler Brothers purchase stock and back Michtom's credit with plush-producing mills: c. **1903-4;** moves to larger premises: **1907;** son, Benjamin Michtom joins firm: **1923;** founder dies, son Benjamin takes over: **1938;** designs change, and name changed to Ideal Toy Corporation, licensed to produce first "Smokey Bear:" **1953;** Lionel Weintraub becomes president: **1962;** becomes publicly held firm, headquartered in Hollis, New York with factory in Newark, New Jersey: **1968;** founder's grandson, Mark Michtom, sells to CBS Toys: **1982;** Hasbro acquires some assets: **1984.**
*Founder:* Morris Michtom.
*Trademark/Identification:* (After 1938) bears marked with a stitched label and paper tag;
*Characteristics:* Early 1900s, lovely appealing faces; wide triangular head which is flat at back; large, round, wide-set ears; medium-length mohair; paw pads taper to point; long muzzle; long, slender body; arms low on body; excelsior stuffing.
*Noteworthy:* Often credited with producing first American teddy bears.

Ideal. Googlie-eyed Bear. Circa 1906. 12in (30cm); apricot mohair; "googlie" eyes; f.j.; e.s.
CONDITION: Good.
**PRICE:** $3,300-$4,000.
*Courtesy Puppenhausmuseum, Basel.*

Ideal. Bear. Circa 1907. 12in (32cm); beige mohair; shoe-button eyes; f.j.; e.s.; five claws.
CONDITION: Good.
**PRICE:** $2,500-$3,500.
*Courtesy Puppenhausmuseum, Basel.*

Right:
(Left to Right) Ideal. Bear. Circa 1950. 13in (33cm); bright cinnamon-colored rayon plush; white rayon plush paw pads and inner ears; vinyl snouts with hand-painted features; plastic eyes; n.j. Label sewn into side seam reads: "Ideal Toy Company."
CONDITION: Excellent.
**PRICE:** $50-$75.
Ideal Bear. 1978. "Collector's Edition." 16in (41cm); caramel colored acrylic plush; short pale caramel colored acrylic plush inset snout; plastic eyes; n.j.
CONDITION: Mint.
**PRICE:** $50-$75.
Ideal Bear. Circa 1939. 12in (31cm); cinnamon-colored mohair; glass eyes; n.j. arms and legs; swivel head; hard resin nose; e.s. head; k.s. body. Cardboard tag attached to bear reads: "An Ideal Ultrafine Animal/Ideal Novelty and Toy Co." To the author's knowledge no pre-1930 Ideal teddy bear has yet been found with its original tag.
CONDITION: Excellent.
**PRICE:** $95-$125.

(Left) Ideal. Bear. Circa 1907. 11in (28cm); apricot mohair; shoe-button eyes; f.j. ("wooden joints"); e.s.
CONDITION: Good.
**PRICE:** $1,300-$1,500.
(Center) Ideal. Bear. Circa 1907. 11in (28cm); golden brown mohair; shoe-button eyes; f.j. ("wooden joints"); e.s.
CONDITION: Good.
**PRICE:** $1,000-$1,200.
(Right) Unknown American Bear. Circa 1907. 10-1/2in (26cm); cinnamon mohair; shoe-button eyes; f.j. "wooden joints"; e.s.
CONDITION: Worn.
**PRICE:** $450-$550.
*Courtesy Martha and Jim Hession.*

Ideal. Bear. Circa 1907. 28in (71cm); honey-colored mohair; large shoe-button type eyes; f.j.; e.s.
CONDITION: Excellent.
**PRICE:** $3,500-$4,000.

Ideal Bears. Circa 1906. 12in (31cm) and 14in (36cm); golden beige mohair; "googlie" eyes; red felt-lined open mouth; f.j.; e.s. Note the close resemblance of these bears' eyes glancing to one side and the open mouth to Clifford Berryman's famous cartoon bear (center illustration).
CONDITION: Good.
**PRICE:** 12in (31cm) $1,500-$1,800, 14in (36cm) $2,000-$2,500.
(Original Clifford Berryman Cartoon)
CONDITION: Mint.
**PRICE:** $500-$600.

Ideal. Bears. Circa 1907. (Left) 15in (38cm); (Right) 18in (46cm); thick pale golden mohair; large black button eyes; f.j.; e.s. Note: same "size" ear pattern on both sizes of bears.
CONDITION: Excellent.
**PRICE:** 15in (38cm) $1,500-$1,800, 18in (46cm) $2,000-$2,500.
*Courtesy Martha and Jim Hession.*

### Knickerbocker Toy Co.
(Albany, New York)

*Important Milestones:* Originated as manufacturer of educational toys: **1850**; introduces teddy bears and other stuffed toys: c. **1920**; company incorporates and permanent labels are introduced : **1930s**, moves to New Jersey, obtains Smokey Bear license c. **1968**; company sold to Lionel: **1979;** Lionel goes bankrupt: **1984;** company resurrected by Louis and Tammy Knickerbocker: **1990.**

*New Founders:* Louis and Tammy Knickerbocker (no relation to original company).

*Trademark/Identification:* "Toys of Distinction" sewn into body seam cloth label; hang tag.

*Characteristics:* Early bears and animals extremely high quality, long mohair (main colors bright cinnamon, gold and white); large cupped ears, amber glass eyes, felt paw pads (later velveteen), vertical stitched oval narrow nose.

Right:
Knickerbocker. Bear. Circa 1930. 18in (46cm); orange mohair; glass "googlie" eyes (glancing to center looking at bug on nose); f.j.; e.s.
CONDITION: Fair.
**PRICE:** $1,000-$1,500.
*Courtesy Puppenhausmuseum, Basel.*

Knickerbocker. Bear. Circa 1930. 10in (26cm); long silky white mohair; short white mohair snout; glass eyes; velveteen paw pads; f.j.; e.s.; label on front seam.
CONDITION: Excellent.
**PRICE:** $450-$500.
*Courtesy Puppenhausmuseum, Basel.*

Knickerbocker. Bear. Circa 1930. 20in (51cm); white silky mohair; glass eyes; f.j.; e.s. and k.s.; hard plastic nose, C.T.
CONDITION: Mint.
**PRICE:** $650-$850.

Knickerbocker. Bear. Circa 1930. 22in (56cm); long gold mohair; short beige inset snout and tops of feet; beige felt lined open mouth; glass eyes; down-turned paws; oversized feet; f.j.; e.s.; replaced foot pads.
CONDITION: Good.
**PRICE:** $550-$650.
*Courtesy Jim and Eleanor Chipman.*

Knickerbocker. "Metal Nose" Bears. Early 1930s. 20in (51cm). (Left) White curly cotton plush, (Right) brown curly cotton plush; amber glass stick pin eyes; f.j.; e.s. heads; k.s. bodies; wide head; large cupped ears; short muzzle; almost straight arms; small oval feet; all characteristics of Knickerbocker from this period.
CONDITION: Excellent.
PRICE: $350-$450 each.
*Courtesy Micki Beston.*

Knickerbocker. Bears. Early 1930s. (Left to Right) 18in (46cm); long silky white mohair. 12in (31cm) long brown silky mohair. 18in (46cm) long golden brown silky mohair; amber glass stick pin eyes; f.j.; e.s. head; k.s. body.
CONDITION: Good.
PRICE: (Left to right) $400, $250, $350.
*Courtesy Micki Beston.*

Left:
Knickerbocker. "Tin Eye" Bears. Mid-1930s. 13in-19in (33cm-49cm); (Left) cinnamon cotton plush; yellow green tin eyes; (Center and right) various colors of long silky mohair; short mohair inset snout; brown tin eyes; black stitched nose and mouth; no claws; velveteen paw pads (with the exception of the brown bear); e.s. heads; k.s. bodies; f.j.
CONDITION: Fair to good.
PRICE: $175-$300 each.
*Courtesy Micki Beston.*

Above:
Knickerbocker. *The Three Bears*. 1938. 9in-11in (23cm-28cm); (Left and right) beige bristly plush; (center) white soft plush; black glass stick pin eyes; red felt tongue; e.s. and k.s. heads; k.s. bodies; cardboard-lined velveteen foot pads; n.j.; cotton and felt clothes. Original Knickerbocker hang tag (Right).
CONDITION: Excellent.
PRICE: $275-$325 (set).
*Courtesy Micki Beston.*

Above:
Knickerbocker. Bear. Late 1940s. 21in (53cm); silky golden brown mohair; beige velveteen inset snout and paw pads; stitched nose; glass eyes; f.j.
CONDITION: Mint.
PRICE: $450-$550.
*Courtesy Nancy Drabek.*

Knickerbocker. Bears. Circa 1940. 20in (51cm); (Left) long silky gold mohair; short gold mohair inset snout; (Right) long dark brown silky mohair; short brown mohair in-set snout; beige velveteen paw pads; glass eyes; f.j.; e.s. head; k.s. body. Knickerbocker cloth tag sewn into front body seam.
CONDITION: Excellent.
PRICE: $450-$550 each.
*Courtesy Nancy Drabek.*

Knickerbocker. Bears. (Left) Circa 1942. 13in (33cm); brown curly plush; inset beige velvet snout; glass eyes; metal nose; velveteen paw pads; jointed head and arms; stationary legs; e.s. and s.s.; (Center) Circa 1942. 18in (46cm); Black curly plush; inset beige velveteen snout; beige velveteen paw pads; jointed head and arms; stationary legs; (Right) Circa 1942. 12in (30cm); long gold mohair; inset beige velveteen snout; beige velveteen paw pads; glass eyes; jointed arms and legs; stationary legs; e.s. and s.s. All bears have wide hips and have cardboard lined feet to enable bears to stand alone.
CONDITION: Fair to excellent:
**PRICE:** $75 -$175 each.
*Courtesy Micki Beston.*

Knickerbocker. Bears. Circa 1940. (Left) 18in (46cm) ; light brown mohair; beige velveteen inset snout; beige velveteen lined ears; glass eyes; n.j. arms and legs; swivel head; e.s. and k.s..
CONDITION: Good.
**PRICE:** $60-75.
(Right) 17in (45cm) white mohair; white velveteen inset snout; white velveteen-lined ears and paw pads; glass eyes; n.j. arms and legs; swivel head; e.s. and k.s.
CONDITION: Excellent.
**PRICE:** $75-$95.
*Courtesy Micki Beston.*

Knickerbocker. Bears. Early 1950s. (Left) 18in (46cm); green alpaca with beige velveteen-lined ears, inset snout and paw pads; beige felt circles behind black painted metal eyes.
CONDITION: Excellent.
**PRICE:** $300-$350.
(Right) 24in (61cm); brown alpaca with beige velveteen lined ears, inset snout and paw pads; rust felt circles behind flat black painted metal eyes; f.j.; e.s. heads; e.s. and k.s. bodies.
CONDITION: Excellent.
**PRICE:** $350-$400.
*Courtesy Micki Beston.*

(Left to right) Knickerbocker. Bears. *Sunshine Bear.* Circa 1985. 16in (41cm); beige synthetic plush; plastic eyes; n.j.
CONDITION: Good.
**PRICE:** $25-$35.
*Pouting Bear.* Circa 1955. 14in (36cm) brown synthetic plush; molded vinyl face; hand painted features; n.j.; s.s.
CONDITION: Good.
**PRICE:** $50-$75.
*Dancing Bear.* Circa 1980s. 8in (20cm); gold synthetic plush; plastic eyes; n.j.; s.s.; key wind mechanism activates bear to move around in dancing motion.
CONDITION: Good.
**PRICE:** $25-$45.
Bear. Circa 1980s; brown synthetic plush; white synthetic plush inset snout and paw pads; plastic eyes; n.j.; s.s.
CONDITION: Good.
**PRICE:** $40-$60.
*Courtesy Emma Stephens.*

Knickerbocker. ***Prayer Bear***. Circa 1981. 10in (25cm); bright cinnamon synthetic plush; inset pale cream synthetic plush snout and inner ears; stitched sleep eyes; plastic nose; n.j.; s.s.
CONDITION: Excellent.
**PRICE:** $40-$50 each.
*Courtesy Emma Stephens.*

Knickerbocker. Dog. Circa 1945. 16in (41cm) high; white and brown mohair; glass eyes; n.j. legs; swivel head; e.s.; Knickerbocker cloth tag sewn in side seam. Replaced collar.
CONDITION: Good.
**PRICE:** $125-$150.
*Courtesy Nancy Drabek.*

Knickerbocker Toy Co. Hanna Barbera Prod. Circa 1959. Characters include: ***Huckleberry Hound, Quick Draw McGraw***, and ***Yogi Bear***. Plush bodies; molded vinyl faces; hand-painted features; n.j.; s.s.; cloth Knickerbocker label stitched into side seam.
CONDITION: Excellent.
**PRICE:** $50-$125 each.
*Private Collection.*

**North American Bear Co., Inc.**
(Chicago, Illinois and New York, New York)
*Important Milestones:* Founded: **1978;** First
creation was *Albert the Running Bear*™©;
**1979;** *Very Important Bears (VIBs)*® intro-
duced **1980**; *VanderBear Family*®: **1983;**
*Muffy VanderBear*®: **1984;** *Hoppy
VanderHare*® **1990;** *Muffy*® Club formed **1990,**
*Muffy*® Kids Club, **1999.**
*Founder:* Barbara Isenberg.
*Trademark/Identification:* Sewn-in label; hang
tag.
*Characteristics:* The 20in (51cm) VIB series
which ended with production of *Mlle.N.Nium*
in 1999, was based on personalities from history, literature or popular culture; names are
always a play on the word, "bear". *Muffy*®, her
*VanderBear Family*® and friends continue to
be the company's most popular collectibles.

North American Bear Co., Inc. *Albert the Running Bear*™©. 1979. (Front) 12in
(33cm); brown synthetic plush head and paws; black plastic eyes and nose; n.j.;
s.s.; various colors of outfits and running shoes are an integral part of body.
Retired Fall 1990.
CONDITION: Excellent.
PRICE: $20 each.
(Center back) 20in (51cm); brown synthetic plush; black plastic eyes and nose;
n.j.; s.s.; removable red jacket; white running shoes. Retired Spring 1991.
CONDITION: Excellent.
PRICE: $30.
*Courtesy Emma Stephens.*

North American Bear Co., Inc. **1998.** *Grand
VanderBall: A FunRaising Gala.*
CONDITION: Mint.
PRICE: (Suggested Retail) *Cornelius*™ $108,
*Alice*™ $100, *Fluffy & Fuzzy*™ $56 each,
*Muffy*® $40, *Hoppy*™ $40, *Lulu*™ (dog) $19,
*Purrlie*™ $10,
*Photograph Courtesy North American Bear
Company, Inc.*

Above: North American Bear Co., Inc. 1999.
VIB *Mlle. N. Nium.* A limited edition of
4,000.
CONDITION: Mint.
PRICE: (Suggested Retail) $150.
*Photograph Courtesy North American Bear
Company, Inc.*

Left: North American Bear Co., Inc. 1999.
*Muffy*® *Polar Bear: North Meets South.*
Holiday Boxed Edition.
CONDITION: Mint.
PRICE: (Suggested Retail) $50.
*Photograph Courtesy North American Bear
Company, Inc.*

North American Bear Co.,
Inc. 1999. *Muffy*® and
*Hoppy*™ In The
Millennium Collection:
*From Dusk to Dawn*.
CONDITION: Mint.
**PRICE:** (Suggested Retail)
$250 set.
*Photograph Courtesy North
American Bear Company,
Inc.*

**Strauss Manufacturing Co. Inc.**
(New York City, New York)
*Important Milestones:* Founded: **1907;** no
longer in business.
*Characteristics:* Rust cotton nose and claws,
pointed muzzle and long, Steiff-like arms and
feet; leather paw pads.

Strauss. Bear. Circa 1907. 13in (32cm); light brown mohair;
shoe-button eyes; f.j; e.s.; fabric nose.
CONDITION: Fair.
**PRICE:** $1,000-$1,500.
*Courtesy Puppenhausmuseum, Basel.*

Strauss. Musical Bear. Circa 1910. 10-1/2in (27cm); beige mohair; glass
eyes; rust stitched nose, mouth and claws; f.j.; e.s.; music plays when han-
dle (porcelain knob) on back is turned.
CONDITION: Good.
**PRICE:** $2,000-$2,500.
*Courtesy Puppenhausmuseum, Basel.*

Strauss. "Self Whistling Bear". Circa 1907. 18in (46cm); white mohair;
shoe-button eyes; rust pearl cotton stitched nose, mouth and claws; f.j.;
e.s.; whistling mechanism is encased in body.
CONDITION: Good.
**PRICE:** $3,000-$4,000.

*Important Milestones:* President William H. Taft adopts Billy Possum as mascot: **1908;** Toy industry begins possum manufacturing: **1909;** known manufacturers: Steiff, Aetna, H. Fisher and Co., Harman Manufacturing Company.
*Characteristics:* Mohair; fully-jointed; shoe button eyes; felt wired tail.

Above: **Billy Possum.** 1909. 10in (25cm); gray mohair; felt ears and tail; glass eyes; f.j.; e.s.
CONDITION: Excellent
PRICE: $1,000-$1,500.
**Billy Possum** metal statue. 1909. 3in (8cm).
CONDITION: Good. PRICE: $150-$200.
(Left) Ideal Bear. Circa 1907. 11in (28cm); golden mohair; shoe-button eyes; f.j.; e.s.
CONDITION: Fair.
PRICE: $900-$1,100.

Roosevelt Bust. Circa 1907. 1-½in (3cm); bronze.
CONDITION: Excellent.
PRICE: $75-$100.
Postcard. "Goodbye Teddy." 1909. Photo of Theodore Roosevelt (Left) and William Taft (Right) can be seen in the corners of this card.
CONDITION: Excellent.
PRICE: $25-$30.

Above: In this rare postcard (postmarked 1907) Taft confidently confronts Roosevelt with his new campaign symbol, Billy Possum, while the defeated looking teddy bear looks on.
CONDITION: Excellent.
PRICE: $100-$125.

Left:
Unknown American manufactured **Billy Possums.** Circa 1909.
CONDITION: Fair.
PRICE: $1,000-$1,200 each.
Possum postcards in background. 1909.
CONDITION: Excellent.
PRICE: $55-$100 each.
*Courtesy Mimi Hiscox.*

## Smokey Bear
### (Ideal Toy Company)

*Important Milestones:* Poster painted by Albert Staehle for Forest Service: **1944;** Rudy Wendelin becomes official "Smokey" artist: **1946;** live symbol of Smokey discovered in New Mexico: **1950;** Ideal Toy Company makes first *Smokey* Teddy Bear: **1953.**

*Characteristics:* First version came with separate hat, blue denim trousers, shovel and silver badge and belt buckle; first plush bear had vinyl head; in second version only face was vinyl; later years bear was completely plush.

**Right:**
Ideal Toy Company. *Smokey Bear* with original box. 1953. 18in (46cm); molded vinyl head; hands and feet stuffed with cotton; brown plush body; plastic eyes; painted features; incised on back of head "c. 1953/Smokey says/Prevent Forest Fires/ Ideal Toy Company." Original *Smokey Bear* sign. *Smokey* came with separate felt hat, blue trousers, blue plastic shovel and silver badge which reads: "Smokey Ranger/Prevent Forest Fires," and a silver belt buckle which reads: "Smokey." First plush *Smokey Bear* design.
CONDITION: Mint.
**PRICE:** $900-up.
*Courtesy Barbara Baldwin.*

**Left:**
(Front Left and Right) Ideal *Smokey Bear*. 1953. 14in (36cm); vinyl molded head, hands and feet; brown synthetic plush upper body; blue denim pants; missing buckle and shovel. First plush *Smokey Bear* design.
CONDITION: Good.
**PRICE:** $200-$300.
Dakin *Woodsy Owl.* Circa 1976. 11in (28cm); brown synthetic plush head and upper body; yellow synthetic plush face; red felt beak; plastic eyes; green fabric hat and pants; n.j.; s.s.
CONDITION: Excellent.
**PRICE:** $50-$75.
Ideal. *Smokey Bear*. 1954. 16in (41cm); brown synthetic plush head and body; vinyl molded face; blue denim pants. Missing plastic yellow hat.
CONDITION: Good.
**PRICE:** $55-$85.
(Back Center) *Smokey Bear* water flask. Vinyl molded *Smokey Bear* head.
CONDITION: Good.
**PRICE:** $30-$45.
*Private Collection.*

**Right:**
Knickerbocker *Smokey Bears*. Circa 1973. (Left to Right) 27in (69cm), 15in (38cm), 33in (84cm); brown synthetic plush; cream plush heart-shaped face; plastic eyes; blue denim pants and foot pads; *Smokey* belt buckle; n.j.; s.s.
CONDITION: Very Good.
**PRICE:** $50-$100 each.
*Private Collection.*

Dakin. **Smokey Bears**. (Left and Center) 1985. 13in (33cm) and 12 in (31cm); brown acrylic plush; beige acrylic plush inset snout and around eyes; glass eyes; plastic noses; n.j. (seated position); blue jeans (an integral part of body); plastic **Smokey** buckle; yellow plastic hat. (Center Right) 1980. 14in (36cm); (Right) 1983. 10in (25cm). Both right and center right are the same design; dark brown acrylic plush; light beige acrylic plush inset snout; plastic eyes; n.j. (standing position); blue jeans (an integral part of body) with plastic **Smokey** buckle; yellow plastic hat.
CONDITION: Mint.
**PRICE:** $30-$50 each.
*Courtesy Richard C. Yokley.*

Miller Antiseptic Company Bear. Circa 1907. 18in (46cm); light golden "nappy wool;" clear glass eyes; f.j.; e.s.; k.s.
CONDITION: Very Good.
**PRICE:** $900-$1,200.
*Courtesy Martha and Jim Hession.*

Three Bears Co. **Smokey Bears**. (Left to Right) 1989, 6in (15cm); 1985, 30 in (76cm); 1985, 12in (31cm); 1985, 15in (38cm). Cinnamon-colored acrylic plush; light beige acrylic plush inset snout and paw pads; brown fabric noses; plastic eyes; n.j. bodies (seated position); blue jeans ( an integral part of body); gold-colored Smokey buckle; floppy beige fabric hat.
CONDITION: Mint.
**PRICE:** (Left) $50; (Center) $250-$300; (Right) $100.
*Courtesy Richard C. Yokley.*

Bears. Circa 1907. (Left) 17in (43cm). (Right) 10in (25cm); golden beige mohair; shoe-button eyes; fabric noses; f.j.; e.s. Wonderful facial and body appeal.
CONDITION: Good.
**PRICE:** (Left) 17in (43cm) $2,500-$3,000; (Right) 10in (25cm) $800-$1,000.
*Courtesy Deborah and Donald Ratliff.*

Right:
Bears. Circa 1907. 13in (33cm); (Left) golden brown mohair; (Right) beige mohair; shoe-button eyes; black twill nose; f.j.; four claws; horsehair and e.s. Note egg-plant-shaped head.
CONDITION: Excellent.
**PRICE:** $1,000-$1,500 each.
*Courtesy Martha and Jim Hession.*

Bear (Possibly Ideal). Circa 1907. 26in (66cm); gold mohair; large black button eyes; f.j.; e.s.
CONDITION: Excellent.
**PRICE:** $2,500-$3,000.
*Courtesy Martha and Jim Hession.*

Right:
(Left) Ideal Bear. Circa 1907. 20in (51cm); golden mohair; large black button eyes; f.j. ("wooden joints"); e.s.
CONDITION: Fair.
**PRICE:** $1,200-$1,500.
(Right) Possible A.S. Ferguson. "Good Bears." Circa 1907. 16in (41cm); deep golden mohair; large black wooden eyes; f.j. "wooden joints"; e.s. The Good Bear Company in 1906 developed into the Uncle Remus Co. by 1907 under Charles Sackman's patent and trademark. The A.S. Ferguson Company was the sole agent for these bears. Ferguson advertised superior quality construction, meaning the unique and time consuming wooden joints and eye attachments (eyes attached through two holes in the neck joint). Attachments tied around center collar pin.
CONDITION: Fair.
**PRICE:** $800-$1,000.
*Courtesy Martha and Jim Hession.*

Bears. (Left and Right Front). Circa 1907. 15in and 24in (38cm and 61cm); (Back Right) Circa 1907. 15in (38cm); mohair; shoe-button eyes; f.j.; e.s. Bears have same three fanned stitched claws.
CONDITION: Excellent.
**PRICE:** 15in (38cm) $800-$1,200. 24in (61cm) $2,800-$3,200.
*Courtesy Martha and Jim Hession.*

Teddy Bear Purse. Circa 1907. 8in (20cm); short honey colored mohair; shoe-button eyes; f.j.; e.s.; metal frame; brown cotton lining, leather handle.
CONDITION: Good.
**PRICE:** $1,500-$2,000.
*Private Collection.*

Bear Muff. Circa 1907. 14in (36cm); white mohair; glass eyes; black fabric nose; beige felt paw and foot pads; n.j. arms and legs; e.s. head; beige fabric lined muff.
CONDITION: Fair.
**PRICE:** $750-$850.
*Private Collection.*

Patriotic Bear. Circa 1907. 12in (31cm); red/white/blue mohair; glass eyes; f.j.; e.s.
CONDITION: Excellent.
**PRICE:** $1,200-$1,500.
*Private Collection.*

Right:
Teddy Doll muffs. Circa 1907. (Left) 10in (25cm); short gold mohair; celluloid face; painted facial features; n.j. arms and legs; swivel head. (Right) 13in (33cm); dark blue and white mohair; beige felt hands and feet; celluloid face; hand painted features; n.j. arms and legs; swivel head.
CONDITION: Very Good.
**PRICE:** 10in (25cm) $250-$350; 13in (33cm) $350-$450.
*Private Collection.*

Teddy Dolls. The Teddy Doll or Eskimo Doll was a distinctive novelty when introduced in America around 1908. They had all the features of a teddy bear body but the doll faces were either celluloid, composition or bisque. Usually a little hood made of the same material as the body surrounded the head. It appears by the advertisement in *Playthings* that the primary manufacturers of these special creations were Hahn and Amberg. New York and Harman Mfg. Co., New York. However, pictured at the top is a teddy doll muff with the original label that reads: "Ideal Baby Mine." Sizes of Teddy Dolls range from 7in-14in (18cm-36cm).
CONDITION: Excellent.
**PRICE:** $125-$600 each.
*Courtesy Dot Gillett.*

Bear. Circa 1908. 24in (61cm); bright red short mohair; wooden painted "googlie" eyes; black "glass" nose; f.j.; e.s. (firm).
CONDITION: Fair.
**PRICE:** $1,500-$2,000.
*Courtesy Deborah and Donald Ratliff.*

"Musical" Bear. Circa 1908. 10in (25cm); short beige mohair head; short red/green mohair arms and legs; glass eyes; felt lined stitched nose; f.j.; e.s.; music box encased in body; music activated by turning small crank on bear's back. Cotton clown outfit.
CONDITION: Good.
**PRICE:** $800-$1,000.
*Courtesy Deborah and Donald Ratliff.*

Bear. Circa 1908. 18in (46cm); grayish white mohair; glass eyes; rusty brown vertical stitched nose with five claws; f.j.; fine e.s.
CONDITION: Excellent.
**PRICE:** $2,500-$3,000.
*Courtesy Martha and Jim Hession.*

Bear. (possibly Ideal.) Circa 1909. 20in (51cm); short gold mohair; glass eyes; twill fabric nose; f.j.; e.s.
CONDITION: Excellent.
**PRICE:** $1,500-$2,000.
*Courtesy Martha and Jim Hession.*

Bear (possibly Ideal). Circa 1910. 24in (61cm); short bristle-type golden mohair; glass eyes; f.j.; e.s. (firm). Note body slightly shorter and head larger than earlier designs.
CONDITION: Excellent.
**PRICE:** $1,200-$1,500.
*Courtesy Martha and Jim Hession.*

Bear. Circa 1910. 26in (66cm); short gold mohair; shoe-button eyes; twill fabric nose; f.j.; e.s. (firm).
CONDITION: Excellent.
**PRICE:** $800-$1,000.
*Courtesy Martha and Jim Hession.*

(Left) Bear. Circa 1910. 24in (61cm); white mohair; brown glass stick pin eyes; pinkish stitched nose; mouth and claws; f.j.; e.s. (firm). CONDITION: Good. **PRICE:** $1,000-$1,200.
(Right) Bear. Circa 1910. 25in (64cm); gold mohair; brown glass stick pin eyes; brown stitched nose and mouth; replaced pads; f.j.; e.s. (firm). Main characteristics of both bears: large head; long mouth stitch and large high humps. CONDITION: Good. **PRICE:** $800-$900. *Courtesy Martha and Jim Hession.*

"Top Stitched" Bear. Circa 1910. 25in (64cm); short gold mohair; glass eyes; f.j.; e.s.; seams are top stitched. CONDITION: Good. **PRICE:** $500-$650. *Courtesy Martha and Jim Hession.*

"Top Stitched" Bears. (Left to Right). Circa 1910, Circa 1925 and Circa 1914. Approximate size 23in (58cm); short golden mohair; shoe-button and glass eyes; f.j.; e.s. Stitching is applied "on top" of seam. Gund is one company known for this sewing procedure. Note the body characteristics of these bears: long torso; long narrow arms and legs; flat heads and back; small feet; felt paw pads with no claws; short bristle-type mohair (predominantly gold); firmly stuffed with excelsior. CONDITION: Very Good. **PRICE:** $550-$750 each. *Courtesy Martha and Jim Hession.*

Far Left:
"Cork Stuffed" Bears (possibly Horsman Company). Circa 1910. 16in -35in (41cm-89cm); beige and gold mohair; shoe-button and glass eyes; cork stuffing; large bear's head stuffed with excelsior. Prior to 1910 in *Playthings* magazine, Horsman Company stated their use of cork stuffing in their bears. Other characteristics are accentuated hump, heart-shaped nose lined with felt; cardboard lined foot pads.
CONDITION: Excellent.
PRICE: $500-$1,500 each.
*Courtesy Martha and Jim Hession.*

Left:
Bears. Circa 1908. (Left) 21in (53cm). (Right) 13in (33cm); golden yellow mohair; shoe-button eyes; f.j.; "cork stuffing;" k.s.; and e.s.
CONDITION: Good.
PRICE: 21in (53cm) $700-$800; 13in (33cm) $200-$300.
*Courtesy Martha and Jim Hession.*

"Long Torso" Bears. Circa 1912. (Right) 21in (53cm). (Left) 23 in (58cm); mohair; glass eyes; f.j. e.s.
CONDITION: Good.
PRICE: $400-$550 each.
*Courtesy Martha and Jim Hession.*

(Left) Bear. Circa 1912. 17in (43cm); golden mohair; shoe-button eyes; f.j.; e.s.
CONDITION: Good.
PRICE: $800-$1,000.
(Right) Long Voice Toy. Bear. Circa 1914. 8-1/2in (21cm); gold mohair; shoe-button eyes; e.s.; jointed head and arms. When toy is released after being pressed down it emits a long drawn-out squeal. It was promoted as "The item for Halloween."
CONDITION: Excellent.
PRICE: $850-$1,100.
Courtesy Deborah and Donald Ratliff.

(Right) "Electric-Eye" Bear. Circa 1907. 18in (46cm); golden brown mohair; glass bulb eyes; f.j.; e.s. Squeezing tummy activates battery (concealed in torso) causing eyes to light up.
CONDITION: Excellent.
**PRICE:** $1,000-$1,200.
(Left) Commonwealth Toy and Novelty Co. Inc. *Feed Me* Bear. Circa 1937. 16in (41cm).
CONDITION: Good.
**PRICE:** $450-$500.

Electric Eye Bear. Circa 1915. 23in (58cm); white mohair; glass light bulb eyes; stationary head and legs; jointed arms; e.s. (firm). By pressing lever in ear eyes light up. Battery enclosed in torso.
CONDITION: Very Good.
**PRICE:** $900-$1,100.
*Courtesy Martha and Jim Hession.*

Bears. Circa 1915. 24in (61cm); (Left) white mohair; (Right) gold mohair; glass eyes; twill fabric nose; f.j.; e.s. (firm).
CONDITION: Excellent.
**PRICE:** $500-$600 each.
*Courtesy Martha and Jim Hession.*

"Moving Eyes" Bear. Circa 1920s. 14in (36cm);
light gold mohair; metal rim surrounds celluloid
"googlie" eyes; f.j.; e.s. and k.s.
CONDITION: Excellent.
**PRICE:** $1,500-$1,700.
*Courtesy Evelyn and Mort Wood.*

Agnes Brush. ***Winnie-the-Pooh and Friends***. Circa 1950. (Center eight char-
acters) All characters are made of felt or cotton; n.j. with s.s.
CONDITION: Excellent.
PRICE: ***Winnie-the-Pooh***: $550-$850; ***Owl***: $350-$550; ***Rabbit***: $350-$550; ***Tigger***: $550-
$750; ***Eeyore***: $450-$750; ***Kanga and Roo***; $650-$950; ***Piglet***: $250-$450.
(Left) Woolnough. ***Winnie-the-Pooh***. Circa 1930. Stamp on right foot.
CONDITION: Mint.
PRICE: $5,000-$8,000.
(Right) Schuco. ***Winnie-the-Pooh***. Circa 1960. Paper tag.
CONDITION: Mint.
PRICE: $1,800-$2,800.
*Courtesy Barbara Lauver.*

Bears with Moveable Eyes. Circa 1924. (Left)
11in (28cm). (Right) 14in (36cm); mohair; cellu-
loid sleep eyes; f.j.; e.s. The National French
Novelty Co. produced bears with sleep eyes.
CONDITION: Excellent.
**PRICE:** $1,000-$1,400 each.
*Courtesy Sherryl Shirran.*

A Georgene Product. ***Uncle Wiggly***. Circa 1943. 12in/18in (31cm/46cm). ***Nurse Jane***. Circa
1943. 12in/18in (31cm/46cm).
CONDITION: Mint.
**PRICE:** 12in (31cm) $500-$600 each; 18in (46cm) $1,000-$1,200 each.
*Courtesy Mimi Hiscox.*

# Chapter Two
# Australian Bears

Australian bear making was healthy and individualistic during the 1920s through 1970s. Bears featured imported English mohair and remarkable glass eyes and frequently had rigid, not jointed, necks. In the late 1960s, almost all Australian toy makers went out of business due to the lifting of import tariffs which opened the door to stiff competition from Asia. Today, there are numerous artists making teddy bears "down under," but this compilation features manufacturers from the hey-day of Australian bear manufacturing.

**Berlex Toys Pty Ltd.**
(Melbourne, Australia)
*Important Milestones:* Founded: early **1930s**; Ceased production: **1970s**.
*Founder:* Lex Bertrand.
*Characteristics:* Rich mohair; chubby body; cream colored, vinyl paw pads; triangular, vertical stitched nose; glass eyes; later bears have stiff, unjointed necks.
*Trademark/Identification:* Cloth tag sewn into right arm with "Berlex Melbourne" printed in red.

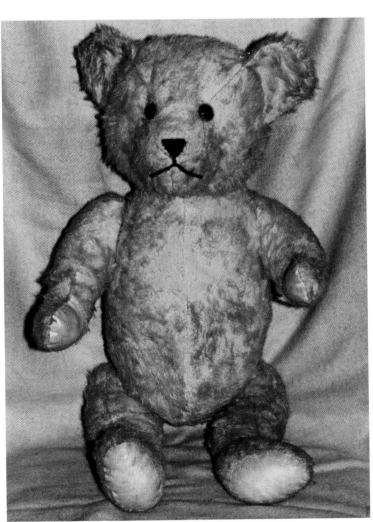

Right:
Berlex Bear. Circa 1950.
16in (41cm); gold mohair;
glass eyes; vinyl paw pads;
f.j.; e.s.
CONDITION: Fair.
**PRICE:** $250-$350.
*Courtesy Romy Roeder.*

Left:
Emil Toys. Bear. Circa 1950. 12in (31cm); gold mohair; glass eyes; vinyl paw pads; f.j.; e.s.
CONDITION: Good.
**PRICE:** $175-$250.
*Courtesy Romy Roeder.*

**Emil Pty Ltd.**
(Melbourne, Australia)
*Important Milestones:* Founded: mid-**1930s**; Ceased production: **1970s**.
*Characteristics:* Early bears (1930s-1940s) used imported mohair, glass eyes; heads are broad with ears placed wide apart; first bears had pointed foot pads of oil cloth and velvet; filled with excelsior/kapok mixture; nose quite distinctive with outside (upward) stitches longer than the inner stitches. Later bears (1960s) did not use as high quality mohair and all have stiff neck; plastic eyes and white vinyl paw pads; nose still distinctive black; some have black claws.
*Trademark/Identification:* Satin label sewn into back or side seam, printed with "Emil Toys made in Australia"; a teddy sits on the "E."

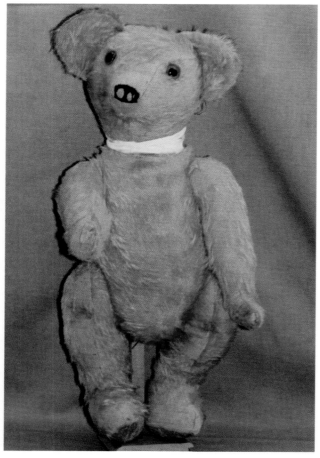

Above:
Fideston Toys. Bear. Circa 1920. 20in (51cm); gold mohair;
glass eyes; leather paw pads; f.j.; e.s.
CONDITION: Fair.
**PRICE:** $500-up.
*Courtesy Romy Roeder.*

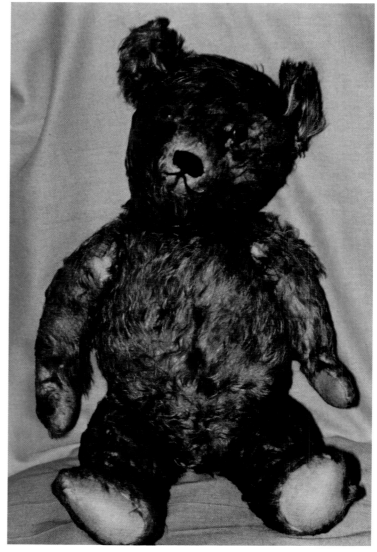

Above:
Fideston Toys. Bear. Circa 1940. 20in (51cm); dark brown tipped mohair;
glass eyes; leather paw pads; f.j.; e.s.
CONDITION: Good.
**PRICE:** $500-up.
*Courtesy Romy Roeder.*

### Fideston Toy Co.
(near Perth, Australia)
*Important Milestones:* Made first commercial teddy bear: **1917;**
Company registered/factory established: **1921;** Made 1000 bears/month:
**1930.**
*Founder:* Richard and Louisa Fiddes.
*Characteristics:* Made two designs; most identifiable has broad head,
large ears and cone-shaped muzzle; actually Fideston bears were often
thought to be German due to high quality.

Left:
Fideston Toys. Bear. Circa 1920. 20in (51cm); faded pale blue mohair;
glass eyes; leather paw pads; f.j.; e.s.
CONDITION: Fair.
**PRICE:** $500-up.
*Courtesy Romy Roeder.*

## Jakas Soft Toys

(Melbourne, Australia)

*Important Milestones:* Founded: **1954;** company registered, moves to Blackburn, Victoria: **1956;** "Big Ted" produced: **1962;** company sold: **1984;** Wendy McDonald buys company: **1989;** merges with Koala Mate; introduces limited-edition lines: **1991.**

*Founders:* Joe and Marion Stanford.

*Characteristics:* Foam rubber stuffing; originally fully jointed; later changed to unjointed.

*Trademark/Identification:* Cloth label on foot reads "Jakas Toys".

## Joy-Toys Pty Ltd.

(Victoria, Australia)

*Important Milestones:* Founded: **1920s;** expands, acquires franchise for Disney characters; produces set of promotional Three Bears: **1937;** Maurice Court joins company: **1935;** Cyclops buys company: **1966;** Ceases business; UK-owned Tube Investments buys company: **1971;** Sandman Pty. Ltd. bought by Maurice Court and Toltoys; last year name Joy-Toys used: **1976;** Court sells his shares to Toltoys: **1979;** Court buys Joy-Toys equipment and trade name for Toltoys: **1980.**

*Founders:* Mr. and Mrs. Gerald Kirby.

*Trademark/Identification:* Embroidered cloth label sewn onto left foot pad: "Joy Toys Made in Australia".

*Characteristics:* Early bears were fully jointed; used English mohair; filled with excelsior; resembled German bears; many Joy-Toy bears are missing original glass eyes; by 1930s more like English bears; stiff neck; pointed up-turned paws; filled with kapok; distinctive vertical nose stitching (two longer outer stitches); large ears wide apart and far back on head; bears from 1940s filled with crumbled up rubber; painted leatherette paw pads; quality of bears deteriorates after 1960.

Jackas Toys. Bear. Circa 1950. 15in (38cm); pale beige mohair; red felt lined open mouth; glass eyes; cloth paw pads; f.j.; e.s.
CONDITION: Excellent.
**PRICE:** $225-$325.
*Courtesy Romy Roeder.*

Jackas Toys. Bears. Circa 1950. 17in and 14-1/2in (43cm and 37cm); black mohair; glass eyes; leather paw pads; f.j.; e.s.
CONDITION: Excellent.
**PRICE:** 17in (43cm) $500-$600; 14-1/2in (37cm) $325 -$475.
*Courtesy Romy Roeder.*

Right:
Joy Toys. Bear. Circa 1930. 24in (61cm); gold mohair; glass eyes; rexine paw pads; f.j.; e.s; label on sole of foot.
CONDITION: Good.
**PRICE:** $500-$750.
*Courtesy Romy Roeder.*

Joy Toys. Bear. Circa 1970. 12in (31cm); bright gold synthetic plush; glass eyes; velveteen paw pads; stationary head; f.j. arms and legs; e.s.; label sewn into seam of foot pad.
CONDITION: Excellent.
**PRICE:** $130-$230.
*Courtesy Romy Roeder.*

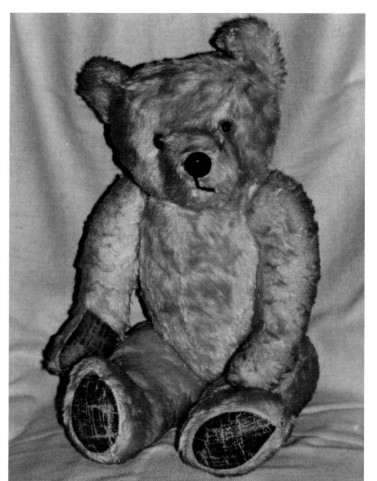

### Lindee Toys
(New South Wales, Australia)
*Important Milestones:* Founded: **1944;** wins "Toy of the Year": **1969;** Founder sells business: **1969;** Ceases business: **1976**.
*Founders:* Mr. and Mrs. Lindenberg.
*Trademark/Identification:* "Lindee Toys the Prestige Name in Soft Toys" inside outline of seated fawn and "Made in Australia".
*Characteristics:* English mohair, jointed and unjointed, glass eyes; brown vinyl and oil cloth paw pads; large noses and black mouths; some have large black claws.

Left:
Lindee Toys. Bear. Circa 1940. 20in (51cm); gold mohair; glass eyes; composition nose; rexine paw pads; f.j.; e.s.; remains of label in seam of foot pad.
CONDITION: Very Good.
**PRICE:** $325-$500.
*Courtesy Romy Roeder.*

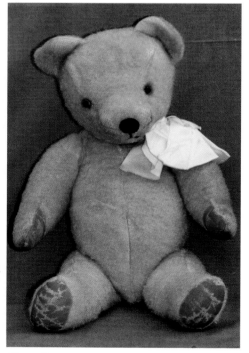

### Verna Toys
(Victoria, Australia)
*Important Milestones:* Established as home-based doll making business: **1941;** Purchased by Arthur Eaton who introduces trade name "Verna" and adds teddy bears to line: **1948;** ceases business: **mid-1980s**.
*Founder:* Eve Barnett.
*Trademark/Identification:* White cloth tag sewn into seam and "Verna Made in Australia" printed in red.
*Characteristics:* Before 1960s, bears were mohair plush, filled with excelsior, cotton flock and were fully jointed; square shaped snout is distinguishing feature; after c. 1960 filling was foam rubber; plastic safety eyes and vinyl pads.

Verna Toys. Bear. Circa 1950. 21in (53cm); blonde mohair; glass eyes; kidney-shaped felt nose; vinyl paw pads; f.j.; e.s.
CONDITION: Excellent.
**PRICE:** $325-$500.
*Courtesy Romy Roeder.*

Verna Toys. Bear. Circa 1940. 15in (38cm); light brown wool plush; glass eyes; round-shaped felt nose; rexine paw pads; f.j.; e.s.
CONDITION: Good.
**PRICE:** $225-$325.
*Courtesy Romy Roeder.*

# Chapter Three
# Austrian Bears

There are not very many Austrian bear manufacturers of note today. One notable company moved to Germany (see Fechter).

### Berg Spielwaren Tiere mit Herz GmbH
#### (Tyrol, Austria)

*Important Milestones:* Teddy Bears made from old army blankets in Tyrolean family farm house: **1946;** business expands as materials become more available: **1951-52;** new trademark introduced:**1957;** new factory built at Admont: **1966;** replica limited editions introduced: **1992;** still in operation.

*Founders:* Broschek family.

*Trademark/Identification:* 1951-57: "Berg" printed on cloth ear tag; 1957: little red heart sewn into chest and *Tiere mit Herz* (Animals with Heart).

*Characteristics:* Used old U.S. Army blankets and buttons from old uniforms until real woven plush and life-like glass eyes were available; first Berg bears identified by small white tag affixed to ear.

Right:
Berg. Bear. Circa 1950. 28in (70cm); yellow mohair; glass eyes; f.j.; e.s.
CONDITION: Mint.
**PRICE:** $700-$1,000.
*Courtesy Puppenhausmuseum, Basel.*

Berg Bear. Circa 1955. 10in (25cm); blond mohair; orange glass eyes; f.j.; e.s.; red metal heart (company trademark) sewn into chest.
CONDITION: Good.
Sold at Horst Poestgens' auction in Germany for approximately $200.
*Courtesy Horst Poestgens Auctioneer, Germany.*

Berg. Bear. Circa 1950. 4in (10cm); pale beige mohair; glass eyes; f.j.; e.s.
CONDITION: Excellent.
**PRICE:** $70-$100.
*Courtesy Puppenhausmuseum, Basel.*

# Chapter Four
# British Bears

Some British collectors contend that teddy bears were named after King Edward VII (whose nickname was "Teddy"). Some early manufacturers were already in the toy business, and made an easy transition to making bears. During the First World War bans on German imports encouraged more British bear makers to set up factories. These early bears, particularly from Harwin, Chad Valley, Merrythought, Chiltern, W.J. Terry and Deans are extremely collectible.

Since there were no rules governing trademarks and logos, many companies employed well crafted "knock-offs" of original German lines of bears. Early bears from this part of the world are very high quality and Yorkshire mohair plush is the fabric of choice for most of them. After the Second World War, the British bear radically changes its look and the "typical" English bears with a flatter face, plump body and short limbs came into its own.

**The Chad Valley Co. Ltd.**
(Birmingham, England)

*Important Milestones:* Founded as printer and bookbinder: **c. 1820;** founder's son Alfred enters business: **1889;** registers Chad Valley trademark, named after Chad Stream near new factory near Harborne: **1897;** first bears produced: **1915;** Alfred Johnson patents toy stuffing machine: **1916;** Wrekin Toy Works (renamed The Chad Valley Co. Ltd.) opens: **1920;** buys Peacock & Co. Ltd. (maker of wooden toys): **1931;** granted Royal Warrant of Appointment as Toymakers to Her Majesty the Queen: **1938;** becomes public company: **1950;** H.G. Stone & Col. Ltd. acquired: **1967;** Palitoy takes over: **1978;** Woolworth's adopts Chad name, production moved to Asia: **1988.**

*Founder:* Anthony Bunn Johnson.

*Trademark/Identification:* Aerolite trademark for kapok-stuffed toys and dolls (until 1926); Chad Valley bears copied Steiff with metal ear buttons; first appeared as metal ring around blue paper disk, covered by celluloid (1920); by the 30s, button was sheet metal with blue outer ring and yellow paper inside with words: "Chad Valley English Hygienic Toys". Prior to the 1930s, bears were also identified with oblong label on foot. Later label depicted the Royal Crest on a square stitched to the foot.

*Characteristics:* Two types of noses: early examples show vertically stitched triangular nose; most prevalent style of coal-shaped nose becomes the norm; widely set, large, flat ears; amber and glass eyes; muzzle is shaved; large, oval foot pads with cardboard inserts; quality mohair, some in vibrant colors.

Chad Valley. Bear. Circa 1930. 17in (43cm); golden beige mohair; glass eyes; f.j.; e.s; celluloid button in ear; oblong cloth label on foot.
CONDITION: Good.
**PRICE:** $700-$1,000.
*Courtesy Puppenhausmuseum, Basel.*

Chad Valley. Bear. Circa 1930. 21in (53cm); pale mohair; glass eyes; f.j.; e.s.
CONDITION: Good.
**PRICE:** $1,300-$1,800.
*Courtesy Puppenhausmuseum, Basel.*

Chad Valley. Bear. Circa 1930. 12in (30cm); yellow mohair; orange glass eyes; f.j.; e.s; celluloid button upper torso; unusual design.
CONDITION: Excellent.
**PRICE:** $700-$1,000.
*Courtesy Puppenhausmuseum, Basel.*

Chad Valley. Bear. Circa 1930. 11in (28cm); pink wool plush; glass eyes; f.j.; e.s; celluloid button in ear; rare color.
CONDITION: Excellent.
**PRICE:** $1,000-$1,300.
*Courtesy Puppenhausmuseum, Basel.*

Chad Valley. Bear. Circa 1938-1953. 16in (40cm); long wavy yellow mohair; glass eyes; f.j.; e.s; square cloth label on foot..
CONDITION: Mint.
**PRICE:** $800-$1,200.
*Courtesy Puppenhausmuseum, Basel.*

### Chiltern
(London, England) – H.G. Stone & Co. Ltd.

*Important Milestones:* Founded: **1908;** made first bear: **1915;** inherited by Leon Reese: **1919;** Reese forms partnership with Harry Stone (H.G. Stone and Co. Ltd.): **1920;** "Chiltern Toys" name appears in journals and "Hugmee" Teddy Bears introduced: **1923;** "Chiltern Toys" registered: **1924;** Panurge Pets taken over: **1925;** first rayon plush teddy, "Silky Teddy," introduced: **1929;** Harry Stone dies: **1934;** second toy factory opened at Pontypool, Wales: **1947;** Leon Reese dies: **1963;** taken over by Chad Valley: **1967.**

*Founders:* Joseph Eisenmann opened Chiltern Toy Works; son-in-law Leon Reese (marketing and sales) and Harry Stone (design) form H.G. Stone & Company.

*Trademark/Identification:* "Chiltern Toys"; Hugmee (originally "Chubby Bears"); Chiltern/Chad Valley; early bears had orange circular cardboard chest tag; cloth labels stitched in side seams or on foot pad: 1940.

*Characteristics:* Early "Hugmee Bears" had clear glass eyes, oblong nose vertically stitched with raised outer stitches, broad smiles, embroidered claws, velveteen paw pads, cardboard-lined foot pads, and large ribbon bow; by 1950s, mohair plush is less luxurious, smile has disappeared, bow is smaller and claws have less thread; still have typically shorter legs and fat thighs; plastic noses were tried in 1960; many Chiltern bears had music and voice boxes.

Right:
Chiltern. Bear. Circa 1930. 26in (65cm); gold mohair; glass eyes; f.j.; e.s.
CONDITION: Excellent.
**PRICE:** $1,300-$2,000.
*Courtesy Puppenhausmuseum, Basel.*

Far Left::
Chiltern. **Master Teddy**. Circa 1915. 7-1/2in (19cm); golden mohair head; paws and feet; painted "googlie" eyes; red stitched tongue; f.j.; e.s.; dressed in original pink and white checked shirt; blue felt trousers with red felt patch and braces.
CONDITION: Good.
Sold at Christie's South Kensington 1997 auction for approximately $2,000.
*Courtesy Christie's.*

Left:
Chiltern. **Tingaling Bruin**. Circa 1950. 13in (32cm); beige mohair; glass eyes; f.j.; e.s.; k.s.; bell in tummy.
CONDITION: Excellent.
**PRICE:** $800-$1,000.
*Courtesy Puppenhausmuseum, Basel.*

Below:
Chiltern. Bear. Circa 1950. 17in (43cm); gold mohair; glass eyes; f.j.; e.s.; k.s.; cloth label on foot.
CONDITION: Excellent.
**PRICE:** $700-$900.
*Courtesy Puppenhausmuseum, Basel.*

Chiltern. Teddy Clown. Circa 1950. 19in (48cm); white mohair head and body; pink mohair arms legs and ears; glass eyes; f.j.; e.s.; rexine paw pads.
CONDITION: Good.
**PRICE:** $500-$600.
*Courtesy Puppenhausmuseum, Basel.*

## Dean's Rag Book Co. Ltd
### (Pontypool, Wales)

*Important Milestones:* Founded: **1903;** Knockabout toy sheets introduced: **1905;** Knockabout teddy bear and Teddy Bear Rag Book introduced; **1908;** first cataloged teddy bears marketed under the name "Kuddlemee" for subsidiary The British Novelty Works: **1915;** fire destroys early products: **1916;** first bears with Dean's logo, "A1 Toys" registered, Evripoze joints patented: **1922;** Merton factory sold, production moved to Rye, Sussex: **1955;** changes name to Dean's Childsplay Toys Ltd.: **1965;** Gwentoys Ltd. is purchased: **1972;** Pontypool is site for all production: **1980;** Neil Miller joins firm: **1987;** firm goes into voluntary liquidation, Miller buys Wendley Ltd and trading rights to Dean's name and logo: **1988;** new line of collector's bears launched: **1991.**

*Founder:* Henry Samuel Dean.

*Trademark/Identification:* Two fighting dogs; Woven and (later) printed label; metal button with Dean's Rag Book Co. Ltd..

*Characteristics:* Glass eyes; traditional claws; vertical stitched nose; felt and velveteen pads; "Evripose" joints on some designs allowed animals to be moved into virtually every position.

Right:
Dean's. Bear. Circa 1930. 12in (31cm); orange mohair; glass eyes; molded nose; f.j.; e.s.; cloth label on foot.
CONDITION: Mint.
**PRICE:** $1,000-$1,200.
*Courtesy Puppenhausmuseum, Basel.*

Dean's. Bear. Circa 1934-1948; 14in (35cm); yellow mohair; glass eyes; f.j.; e.s.; cloth label on foot.
CONDITION: Good.
**PRICE:** $1,000-$1,500.
*Courtesy Puppenhausmuseum, Basel.*

Dean's. Bear. Circa 1937-1939. 16in (40cm); orange mohair; glass eyes; f.j.; e.s.;
CONDITION: Good.
**PRICE:** $900- $1,200.
*Courtesy Puppenhausmuseum, Basel.*

Dean's. *Tru-to-Life* Bear. Circa 1950. 22in (56cm); black mohair; white plush muzzle; glass eyes; internal rubber face mask with rubber eye sockets; large wide apart ears; black molded rubber nose; pink molded rubber paws and claws; s.s. and e.s. Creation of Sylvia R. Wilgoss, chief designer for Dean's from the 1950s.
CONDITION: Excellent.
Sold at Christie's South Kensington 1997 auction for approximately $5,200.
*Courtesy Christie's.*

Dean's. *Dismal Desmond* riding on a horse. Circa 1923. 10-1/2in (26cm) tall. *Dismal Desmond* (Dalmatian dog); black spotted velveteen; pink felt tongue; n.j.; e.s. Horse; white felt airbrushed markings; glass eyes; n.j.; e.s.; s.s.
CONDITION: Excellent.
PRICE: $800-$900.
*Courtesy Deborah and Donald Ratliff.*

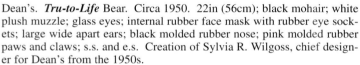

### Ealontoys Ltd.
(East London, England)
*Important Milestones:* Founded as East London Federation Toy Factory: **1914**; changes name to East London Toy Factory: **c. 1921**; teddy bears first mentioned in ads: **1924**; trade name Ealontoys registered: **1926**; name changes to Ealontoys Ltd.: **1948**; ceases business: **early 1950s**.
*Founders:* Sylvia Pankhurst.
*Trademark/Identification:* Seated, shaggy dog beneath Ealontoys with "Made in England"; cloth label stitched to foot.
*Characteristics:* Round head, short snout, short arms; thin tapering paws; small feet.

Ealontoys. Bear. Circa 1950. 20in (50cm); gold mohair; glass eyes; f.j.; e.s. and k.s.
CONDITION: Excellent.
PRICE: $600-$800.
*Courtesy Puppenhausmuseum, Basel.*

## J.K. Farnell and Co. Ltd.
(London, England)

*Important Milestones:* Founded: **1840;** originally made small items such as pin cushions and tea cozies; moved to Acton, Henry Kirby and Agnes Farnell (founder's family) make soft toys from rabbit skins: **1897;** produce first teddy bears: **1908;** H.C. Janisch (later with Merrythought) joins as sales manager, Agnes Farnell designs toys with Sybil Kemp: **1921;** Alpha registered as Trademark/Identification: **1925;** Anima wheeled toys introduced: **1927;** Agnes Farnell dies: **1928;** fire destroys factory and stock: **1934;** reintroduction of Alpha and Teddy lines of bears, move to larger showrooms: **1935;** production moves to Hastings, subsidiary company, Acton Toycraft Ltd., takes over Alpha Works lease, renamed Twyford Works: **1964;** bought by finance company: **1968.**

*Founder:* John Kirby Farnell.

*Trademark/Identification:* "A Farnell Alpha Toy Made in England", white woven label attached to foot; after WWII, printed label reads: "Alpha" in a shield shape.

*Characteristics:* Highly-regarded for high quality; machine seamed; very appealing faces with long shaved muzzle on early designs; early bodies have long curved arms, long legs and large feet; percentage have webbed stitched paw designs; mohair is predominantly long and silky.

J.K. Farnell. Bear. Circa 1920. 20-1/2in (52cm); yellow mohair; glass eyes; f.j.; e.s.; webbed paw stitching.
CONDITION: Good.
**PRICE:** $2,500-$3,000.
*Courtesy Puppenhausmuseum, Basel.*

J.K. Farnell. Bear. Circa 1920. 20in (50cm); yellow mohair; glass eyes; f.j.; e.s.; webbed paw stitching.
CONDITION: Excellent.
**PRICE:** $2,700-$3,300.
*Courtesy Puppenhausmuseum, Basel.*

Right:
Farnell. Bears. (Back) Circa 1930. 27in (69cm); long white mohair; large glass eyes; tan stitched nose; mouth and claws; f.j.; e.s.; rexine paw pads.
CONDITION: Excellent.
**PRICE:** Approximately $3,200.
(Center) Circa 1930. 27in (69cm); long gold mohair; large glass eyes; f.j.; e.s.; rexine paw pads.
CONDITION: Excellent.
**PRICE:** Approximately $1,700.
(Front) Circa 1930. 13in (33cm); dense long golden mohair; glass eyes; f.j.; e.s.; linen paw pads; cardboard lined feet.
CONDITION: Excellent.
**PRICE:** Approximately $1,500.
Sold at Christie's South Kensington 1998 auction for the approximate values printed.
*Courtesy Christie's.*

Left:
J.K. Farnell. Bear. Circa 1930. 25in (64cm); brown tipped pale beige wavy mohair; glass eyes; f.j.; e.s.; cloth label on foot.
CONDITION: Excellent.
**PRICE:** $5,500-$7,500.
*Courtesy Puppenhausmuseum, Basel.*

Bottom Left:
J.K. Farnell. Bear. Circa 1930. 12in (30cm); white wool plush; glass eyes; f.j.; e.s.; "Farnell's 'ALPHA Toys' " fabric label on foot.
CONDITION: Excellent.
**PRICE:** $2,000-$3,000.
*Courtesy Puppenhausmuseum, Basel.*

Below:
J.K. Farnell. Bear. Circa 1965. 29in (74cm); long wavy cinnamon mohair; glass eyes; f.j.; artificial leather paws; e.s. One of last three bears manufactured by Farnell.
CONDITION: Excellent.
**PRICE:** $1,000-$1,700.
*Courtesy Puppenhausmuseum, Basel.*

### Harwin & Co. Ltd

(North London, England)

*Important Milestones:* Founded: **1914;** made first bears: **1915;** launched mascot Ally Bears at London Fair: **1916;** ceases business: **c. 1930.**
*Founder:* G.W. Harwin.
*Trademark/Identification:* Intertwined letters DOTS inside circle with words "British Made".
*Characteristics:* Quality mohair; shoe button eyes; dressed bears.

### Invicta Toys Ltd.

(North West London, England)

*Important Milestones:* Founded: **1935;** with retirement of co-founder, Beer, closed down: **1954.**
*Founders:* G.E. Beer; T.B. Wright.
*Trademark/Identification:* Woven label stitched to foot.
*Characteristics:* Many of the same characteristics as Farnell; wide range of toys included animals on wheels, bears, cats, dogs, monkeys.

### Merrythought Ltd.

(Shropshire, England)

*Important Milestones:* Founded: **1919;** Dyson Hall & Co. Ltd., a mohair-plush weaving factory purchased: **1920s;** Merrythought company formally founded and trademark registered: **1930;** produces first catalog with former Chad Valley designer Florence Atwood **1931;** *Bingie* line of bears primarily produced: **1931-38;** factory expansion: **1935;** produces first panda bear: **1939;** war work: **1940-43;** production resumes but prewar samples and supplies destroyed by flood: **1946;** C.J. Rendle and Florence Atwood die, B.T. Holmes (son of founder) joins company: **1949;** factory premises purchased from Coalbrookdale Company: **1956;** Oliver Holmes (son of B.T. Holmes) joins company: **1972;** collaborates with Tide-Rider Inc. (Baldwin, NY) to export new collector's line to U.S.A.: **1982;** Merrythought shop and museum opens: **1988.**
*Founders:* W.G. Holmes and G.H. Laxton.
*Trademark/Identification:* A wishbone and company name appearing on a printed celluloid covered metal button; embroidered label on foot pre-WWII; later labels were printed; (Merrythought: old 17th-century English word for wishbone); "Regd trademark HYGIENIC MERRYTHOUGHT TOYS/MADE IN ENGLAND".
*Characteristics:* Until World War II, both a woven and paper labels; a clear, celluloid-covered metal button appeared on the inside of the left ear; later buttons were affixed to back of bears; after 1947, label sewn into foot and used on its own; printed label says "Merrythought Ironbridge, Shrops. Made in England"; currently, Merrythought uses embroidered label; early and highly collectible creations were jointed, high quality mohair (or "art silk plush"); brown glass eyes and kapok stuffing are further used to identify bears from this manufacturer; certain of these bears can be determined by unusual design of webbed paw stitching and wide vertically stitched nose.

Right:
Harwin & Co. Ltd. *Lord Kitchener.* Circa 1916. 12in (30cm); beige mohair; shoe-button eyes; f.j.; e.s.; original military outfit.
CONDITION: Excellent.
**PRICE:** $2,500-$3,000.
*Courtesy Puppenhausmuseum, Basel.*

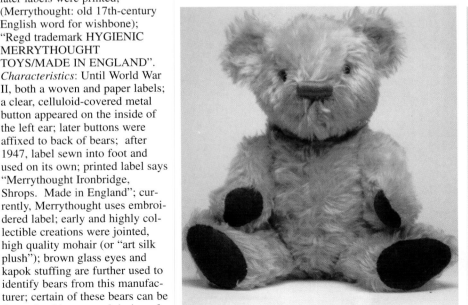

Invicta. Bear. Circa 1930. 17in (42cm); orange mohair; glass eyes; f.j.; e.s.; k.s.; brown cloth paw pads.
CONDITION: Excellent.
**PRICE:** $500-$600.
*Courtesy Puppenhausmuseum, Basel.*

Merrythought. Bear. Circa 1930. 20in (50cm); gold mohair; glass eyes; f.j.; webbed paw stitching; e.s.; fabric label on foot.
CONDITION: Excellent.
**PRICE:** $1,200-$1,700.
*Courtesy Puppenhausmuseum, Basel.*

Merrythought. *Bingie*. Bear. Circa 1930. 20in (50cm); light beige mohair; glass eyes; f.j.; e.s.; original Scottish outfit.
CONDITION: Excellent.
**PRICE:** $5,500-$6,500.
*Courtesy Puppenhausmuseum, Basel.*

Merrythought. Bear. Circa 1930. 19in (48cm); green artificial silk plush; glass eyes; f.j.; e.s.; cloth label on foot; rare color.
CONDITION: Good.
**PRICE:** $1,000-$1,500.
*Courtesy Puppenhausmuseum, Basel.*

Merrythought. *Cheeky*. Bear Muff. Circa 1970. 13in (33cm); gold mohair head and legs; inset gold velvet snout; white mohair muff; glass eyes; n.j. legs; swivel head; e.s.; k.s.; bell in ears; fabric label on foot.
CONDITION: Excellent.
**PRICE:** $300 -$400.
*Courtesy Puppenhausmuseum, Basel.*

Merrythought. (Top Left to Right) *Cheeky*. Bear. Circa 1950. 27in (69cm).
CONDITION: Excellent.
**PRICE:** Approximately $1,400.
*Mrs. Twisty. Cheeky Bear*. Circa 1966. 10in (25cm).
CONDITION: Excellent.
**PRICE:** Approximately $1,300.
*Mr. Twisty. Cheeky Bear*. Circa 1966. 10in (25cm).
CONDITION: Excellent.
**PRICE:** Approximately $1,200.
(Center) *Twisty*. Bear. Circa 1966. 10in (25cm).
CONDITION: Excellent.
**PRICE:** Approximately $440.
(Bottom Left to Right) *Punkinhead*. Bears. Circa 1950. 15in (38cm); 10in (25cm); 13in (33cm).
CONDITION: Good.
**PRICE:** (Left to Right) Approximately $2,800, $1,600, $3,200.
Sold at Christie's South Kensington auction for the approximate prices printed. *Courtesy Christie's.*

## Peacock & Co. Ltd.

(London, England)

*Important Milestones:* Established as Peacock & Sons, London: **1853**; listed as William Peacock & Co.: **1904**; purchased by Chad Valley: **1931**; last mentioned in trade director as A. & A. Peacock Ltd., : **1939**.

*Founder:* William Peacock (1904).

*Trademark/Identification:* White cloth label with red embroidered company name; original trademark was an open-tailed peacock.

*Characteristics:* Black horizontally stitched noses, fairly straight arms and legs, woven fabric paw pads, similar stylistically to Magna Bear (Chad Valley); other features akin to Chad Valley: large cupped ears, four stitched claws on foot pads, large chest, long arms, legs are larger at top/thigh area.

## Pedigree Soft Toys Ltd.

(Merton, Southwest London, England)

*Important Milestones:* Established as wooden toy and baby carriage manufacturer: **mid 19th centurby**; Lines Bros. Ltd. founded: **1919**; "Pedigree" registered as trademark for baby carriages: **c. 1931**; produces first Pedigree Soft Toy catalog offering "Pedigree Pets" (stuffed toys) and "Pedigree Dolls;" **1937**; Lines buys Australian-owned Joy-Toys Ltd. factory in New Zealand, begins manufacturing in Ireland: **1946**; merges activities of soft toy and plastic subsidiaries: **1950**; Lines Bros. ceases bear production, transfers to Canterbury: **1971**; Lines ceases business: **1988**.

*Founders:* Original 19th century founders: George and Joseph Lines; 20th century founders: William, Arthur and Walter.

*Trademark/Identification:* Printed label.

*Characteristics:* Better known for dolls; factory in Belfast, Ireland produced both jointed and unjointed mohair bears; mid-1950s produced bear with vertical central front head seam and top of head horizontal seam; edges of tops of ears folded over; separate muzzles appeared after 1960 as well as synthetic materials; some bears had musical boxes.

## H.G. Stone & Co. Ltd. (see Chiltern)

## W.J. Terry

(North London, England)

*Important Milestones:* Founded: **1890**; opens large new factory as a "skin merchant" and soft-toy manufacturer: **1909**; introduces *"Billy Owlet"* to challenge "supremacy" of the teddy bear: **1913**; produces teddy bears with webbed claws: **c. 1919**; "Ahsolight" trademark used; kapok first used: **1921**; William Terry dies, son Frederick B. Terry continues business: **1924**; ceases business: **WWII**.

*Founder:* William J. Terry.

*Trademark/Identification:* "I am Caesar" tag on toy stuffed dog; "Ahsolight" when kapok was used.

*Characteristics:* Long, silky mohair; large glass eyes, elongated limbs.

Peacock. Bear. Circa 1930. 28in (70cm); gold mohair; glass eyes; f.j.; e.s. cloth label on foot.
CONDITION: Excellent.
**PRICE:** $1,200-$1,700.
*Courtesy Puppenhausmuseum, Basel.*

Pedigree. Bear. Circa 1950. 20in (50cm); yellow mohair; glass eyes; f.j.; e.s.; k.s.; fabric label on foot.
CONDITION: Very Good.
**PRICE:** $500-$700.
*Courtesy Puppenhausmuseum, Basel.*

William J. Terry. Bear. Circa 1920. 18in (46cm); golden mohair; large clear glass eyes painted brown on reverse; f.j.; e.s.; linen paw pads; webbed paw claws and flat cardboard lined feet.
CONDITION: Very Good.
Sold at Christie's South Kensington 1997 auction for approximately $3,600.
*Courtesy Christie's.*

William J. Terry. Bear. Circa 1921. 23-1/2in (60cm); gold mohair; glass eyes; f.j.; e.s..
CONDITION: Worn.
**PRICE:** $400-$500.
*Courtesy Puppenhausmuseum, Basel.*

**Unidentified and Miscellaneous British Manufactured Bears**

Unidentified Manufacturer. Bears. Circa 1920 to 1940. 18in (46cm); golden mohair; glass eyes; f.j.; e.s. Note these two bears portray the most common distinguishing features of British bears produced during the 1920 to 1940 era. Large wide head; short nose; fairly large ears; plump body and short arms. Note the rexine (painted oilcloth) paw pads on the bear on the right.
CONDITION: Worn
PRICE: $300-$400 each.

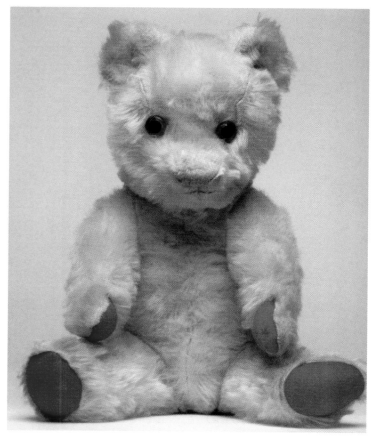

Twyford. Bear. Circa 1960. 12in (32cm); white mohair; glass eyes; f.j.; e.s.; red felt paw pads; fabric label in side seam.
CONDITION: Excellent.
**PRICE:** $500-$700.
*Courtesy Puppenhausmuseum, Basel.*

(Left) Gabrielle Designs. *Paddington Bear*. 1981. 14in (36cm); white synthetic plush; plastic eyes; s.s.; wearing red duffel coat and red rubber boots.
CONDITION: Excellent.
**PRICE:** $75-$110.
(Right and Center) Eden Toys Inc. *Paddington Bear*. Circa 1982. 9in-14in (23cm-36cm); beige synthetic plush; plastic eyes; n.j.; s.s.; blue duffle coats; yellow and red felt bush hats.
CONDITION: Excellent.
**PRICE:** $30-$65 each.
*Courtesy Emma Stephens.*

# Chapter Five
# French Bears

France is best known for its mechanical toys. The first teddy bears were presented around 1911. When mohair was introduced a few companies began producing bears, but the real "bear boom" came in the 1950s when more than 25 firms jumped on the "bear-wagon!" Because so many bear makers moved from firm to firm, French bears mostly share the same characteristics of displaying short mohair, bright colors, narrow torsos, straight arms and legs, simple jointing and almost pouting mouths. Even though teddy bears are extremely popular in France, very few bear manufacturers remain in business today. Early French bears are exceptionally rare.

### M. Pintel Fils
(Paris, France)
*Important Milestones:* First bears in catalog: **1911;** Marcel Pintel begins making bears for father's firm, trademark registered: **1913;** new line of stuffed dolls and animals: **1919;** first mohair bears: **1920;** business closes: **1976.**
*Founders:* Marcel Pintel and father.
*Trademark/Identification:* Two embracing bears.
*Characteristics:* Short mohair; stuffed firmly, tapered limbs; clear glass painted eyes; vertical stitched nose; until 1930s have metal button on chest.

### F.A.D.A.P.
(Divonne-les-Bains, France)
*Important Milestones:* Founded: **1920;** new colors introduced: **c.1925;** rayon plush introduced: **1930s;** collaboration with US Ideal Toy Corporation: **1950s;** ceases business: **1970s.**
*First Designer:* Celebrated illustrator: Benjamin Rabier.
*Trademark/Identification:* Embossed metal button and paper tag in left ear.
*Characteristics:* First bears are golden mohair with shoe-button eyes, bat-shaped nose, down turned mouth, four claws; as company matures, red, white and blue colors are introduced; now three claws; some jointed externally with wire; luxury models employ glass eyes, felt pads with four claws; bears have large, pear-shaped bodies; during the Second World War, company makes flannelette bears with button eyes; during the 50s, firm creates new range of bears using a soft molded vinyl head, mask or muzzle.

Pintel. Bear. Circa 1930. 12in (32cm); white mohair; glass eyes; f.j.; e.s. metal tag affixed to chest.
CONDITION: Fair.
**PRICE:** $1,200-$1,700.
*Courtesy Puppenhausmuseum, Basel.*

Pintel. Bear. Circa 1910. 14in (36cm); gold mohair; shoe-button eyes; f.j.; e.s. metal tag affixed to chest.
CONDITION: Fair.
**PRICE:** $1,200-$1,700.
*Courtesy Puppenhausmuseum, Basel.*

Right:
F.A.D.A.P. Bear. Circa 1925. 18in (46cm); white mohair; shoe-button eyes; f.j.; e.s. label in ear.
CONDITION: Good.
**PRICE:** $1,700-$2,200.
*Courtesy Puppenhausmuseum, Basel.*

Far Right:
F.A.D.A.P. Bear. Circa 1925. 22in (57cm); beige mohair; shoe-button eyes; f.j.; e.s. button in ear.
CONDITION: Fair.
**PRICE:** $700-$1,000.
*Courtesy Puppenhausmuseum, Basel.*

Roullett et Decamps. Mechanical (Key Wound) Bears. Circa 1900.
(Left) Bear. 16in (41cm); brown fur; wooden paws and feet; shoe-button
eyes. Head moves and arm rings bell.
CONDITION: Excellent.
**PRICE:** $2,000-$3,000.
(Right) Polar Bear. 18in (45cm); white mohair; glass eyes. Open and
closes mouth as if breathing and nods head.
CONDITION: Excellent.
**PRICE:** $3,500-$5,000.
*Courtesy Helen Sieverling.*

Roullett et Decamps. Mechanical (Key Wound) Bears. Circa 1900.
(Left) Drinking Koala. 15in (38cm); dark brown and white fur; glass
eyes. Koala pours from a bottle into cup and drinks.
CONDITION: Excellent.
**PRICE:** $1,500-$2,000.
(Right) Drinking Polar Bear. 14in (36cm); white fur; glass eyes. Pours
from bottle, raises cup to drink. R.D. on key.
CONDITION: Excellent.
**PRICE:** $2,000-$3,000.
*Courtesy Helen Sieverling.*

Murcy France. Bear. Circa 1940. 22in (56cm); yellow
mohair; glass eyes; f.j.; e.s.; button in ear.
CONDITION: Fair.
**PRICE:** $700-$1,000.
*Courtesy Puppenhausmuseum, Basel.*

### Roullet et Decamps
(France)
*Important Milestones:* Company
formed: **19th century;** catalog with
variety of mechanical toy animals
produced: **1911.**
*Founders:* Jean Roullet and Ernest
Decamps.
*Trademark/Identification:* RD on key.
*Characteristics:* Real fur key-wind
mechanical bears and animals.

### Miscellaneous French Manufactured Bears

Left:
J.R.M. Massy. Bear. Circa 1950.
5in (14cm); beige artificial plush; red
mohair lined ears; red glass eyes; f.j.;
e.s.; heart-shaped label.
CONDITION: Mint.
**PRICE:** $100-$200.
*Courtesy Puppenhausmuseum, Basel.*

Steevans. Bear. Circa 1918. 12in (30cm); raspberry colored mohair; shoe-button eyes; f.j.; e.s.; bell in tummy; metal tag in ear.
CONDITION: Fair.
**PRICE:** $800-$1,000.
*Courtesy Puppenhausmuseum, Basel.*

Fleischmann Bloedel. Bear. Circa 1920. 28in (70cm); light brown mohair; shoe-button eyes; f.j.; e.s.; metal tag.
CONDITION: Very Good.
**PRICE:** $2,000-$2,700.
*Courtesy Puppenhausmuseum, Basel.*

Lias. ***Teddy Baby***. Circa 1960. 24in (60cm); long wavy beige artificial plush; white silk plush inset snout; felt-lined open mouth; glass eyes; f.j.; e.s.; collar with label.
CONDITION: Excellent.
**PRICE:** $500-$700.
*Courtesy Puppenhaus museum, Basel.*

Tara. Bear. Circa 1960. 16in (41cm); yellow mohair; glass eyes; f.j.; e.s.; k.s.; label sewn into foot seam.
CONDITION: Very Good.
**PRICE:** $500-$800.
*Courtesy Puppenhausmuseum, Basel.*

# Chapter Six
# German Bears and Friends

Germany is rich in the heritage of creating dolls and plush animals. The "Garden of Eden" for these special toys is Sonneberg, in the southern hills of the state of Thuringia. Except for Steiff, a preponderance of German teddy bear manufacturers are somehow linked to this lovely area. A large number of German families produced incredibly high quality teddy bears from cottage industries based in their homes during the early 1920s. Of those that survived World War II, many continue in business to this day.

**Anker Plüschspielwarenfabrik GmbH**
(München-Pasing, Germany)
*Important Milestones:* Founded: **c.1954;** firm buys stuffed-toy company owned by son of Johann Hermann known as J. Hermann Nachf. Inf. Artur Hermann: **1954;** makes plush glove puppets and animals: **early 1960s;** unsuccessful collaboration with Hegi (part of Schuco): **1976;** ceases business: **1977.**
*Founder:* Ernst Bäumler.
*Trademark/Identification:* Bear holding anchor (1955); anchor superimposed on lion (1957); hang tags.
*Characteristics:* Fully-jointed traditional style and non-jointed novelty mohair bears with open and closed mouths. Co-founder Gisela Diehl had no function herself but association allowed husband, a painter named Hermann Diehl to become designer; popular creations included laughing donkey *"Mufti"*, range of traditional mohair and Dralon teddy bears, standing bears with chains through noses; open mouth *Zotty*-style bears and *"Drolly"*, a grotesque short-legged bear with large paws and "Puck" the dancing bear.

Anker Bear. Circa 1960. 18in (46cm); short beige mohair; glass eyes; f.j.; e.s. C.T.
CONDITION: Mint.
**PRICE:** $350-$400.
*Courtesy Kay and Wayne Jensen.*

Anker Terrier. Circa 1955. 8in (20cm) tall; white, brown and black mohair; n.j. legs; swivel head; e.s. Paper/Foil tag reads: "Anker Pluschtiere Aus Muchen."
CONDITION: Excellent.
**PRICE:** $100-125.
*Courtesy Nancy Drabek.*

(Left) Anker. Bear. Circa 1960. 11in (28cm); light brown draylon; inset beige synthetic plush snout; glass eyes; f.j. e.s; Anker medallion
CONDITION: Fair.
**PRICE:** $50-$75.
(Right) Anker Donkey. Circa 1960. 8in (20cm); gray mohair; glass eyes; open felt-lined mouth; n.j.; e.s.; Anker medallion.
CONDITION: Mint.
**PRICE:** $50-$75.
*Courtesy Renee Koch.*

### Gebrüder Bing
(Nuremberg, Germany)

*Important Milestones:* Founded: **1863;** Adolph Bing leaves company, brother Ignaz is chairman: **1895;** starts producing toys: **1907;** produces teddy bears in dark brown, gold and white; employs 3,000 workers: **1908;** legal battle with Steiff over "button in ear": **1909;** lawsuit with Steiff over somersaulting bear: **1911-1915;** bears with clockwork mechanism: **1909;** Heinrich Müller joins firm: **1909-12;** Ignaz Bing dies: **1918;** Stephen Bing (Ignaz' son) takes over as director general, name changes to Bing Werke: **1919;** firm goes into receivership, departments sold off: **1932.**

*Founders:* Ignaz and Adolf Bing.

*Trademark/Identification:* Initially used metal button affixed to right ear or under arm with initials G.B.W. (1907-1908); Steiff objected to Bing advertising its trademark words "Button in Ear", Bing changes to a metal label (flag) with printed GBN in diamond (1910); later metal mark (painted orange or green with black lettering) with BW (Bing Werke [Bing Works]) with either "Made in Bavaria" or "Made in Germany" affixed to arm or body (1920s).

*Characteristics:* Early bears are similar to Steiff with shoe button eyes; changed design c. 1920 to wide head with glass eyes; long arms, large oval feet; long snout with distinctive nose stitching and broad smile; long, wavy mohair; mechanical bears' small features mainly covered with short beige or brown mohair; many dressed in colorful felt and silk outfits; "Acro" bears turned somersaults and hung on trapeze.

Bing. Mechanical. Bear with ball. Circa 1912. 8in (20cm); brown mohair; shoe-button eyes; f.j.; e.s.; when wound with key bear turns around with ball; original cardboard box.
CONDITION: Excellent.
**PRICE:** $6,000-$8,000.
*Courtesy Puppenhausmuseum, Basel.*

Bing. Skating Bear. Circa 1912. 9in (23cm); short cinnamon mohair; shoe-button eyes; f.j.; e.s.; Key wind mechanism activates skating action; metal orange/black tag reads: "BW, Made in Bavaria."; felt outfit.
CONDITION: Very Good.
**PRICE:** $4,000-$4,500.
*Courtesy Deborah and Donald Ratliff.*

Bing. Walking Bear. Circa 1912. 8in (20cm); short brown mohair; shoe-button eyes; f.j.; e.s.; Bear rocks back and forth when wound with key.
CONDITION: Very Good.
**PRICE:** $4,500-$6,000.
*Courtesy Puppenhausmuseum, Basel.*

Bing. Tumbling Bear. Circa 1912. 10in (25cm); short gold mohair; felt outfit; shoe-button eyes; f.j.; e.s.; turns somersaults when the arms are wound.
CONDITION: Excellent.
**PRICE:** $4,000-$5,000.
*Courtesy Puppenhausmuseum, Basel.*

Bing. Mechanical Head. Bear. Circa 1910. 11-1/2in (30cm); light brown mohair; shoe-button eyes; f.j.; e.s.; head turns when wound with key. Button on side 'GBN.' CONDITION: Good.
PRICE: $4,700-$5,300.
*Courtesy Puppenhausmuseum, Basel.*

Bing. (Left) Monkey. Circa 1908. 7in (18cm); short golden brown mohair; beige felt face, hands and feet; shoe-button eyes; f.j.; e.s.; metal button incised "DRP/DRGM" affixed to side of body; metal tag in ear marked: "GBN"; key wind mechanism activates jumping action.
CONDITION: Mint.
PRICE: $500-$700.
(Center) "Acro Bear." Circa 1909. 8in (20cm); short cinnamon mohair; shoe-button eyes; f.j.; e.s.; metal button marked "DRP/DRGM" affixed to side of body and metal tag in ear marked "GBN."
CONDITION: Mint.
PRICE: $2,500-$3,000.
(Right) Bear. Circa 1912. 13in (33cm); honey-colored medium length mohair; shoe-button eyes; f.j.; e.s.; metal button marked: DRP/DRGM affixed to side of body.
CONDITION: Excellent.
PRICE: $3,000-$3,500.
Child's record player. Circa 1900.
CONDITION: Mint.
PRICE: $750-$850.
*Courtesy Jim and Eleanor Chipman.*

Bing. Bears. (Back) Circa 1920. 15in (38cm); golden mohair; glass eyes; f.j.; e.s.
CONDITION: Good.
PRICE: Approximately $1,600.
(Center) Circa 1920. 28in (71cm); beige mohair tipped with black (faded); glass eyes; f.j.; e.s.
CONDITION: Good.
PRICE: Approximately $2,000.
(Front) Circa 1920. 14in (35cm); golden brown mohair; glass eyes; f.j.; e.s.
CONDITION: Good.
PRICE: Approximately $1,200. Sold at Christie's South Kensington 1998 auction for the approximate prices printed.
*Courtesy Christie's.*

Right:
Bing. Bear. Circa 1920. 18in (46cm); long wavy grayish beige mohair; glass eyes; dark brown stitched nose, mouth and claws; f.j.; e.s.; red/black metal Bing tag on right arm.
CONDITION: Excellent.
PRICE: $5,000-$6,000.
*Courtesy Deborah and Donald Ratliff.*

Bing. Bear. Circa 1920. 24in (61cm); pale gold long wavy mohair; glass eyes; f.j.; e.s.
CONDITION: Excellent.
**PRICE:** $6,000-$8,000.
*Courtesy David Douglas.*

Bing. Bear. Circa 1920. 32in (81cm); long wavy white mohair; glass eyes; rust embroidered nose, mouth and claws; f.j.; e.s. Impressive bear with wonderful facial expression, full of character.
CONDITION: Excellent.
**PRICE:** $10,000-up.
*Photograph courtesy Horst Poestgens Auctioneer, Germany.*

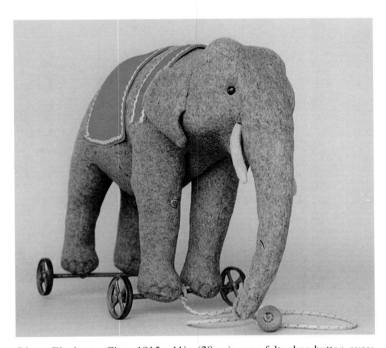

Bing. Elephant. Circa 1915. 11in (28cm); gray felt; shoe-button eyes; n.j.; e.s.; metal frame and wheels; yellow/black "BW" metal tag affixed to right front leg.
CONDITION: Mint.
**PRICE:** $1,500-$2,000.
*Courtesy Deborah and Donald Ratliff.*

Bing. St. Bernard dog on wheels. Circa 1920. 8-1/2in (24cm) tall; off-white and light brown mohair; glass eyes; n.j.; e.s.; Bing's red metal tag affixed to leg; metal frame and wheels.
CONDITION: Excellent.
**PRICE:** $750-$1,000.
*Courtesy Nancy Drabek.*

Clemens. Bear. Circa 1950. 16in (41cm); beige mohair; glass eyes; f.j.; e.s.; metal hang tag.
CONDITION: Excellent.
**PRICE:** $300-$350.

Above:
Group of Clemens Bears. Circa 1950. Sizes range from 9in (23cm) - 20in (51cm); various shades and types of mohair; glass eyes; f.j.; e.s. Larger bears have short mohair inset snouts. Note the red felt lined open mouths, a popular 1950s design.
CONDITION: Excellent.
**PRICE:** $125-$400 (each).
*Photograph courtesy Horst Poestgens Auctioneer, Germany.*

### Hans Clemens
(Kirchardt/Baden, Germany)
*Important Milestones:* Founded: **1947;** Clemens registers for Toy Fair: **1952;** Peter Clemens joins company: **1953;** Peter takes over management: **1983**.
*Founder:* Hans Clemens.
*Trademark/Identification:* Paper pendant: 1949-1955; triangular metal chest tag 1952-57; wooden triangular red tag: 1960; later metal triangular tag reintroduced.
*Characteristics*: Traditional-style bears.

Clemens. Bear. Circa 1950; 4in (9cm); white mohair; glass eyes; f.j.; e.s.; U.S. Zone Germany tag under arm.
CONDITION: Very Good.
**PRICE:** $100-$300.
*Courtesy Puppenhausmuseum, Basel.*

Clemens. Panda. Circa 1950; 8-½in (21cm); black and white mohair; glass eyes; pink felt lined open mouth; f.j.; e.s.; Clemens tag.
CONDITION: Excellent.
**PRICE:** $500-$700.
*Courtesy Barbara Lauver.*

## Eduard Crämer
### (Schalkau, Germany)

*Important Milestones:* New founding: **1896;** Hermann Crämer joins company: **1901;** machines brought in: **1905;** limited partnership created by Eduard and Hermann Crämer and sons in-law Walter Macheleidt and Heinrich Löhr: **c. 1920;** most products shipped to England and America: **1928;** Eduard Crämer dies: **1945;** Hermann Crämer leaves company: **1952;** Crämer's descendants made license agreement with Schildköt-Puppen u. Spielwaren GmbH to manufacture the complete Crämer line and to bring new editions of former plush items; today, limited editions of the old-designed EDUCA-teddy bears made by Raby, Rauenstiner Spielzeug GmbH.

*Founder:* Eduard Crämer (took over father-in-law's toy factory).

*Trademark/Identification:* "EDUCA" established in 1915; "Eduard Crämer above the word Schalkau appears in banner above triangle in 1920s; letters E / C used prior to 1928; word "Educa" in script over words "Qualitäts-Marke" appear with drawing of monkey centered in top corner of modified triangle c. 1930; keyhole design with "Qualitäts-Marke" on top of "EDUCA" which is placed above Made in Germany during the 1930s;

*Characteristics:* "Heart shaped" facial insert, with short shaved mohair nose; open (felt-lined) and closed mouths; closed mouths may have small embroidered, red tongue; big feet; voice box and mechanical musical devices from 18in (46cm) and up; glass eyes; wood-wool and kapok fillings; walking animals with moving mechanisms.

Right:
Eduard Crämer. Bear. Circa 1930. 28in (70cm); cream colored long wavy mohair tipped with brown; glass eyes; f.j.; e.s.; tag on chest.
CONDITION: Mint.
**PRICE:** $16,000-up.
*Courtesy Puppenhausmuseum, Basel.*

Right:
Eduard Crämer. Bear. Circa 1930. 20in (51cm); long white wavy mohair; short mohair inset shield-shaped face; felt lined open mouth with pink felt tongue; f.j.; e.s.
CONDITION: Excellent.
**PRICE:** $3,500-up.
*Courtesy David Douglas.*

Far Right:
Eduard Crämer. Bear. Circa 1930. 20in (51cm); blonde mohair; glass eyes; f.j.; e.s.
CONDITION: Excellent.
**PRICE:** $3,500-up.
*Courtesy Puppenhausmuseum, Basel.*

Eduard Crämer. Bear. Circa 1930. 24in (61cm); long blonde mohair; short mohair inset shield-shaped face; pink embroidered mouth and tongue; f.j.; e.s.
CONDITION: Mint.
**PRICE:** $3,800-up.
*Courtesy David Douglas.*

Eduard Crämer. *Bearkin.* Circa 1930. 8in (20cm); brown tipped blonde mohair; short mohair snout; red stitched mouth and tongue; glass eyes; f.j.; e.s.; felt jacket and pants. Manufactured for Toy Shop; FAO Schwarz.
CONDITION: Excellent.
**PRICE:** $2,700-up.
*Courtesy Puppenhausmuseum, Basel.*

Wind Up Mother and Baby Bear (probably Eduard Crämer). Circa 1930. 12in (31cm); gold mohair; short mohair inset shield-shaped face; glass eyes; mechanical mechanism encased in body. Bear rolls sideways on wheels when key is wound in back of bear.
CONDITION: Excellent.
**PRICE:** $2,900-up.
*Courtesy David Douglas.*

Eduard Crämer. Bears. (Left to right) 7in (18cm); blonde mohair; short mohair inset heart-shaped face; red stitched mouth and tongue; glass eyes; f.j.; e.s.
CONDITION: Good.
**PRICE:** $1,000-up.
17in (43cm); brown tipped blonde mohair; short beige mohair inset heart-shaped face; brown stitched nose, mouth and claws; glass eyes; f.j.; e.s.
CONDITION: Good.
**PRICE:** $2,500-up.
8in (20cm); cinnamon mohair; short beige mohair inset heart-shaped face; red stitched mouth and tongue; short beige mohair tops to feet; glass eyes; f.j.; e.s.
CONDITION: Good.
**PRICE:** $1,200-up.
*Courtesy Mimi Hiscox.*

Eduard Crämer. Rabbit. Circa 1930. 8in (20cm); beige and tan fabric; outfit an integral part of the body; glass eyes; f.j.; e.s.
CONDITION: Mint.
**PRICE:** $750-$950.
*Courtesy David Douglas.*

Eduard Crämer. Bear. Circa 1930. 15in (38cm); green-tipped blonde mohair; glass eyes; f.j.; e.s.; Rare color.
CONDITION: Excellent.
**PRICE:** $8,000-$10,000.
*Courtesy Puppenhausmuseum, Basel.*

Eduard Crämer. Dachshund Dog. Circa 1930. 10in (25cm); black and tan mohair; glass eyes; f.j.; e.s.
CONDITION: Mint.
**PRICE:** $650-$800.
*Courtesy David Douglas.*

### Richard Diem

(Sonneberg, Germany)

*Important Milestones:* Founded: **1896;** daughter-in-law, Lise-Lotte Diem, becomes owner: **1953.**

*Founder:* Richard Diem.

*Trademark/Identification:* Circular seal with words "Diem Stoff Spiel Zeug"; outer ring includes words Est. 1896.

*Characteristics:* Very good quality; excellent plush; well-embroidered noses; big glass eyes; inset short mohair snout, pads are short plush; used cardboard to reinforce soles.

### Fechter Co.

(Neustadt near Coburg, Germany)

*Important Milestones:* Founded: **1939;** exhibits Vienna Toy Fair: **1950;** Berta Bohn dies: **1973;** business discontinues: **1979;** antique dealer buys Fechter warehouse stock and imports to U.S.: **1984;** Wilhelm Fechter dies: **1985.**

*Founders:* Wilhelm Fechter and Berta Bohn.

*Trademark/Identification:* Cloth label stitched in edge of ear seam.

*Characteristics:* Shield-shaped, embroidered nose with downward crescent at top; large, erect ears with contrasting lining; red felt tongue in open mouth versions.

Diem Bear. Circa 1950. 14in (36cm); cinnamon-tipped blonde mohair; short blonde mohair inset snout and paw pads; glass eyes; f.j.; e.s. Bears of this design were previously attributed to Schreyer and Co.
CONDITION: Excellent.
**PRICE:** $800-$1,000.
*Courtesy David Douglas.*

Fechter Bear. Circa 1960. 16in (41cm); gold mohair; short mohair inset snout, felt lined open mouth; glass eyes; f.j.; e.s. Fechter cloth label sewn into ear.
CONDITION: Excellent.
**PRICE:** $400-$500.
*Courtesy Kay and Wayne Jensen.*

Group of Diem Bears. Circa 1950. (Left to Right) 25in (64cm); golden yellow mohair; 24in (61cm); gray mohair; 20in (51cm); golden yellow mohair; 24in (61cm); blonde mohair. All bears have inset short mohair snouts; short mohair paw pads (soles of feet reinforced with cardboard); black embroidered noses (some have two stitches extended down each side of vertically stitched nose); f.j.; e.s. Until recently these bears were attributed to Schreyer & Co. (Schuco).
CONDITION: Very Good.
**PRICE:** $800-$1200 (each).
*Photograph Courtesy Horst Poestgens, Auctioneer, Germany.*

Fechter. (Left to Right) Bear. Circa 1970. 13in (33cm); grayish beige mohair; white mohair snout, ears, tops of paws and feet (cuffs); felt-lined open mouth; glass eyes; f.j.; e.s.; Fechter cloth tag sewn onto ear.
CONDITION: Excellent.
**PRICE:** $350-$450.
Bear. Circa 1970. 10in (25cm); mohair; glass eyes; f.j.; e.s.; Fechter cloth tag sewn onto ear.
CONDITION: Excellent.
**PRICE:** $200-$300.
Cat. Circa 1970. 12in (31cm); rusty brown mohair; white mohair inset snout, paws and feet (cuffs); Fechter tag sewn into ear.
CONDITION: Excellent.
**PRICE:** $200-$250.

## Grisly Spielwaren GmbH & Co. KG
### (Rheinphalz, Germany)

*Important Milestones:* Founded: **1954;** metal button trademark replaced by paper tag: **1964;** founder dies, son Hans-Georg and daughter Hannelore Wirth take over: **1980;** Hans-Georg Unfrecht dies: **1994;** management transferred to Daniela Eibofner and Olver Lederle: **1995.**
*Founder:* Karl Theodor and Luise Unfricht.
*Trademark/Identification:* Needle and thread superimposed upon grizzly (German: "Grisly"); first appears on small black metal button inside gold quadrangle with name printed in red, a bear on all-fours is below.
*Characteristics:* Oversized head; traditional-style bears.

## Bernard Hermann/Gebrüder Hermann KG
### (Hirschaid, Germany)

*Important Milestones:* Founded: **1912;** Small trading firm "Be-Ha" founded in Sonneberg: **post WWI;** founders' sons, Hellmut, Artur, Werner and Horst help in business: **1930s;** brothers go into military, Horst dies: **WWII;** production transferred, company reforms as Gebrüder Hermann: **1948;** Bernard dies, his three sons take over management of company, Artur becomes sales administration manager, Werner handles production/design and Hellmut directs operations: **1959;** Hellmut retires: **1980;** limited edition bears produced: **1984;** Hellmut dies, eventually brothers' daughters manage firm: **1985;** Artur dies: **1990;** company named Teddy-Hermann GmbH: **1994;** daughters of the three brothers Marion Mehling and Margit Drolshagen manage the firm and Traudi Mischer is the designer.
*Founder:* Bernard Hermann (1912); Hellmut, Artur, and Horst Hermann (1948).
*Trademark/Identification:* Sphere with toy dog, letters "BEHA" inside circle (1920s); circle with words: BE HA QUALITY GERMANY (1930s); circle with "Teddy" in script surrounded by words "Marke BE HA bürgt (1940s); circle with "Teddy" in script (silver/green pendant) (1950s/60s); circle with HERMANN® ORIGINAL "Teddy" in (red plastic/white writing) script (present time).
*Characteristics:* In 1920s, teddy bears were 4in(10cm) to 31in(80cm) with press voices or growlers, disk jointing; most early bears have short mohair and shaved mohair inset plush muzzle; early bears displayed large, round head and ears with narrow limbs; upturned paws, three black claw stitches are characteristics of early Hermann bears; later bears made in the same tradition; include plush toys with and without clockwork mechanisms; still use funnel to hand-stuff bears with excelisior; hand-stitched noses.

Grisly. Bear. Circa 1960. 22in (56cm); beige mohair; glass eyes; f.j.; k.s.; paper tag reads: "Grisly/ Made in Western Germany."
CONDITION: Mint.
**PRICE:** $400-$500.
*Courtesy Kay and Wayne Jensen.*

Grisly. Rabbit. Circa 1960. 15in (38cm); gold mohair; short mohair face and paw pads, felt lined open mouth; wired ears; f.j.; e.s. and s.s. Grisly metal button on chest.
CONDITION: Mint.
**PRICE:** $150-$175.
*Private Collection.*

Bernhard Hermann. Bear. ***Teddy Baby***. Circa 1930. 12in (30cm); maize wool plush; pink felt tongue; glass crossed eyes; f.j.; wired arms; e.s.; original baby's pacifier.
CONDITION: Good.
**PRICE:** $1,000-$1,700.
*Courtesy Puppenhausmuseum, Basel.*

A selection of early original Hermann Bears.
CONDITION: Good.
**PRICE:** $300-$800 each.
*Courtesy Hermann Teddy Original.*

Hermann Bear. Circa 1940. 20in (50cm); black tipped white mohair; short beige mohair snout and ear linings; glass eyes; f.j.; e.s. Hermann chest tag.
CONDITION: Excellent.
**PRICE:** $600-up.
*Courtesy Hermann Teddy Original.*

Left:
Hermann Teddy Original. 1980. (Center and Right) 12in-23in (31cm-59cm); short beige mohair; amber plastic safety eyes; f.j.; s.s. (stuffed firm). (Right) 11in (28cm); brown tipped blonde mohair; amber plastic safety eyes; f.j. s.s. (stuffed firmly). Hang tag reads: "HERMANN-Teddy Original. MADE IN WEST GERMANY."
CONDITION: Mint.
**PRICE:** $85-$200 each.
*Courtesy Micki Beston.*

### Hermann-Spielwaren GmbH
(Cortendorf, Germany)

*Important Milestones:* Founded: **1920;** moves to Sonneberg and trades as Max Hermann: **1923;** first Max Hermann Teddy Bear Catalog appears: c. **1920:** participates in Sonneberg toy exhibit: **1936;** first peace time teddy bears produced, exhibited at Leipzig Fair: **1947;** name changed to Max Hermann & Sohn: **1948;** Max Hermann dies, son Rolf Hermann leads business with wife Dora-Margot responsible for design: **1955;** animals now stuffed with Dralon-woven fur: **1958;** swing tag introduced: **1968;** becomes private limited company: **1979;** limited editions introduced, reunification of Germany allows family to research archives in Sonneberg, replicas of old designs made: **1990;** Rolf Hermann dies, daughter Dr. Ulla Hermann and son Martin continue business: **1995.**
*Founder:* Max Hermann.
*Trademark/Identification:* "Maheso" with bear and dog logo in green triangle (1933-1940s); metal triangular labels (1950s); hard cardboard swing tags (1960s); triangle logo set in circle 1968).
*Characteristics:* Early bears used shorter mohair; after WWII, limbs of Hermann bears are shorter; lower priced bears have rigid heads with arms and legs connected by wire; better versions are fully jointed.

### Heunec Plusch Spielwaren Fabrick KG
(Neustadt near Coburg, Germany)

*Important Milestones:* Established: **1891;** moves to West Germany and changes name: **c. 1947;** becomes manufacturer of plush toys: **1972.**
*Founder:* Hugo Heubach; newly established: Otto Eichhorn.
*Trademark/Identification:* Teddy bear encircled with "HEUNEC MOHAIR PLÜSCH GERMANY".
*Characteristics:* Talking bear says, "I am the talking bear," short plush fur; wood-wool stuffing, ring on back starts voice.

Group of Hermann Bears. Circa 1950. (Back Left to Right) Max Hermann. (triangle metal green/gold chest tag). 16in (40cm). Hermann 23in (58cm). Max Hermann (triangle metal green/gold chest tag) 17in (43cm). (Front center) Hermann 19in (48cm). All bears are beige-tipped brown mohair; inset short beige mohair snouts; glass eyes; f.j.; e.s.; Hermann Bears on Tricycles. Circa 1960. 10in (25cm) tall.
CONDITION: Excellent.
**PRICE:** $200-$600 each.
*Photograph courtesy Horst Poestgens, Auctioneer, Germany.*

Max Hermann and Son (Maheso). *Felix the Cat.* 1950. 8in (20cm); black mohair; white mohair face; black button eyes and nose; f.j.; e.s. Max Hermann and Son hang tag.
CONDITION: Mint.
**PRICE:** $700-$800.
*Courtesy David Douglas.*

Heunec. Talking Bear. Circa 1960. 18-1/2in (47cm); gold mohair; glass eyes; f.j.; e.s.; talks a few sentences when cord is pulled.
CONDITION: Mint.
**PRICE:** $600-$900.
*Courtesy Puppenhausmuseum, Basel.*

## Petz

(Neustadt near Coburg, Germany)

*Important Milestones:* Founded: **1859**; produced teddy bears and animals: **1921**; teddy bear school is hit of Nuremberg Toy Fair: **1949**; rabbit school added to line: **1950**; founder dies, widow (Ernestine) and children Charlotte and Gerhard) take over: **1955**; closed: **1967**.

*Founder:* Anton Kiesewetter.

*Trademark/Identification:* Reclining teddy bear holds sign with intertwined lines in form of cross with the name "PETZ;" protected white glass button with red letters.

*Characteristics:* All eyes were inserted with yarn, firmly attached with special glue; all jointed with discs; both dense, short-hair plush and shaggy plush used; blond color particularly characteristic.

Petz. Bear. Circa 1940. 12-1/2in (32cm); brown artificial silk; glass eyes; f.j.; e.s.; Petz glass button affixed to chest.
CONDITION: Good.
**PRICE:** $600-$800.
*Courtesy Puppenhausmuseum, Basel.*

Petz. Bear. Circa 1930. 24in (60cm); brown-tipped blonde mohair; glass eyes; f.j.; e.s.; Petz glass button affixed to chest.
CONDITION: Good.
**PRICE:** $1000-$1,500.
*Courtesy Puppenhausmuseum, Basel.*

Left:
Petz. Bear. Circa 1950. 20in (51cm) long; gold mohair; white wool plush inset snout and tops of feet; orange/yellow glass eyes; f.j.; e.s.; cardboard lined footpads.
CONDITION: Good.
PRICE: $700-$1,000.
*Courtesy Horst Poestgens, Auctioneer, Germany.*

Right:
Petz. Bear. Circa 1950. 28in (71cm); yellow mohair; brown tipped dual plush mohair; short blonde mohair inset snout; glass eyes; f.j.; e.s.; Petz cloth tag sewn into under arm seam.
CONDITION: Excellent.
**PRICE:** $800-$1,200.
*Courtesy Horst Poestgens, Auctioneer, Germany.*

### Josef Pitrmann "JoPi"
(Nuremberg, Germany)

*Important Milestones:* Founded: **1910;** legally protected Trademark: **1921;** founder dies, wife Maria and daughter Hilde take over: **1938;** last exhibited at Nuremberg Toy Fair: **1959**.

*Founder:* Josef Pitrmann.

*Trademark/Identification:* "JoPi" on hemisphere with Nuremberg in background and teddy bear holding a Christmas tree at top (1922); "JoPi" with horse, rider and whip (mid-1920); "JoPi" with stylized horse, rider and whip (1930s).

*Characteristics:* Large glass eyes; large cupped ears placed high on head; long silky mohair; many brightly colored dual plush; musical devices encased in body or head.

Right:
Jopi (Josef Pitrmann). Bear. Circa 1930. 14in (36cm); pale gold mohair; large glass eyes; large ears; f.j.; e.s.; cardboard/foil "*Jopi*" hang tag.
CONDITION: Mint.
**PRICE:** $3,000-up.
*Courtesy David Douglas.*

Jopi (Josef Pitrmann). Musical Bear. Circa 1930. 16in (41cm); long wavy thick blonde mohair; large glass eyes; f.j.; e.s.; squeeze-type music box is encased in tummy. Oversized head and ears are characteristics of *Jopi.*
CONDITION: Excellent.
**PRICE:** $3,500-up.
*Courtesy David Douglas.*

Right:
Jopi (Josef Pitrmann). Musical Bear. Circa 1930. 16in (40cm); pink mohair; glass eyes; f.j.; e.s.; squeeze-type music box is encased in tummy. Rare color.
CONDITION: Good.
**PRICE:** $3,500-up.
*Courtesy Puppenhausmuseum, Basel.*

Jopi (Josef Pitrmann). Bear. Circa 1930. 17in (43cm); reddish brown tipped blonde mohair; glass "googlie" (each eye glancing to center) eyes; f.j.; e.s.
CONDITION: Excellent.
**PRICE:** $3,500-up.
*Courtesy Puppenhausmuseum, Basel.*

Jopi (Josef Pitrmann). Musical Bear. Circa 1920. 22in (56cm); white tipped with dark brown mohair; large glass eyes; f.j.; e.s.; squeeze-type music box encased in tummy.
CONDITION: Excellent.
Sold at Christie's South Kensington 1998 auction for approximately $15,300.
*Courtesy Christie's.*

Jopi (Josef Pitrmann). Baby Bear. Circa 1930. 8in (20cm); blonde wool plush; large glass eyes; f.j.; downturned paws; e.s.; red stitch outlines black stitched nose; red stitched mouth; tiny red felt tongue.
CONDITION: Excellent.
**PRICE:** $1,000-$1,200.
*Courtesy David Douglas.*

### Schreyer & Co. / Schuco
(Nuremberg, Germany)

*Important Milestones:* Founded: **1912;** ad for "Tipp-Tapp-Tiere" wheeled bears appears: **1913;** Adolph Kahn becomes partner: **1919;** "Schuco" abbreviation adopted as trademark, "Piccolo", "Acrobato" and yes-no bears introduced: **1921;** turning and nodding movement introduced: **1922;** to escape Hitler, Kahn emigrates to England and then USA: **1936;** Kahn and son establish Schuco Toy Co. in U.S.: **1947;** Müller dies, son takes over business with manager Alexander Girz : **1958;** "Trickey-Bären" sold: **1952;** "Janus-bear" sold: **1954;** firm sells toys (including "bigo-bello" speaking bears) produced by Herta Girz & Co. ("Hegi" logo):**1960s-70s;** Hegi and Anker collaborate with Schuco selling toys, company sold to Dunbee-Combex Marx: **1976;** auction held, Karl Bär acquires tools to make miniature bears.

*Founders:* Heinrich Müller and Heinrich Schreyer.

*Trademark/Identification:* Hang tag, tumbling man clasping his feet; in 1921, "Schuco" officially added to logo.

*Characteristics:* Mechanical bears close in design to Gebrüder Bing; small facial features, head, ears, slightly upturned snout, slim body, narrow straight arms with slightly curved paws, round small feet, shoe-button and eyes cut like diamonds to sparkle (1925); non-mechanical bears have wide head, large ears, deep and closely set eyes are frequently clear; later muzzles and paw pads were sheared; miniature bears were often made of tin-plate covered with mohair, some made with felt integral clothes.

Schuco. Automaton Bear. Circa 1920. 10in (25cm); gold mohair; shoe-button eyes; f.j.; e.s.; mechanical bear; walks forward and backward with key; circles to right or left; original box.
CONDITION: Excellent.
**PRICE:** $4,000-$5,000.
*Courtesy Puppenhausmuseum, Basel.*

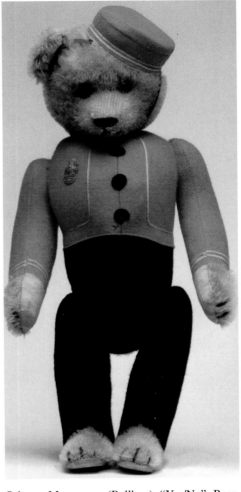

Schuco Messenger (Bellhop) "Yes/No" Bear. Circa 1920/1930. Short gold mohair head; paws and feet; glass eyes; red felt jacket and hat; black felt pants (clothes are an integral part of body); f.j.; e.s.; head nods "yes" or " no" when tail is moved (missing leather message pouch).
CONDITION: Excellent.
**PRICE:** 8in (20cm) $2500-up, 12in (31cm) $3,000-up, 17in (43cm) $4,000-up, 20in (51cm) $5,000-up.
*Photograph courtesy of Puppenhausmuseum, Basel.*

Schuco. Acrobatic Bear. Circa 1920. 10in (25cm); gold mohair; shoe-button eyes; f.j.; e.s.; turns around (somersaults) in circular motion.
CONDITION: Excellent.
**PRICE:** $2,300-$3,000.
*Courtesy Puppenhausmuseum, Basel.*

Schuco. "Yes/No" Bear. Circa 1920s. 12in (30cm); gold short mohair; glass eyes; f.j.; e.s.; head nods "yes" or " no" when tail is moved. CONDITION: Mint.
PRICE: $1,200-$2,000.
*Courtesy Puppenhausmuseum, Basel.*

Above:
Schuco. "Yes/No" Bear. Circa 1920s. 11in (28cm) short gold mohair; shoe-button eyes; f.j.; e.s.; head nods "yes" or " no" when tail is moved; replaced paw pads. CONDITION: Good.
PRICE: $1,200-$2,000.
*Courtesy Puppenhausmuseum, Basel.*

Right:
Schuco. "Yes/No" Bear. Circa 1920s. 11in (27cm); blue tipped white mohair; glass eyes; f.j.; e.s.; head nods "yes" or " no" when tail is moved. Rare color.
CONDITION: Excellent.
PRICE: $7,000-$8,000.
*Courtesy Puppenhausmuseum, Basel.*

Schuco. Bear. Circa 1920s. 5in (12cm); yellowish-green mohair covers metal body; metal eyes; f.j.; metal spectacles.
CONDITION: Good.
PRICE: $700-$1,300.
*Courtesy Puppenhausmuseum, Basel.*

Right:
Schuco. "Yes/No" Bear
Bicycle Lamp. Circa
1930. 5in (13cm); short
gold mohair covers metal
body; tiny black metal
eyes; head nods "yes"
and "no" when tail is
moved up and down and
back and forth.
CONDITION: Excellent.
**PRICE:** $5,000-$5,500.
*Courtesy David Douglas.*

Schuco. Bear on a Scooter. Circa 1930. 5in (12cm); yellow mohair
covers metal body; brown pants are an integral part of body; metal
eyes; f.j.; e.s.; key wind mechanism activates movement.
CONDITION: Good.
**PRICE:** $1,200-$1,800.
*Courtesy Puppenhausmuseum, Basel.*

Right:
Schuco. Tricky "Yes/No" Bear. Circa 1950. Beige mohair; glass eyes;
f.j.; e.s.; head nods "yes" or "no" when tail is moved. Red plastic tag
reads: "Schuco 'Tricky' Patent ANG." Reverse of tag: "D.B. Pat. ang.
IND. Patents pending/ Made in U.S. Zone Germany."
CONDITION: Excellent.
**PRICE:** 8in (20cm) $1,000-up, 12in (31cm) $1,200-up, 17in (43cm)
$2,000-up, 20in (51cm) $2,500-up.

Left:
Schuco. Miniature Bears. (Left to Right) *Janus* (Two Faces). Circa 1950; 3-½in (9cm); short gold mohair covers metal head and body; black metal eyes; f.j.; twisting brass knob at base of body changes faces.
CONDITION: Mint.
**PRICE:** $800-up.
Bear (perfume). Circa 1920. 3-1/2in (9cm); short gold mohair covers metal body; black metal eyes; f.j. Removing head discloses perfume bottle.
CONDITION: Mint.
**PRICE:** $400-up.
Bears (Compact). Circa 1920. 3-1/2in (9cm); short lavender mohair and short red mohair covers metal body; black metal eyes; f.j. Removing head discloses compact.
CONDITION: Excellent.
**PRICE:** $1,200-up.
Not pictured. Miniature Schuco Bear without novelty designs (basic bear).
CONDITION: Excellent.
**PRICE:** $150-$200. Rare colors command higher prices.
Miniature Schuco. *Panda.*
CONDITION: Excellent.
**PRICE:** $250-$350.

Schuco. "Yes/No" Musical Bear. *Tricky.* Circa 1950. 20in (52cm); caramel mohair; glass eyes; f.j.; e.s.; head nods "yes" or "no" when tail is moved; music plays when wound with key; red plastic tag.
CONDITION: Mint.
**PRICE:** $3,000-$3,500.
*Courtesy Puppenhausmuseum, Basel.*

Schuco "Yes/No" Pandas. Circa 1950. 12in (31cm); black and white mohair; glass eyes; f.j.; e.s.; red plastic Schuco tag; head nods "yes" or "no" when tail is moved.
CONDITION: Mint.
**PRICE:** $2,500-up each.
*Courtesy Donna Harrison-West.*

(Left to Right) Schuco. Acrobat Bear. Circa 1950. 5in (13cm); short gold mohair covers metal body; glass eyes; key wind mechanism activates tumbling action.
CONDITION: Excellent.
**PRICE:** $700-$1,000.
Schuco *Rolly* Bear. Circa 1950. 9in (23cm); short beige mohair; glass eyes; f.j.; e.s.
CONDITION: Excellent.
**PRICE:** $1,000-$1,500.
Schuco Acrobat Mouse. Circa 1950. 4in (10cm); gray velveteen covers metal body; key wind mechanism activates tumbling motion.
CONDITION: Excellent.
**PRICE:** $200-$300.
Schuco "Yes/No" Cat. Circa 1950. 8in (20cm); gray mohair; black mohair ears; glass eyes; f.j.; moving tail activates head to nod "Yes" or "No".
CONDITION: Excellent.
**PRICE:** $500-$750.
*Photograph courtesy Horst Poestgens, Auctioneer, Germany.*

Schuco "Yes/No" Baby Bear. Circa 1950. 8in (20cm); beige wool plush; glass "googlie"-type eyes; brown felt lined open mouth; red felt tongue; f.j.; e.s.; felt and cotton outfit; head nods "Yes" or "No" when tail is moved.
CONDITION: Excellent.
**PRICE:** $2,500-$2,800.
*Courtesy David Douglas.*

Schuco "Yes/No" Boy and Girl Bear. Circa 1950. 8in (20cm); beige mohair; glass eyes; f.j.; e.s.; felt and cotton outfit; "Schuco Tricky" tag affixed to body; head nods "Yes" or "No" when tail is moved.
CONDITION: Excellent.
**PRICE:** $1,500-$2,000 each.
*Courtesy David Douglas.*

Schuco. Bigobello Bear. Circa 1950. 20in (50cm); caramel mohair; beige mohair inset snout; felt lined open mouth; glass eyes; f.j.; e.s.;
CONDITION: Excellent.
**PRICE:** $400-$700.
*Courtesy Puppenhausmuseum, Basel.*

(Left) Schuco. *Molly*. Bear. Circa 1950. 13in (33cm); light beige mohair; glass eyes; hard rubber nose; n.j.; foam rubber stuffing; rubber chest tag reads: "Schuco." Molly bears were advertised in Schuco's 1950 catalog as having bodies that "twist and turn amusingly."
CONDITION: Good.
PRICE: $250-$350.
(Right) Schuco. Bear. Circa 1960. 13in (33cm); honey colored mohair; glass eyes; n.j. body; swivel head; cloth label attached to leg reads "Schuco/ Made in Western Germany." Reverse side of label reads: "Bigo Bello, Hegi Production."
CONDITION: Good.
PRICE: $250-$350.

(Right) Schuco. "Yes/No" Monkey. Circa 1927. 12in (13cm); yellow mohair; white mohair beard; beige felt face, ears, paws and feet; glass eyes; f.j.; e.s. head nods "Yes" or "No" when tail is moved.
CONDITION: Excellent.
PRICE: $400-$600.
(Left) Schuco. "Yes/No" Bellhop Monkey. Circa 1926; short brown mohair; beige felt face and paws; red felt jacket and hat; black felt pants (clothes are an integral part of body); glass eyes; f.j.; e.s. Head nods "Yes" or "No" when tail is moved.
CONDITION: Excellent.
PRICE: 8in (20cm) $375-up, 12in (31cm) $475-up, 17in (43cm) $550-up, 20in (51cm) $675-up.
*Photograph courtesy of Mimi Hiscox.*

Left:
(Left) Schuco. Disappearing Monkey. Circa 1920. 3in (8cm); green mohair covers metal head and body; beige flocked face; beige felt paws; glass eyes; f.j. Magic Box.
CONDITION: Mint.
PRICE: $800-$1,000.
(Right) Schuco "Yes/No" Gnome. 1920. 9in (23cm); beige felt face; white mohair hair and beard; glass eyes; felt body; felt clothes; metal spectacles; f.j.; e.s.; Schuco chest tag. Head nods "Yes" or "No" when tail is moved.
CONDITION: Mint.
PRICE: $850-$950.
*Courtesy Mimi Hiscox.*

(Left to Right) Schuco. ***My Darling***. Disappearing Monkey. Circa 1924. 3in (8cm); red mohair covers metal frame; flocked face; beige felt paws. Original magic box.
CONDITION: Mint.
**PRICE:** $800-$1,000.
Schuco "Yes/No" Gnome. Circa 1929. 9in (23cm); red mohair hat; green felt jacket and black felt pants cover metal body; beige flocked face; white mohair beard; glass eyes; f.j.; tiny tag reads: "Made in Germany."
CONDITION: Mint.
**PRICE:** $750-$800.
Schuco Mouse in Car. ***Sonny*** 2005. Circa 1950. 3in x 8in (8cm x 20cm). Mouse; gray felt covers metal head and body; black metal eyes; jointed arms and legs; holding a balloon; riding in a yellow metal car.
CONDITION: Mint.
**PRICE:** $400-$600.
Schuco. Pecking Bird. Circa 1928. 2in (5cm); short mohair covers metal body. Clockwork mechanism concealed in body. When wound with key bird moves in pecking motion.
CONDITION: Mint.
**PRICE:** $150-$295.
*Courtesy Mimi Hiscox.*

(Left) Schuco Dancing Poodle. Circa 1926. 5in (13cm); gray curly wool covers metal head and upper torso; tiny black metal eyes; black metal feet; jointed arms; stationary head; red felt pants; black metal top hat. Clockwork mechanism concealed in body. When wound with key, dog dances in circular motion. (Right) Schuco Monkey Riding-Roller. Circa 1927. 5in (13cm); short cinnamon mohair head; flocked beige face; beige felt paws, red felt jacket; black felt pants covers metal legs and torso; glass eyes; f.j. Riding a clockwork metal scooter.
CONDITION: Excellent.
**PRICE:** $1,000-$1,400 each.
*Courtesy Mimi Hiscox.*

Schuco. ***Three Little Pigs***. Circa 1934. 4-1/2in (11cm); pink felt face and felt outfits cover metal head and bodies. Each Little Pig plays a different instrument. Key wound mechanism activates motion.
CONDITION: Mint.
**PRICE:** $1,500-$1,800 (set).
*Courtesy Mimi Hiscox.*

Schuco. Tricky "Yes/No" Monkey. Circa 1950. Dark brown mohair; white mohair chin; beige felt face and paws; glass eyes; f.j.; e.s. head nods "Yes" or "No" when tail is moved. Red plastic tag reads: "Schuco 'Tricky' Patent ANG." Reverse of Tag: "D.B. Pat. ang. IND. Patents pending/Made in U.S. Zone Germany.
CONDITION: Excellent.
**PRICE:** 8in (20cm) $175-up; 12in (31cm) $250-up; 17in (43cm) $325-up; 20in (51cm) $425-up.
*Photograph Courtesy Kay and Wayne Jensen.*

Schuco. Bears, Animals, Comic Figure and Doll. Circa 1950-1960. Sizes 2-½in (7cm)-7in (18cm).
CONDITION: Mint.
PRICE: $150-$300 each.
*Photograph courtesy Horst Poestgens, Auctioneer, Germany.*

(Back) Schuco. Bendy Animals. Circa 1970. 6in (15cm); mohair heads; wired bendable bodies; glass eyes; original clothes.
CONDITION: Mint.
PRICE: $400-$600 each.
(Front) Steiff Chicks. Circa 1950. Ranging from 1-½in (4cm); yellow wool; glass eyes; metal feet; R.S.B.
CONDITION: Mint.
PRICE: $100-$150.
*Photograph courtesy Horst Poestgens, Auctioneer, Germany.*

Schuco. Bears, Animals and Dolls. (Top row left to right) Bear. 1970. 10in (25cm); beige plush; glass eyes; n.j.; s.s.; Bigo-bellow/Hegi tag.
CONDITION: Mint.
PRICE: $250-$350.
*Tripp-Trapp* Poodle. Circa 1950. 8in (20cm); long black mohair; glass eyes; n.j.; e.s.; metal wheels.
CONDITION: Excellent.
PRICE: $350-$400.
*Parlo-Teddy.* Circa 1970. 16in (41cm); caramel mohair; beige mohair lower face; pink lined felt open mouth; glass eyes; n.j.; s.s.
CONDITION: Mint.
PRICE: $350-$400.
Bear. Circa 1970. 10in (25cm); beige plush; glass eyes; n.j.; s.s.; Bigo-bello/Hegi tag.
CONDITION: Mint.
PRICE: $250-$350.
(Front row left to right) Schuco Bigo-bellow. Doll, Cat, Bear, Wolf and Doll. Circa 1960. 10in (23cm).
CONDITION: Mint.
PRICE: $200-$350 each.
*Photograph courtesy Horst Poestgens, Auctioneer, Germany.*

Schuco. Disney Characters. Circa 1970. All characters are made of mohair with glass eyes; flexible limbs; s.s.; original clothes.
CONDITION: Mint.
PRICE: (Left to right) *Mickey Mouse* $700-up; *Lupo* $800-up; *Pluto* $500-up; *Goofy* $600-up.
*Photograph courtesy Horst Poestgens, Auctioneer, Germany.*

### Margarete Steiff GmbH
(Giengen/Brenz, Germany)

*Important Milestones:* Margarete Steiff opens company to make felt clothes: **1877;** adapts little felt elephant pin cushion, introduces animal toys: **1880;** moves to larger premises: **1889;** registers business as "Felt Toy Company:" **1893;** nephew Richard Steiff joins company: **1897;** experiments with jointed bear design, legendary "55 PB" produced: **1902;** first bear presented at Leipzig Spring Fair: **1903;** Bär 35 PB registered: **1904;** Trademark metal button with embossed elephant and "button in ear" registered: **1904;** factory expands three times, company calls era *Bärenjahre* (Bear Years): Bear 28 PB (jointed with metal rods), available for one year: **1904;** Bear 35 PAB (disc-jointed) introduced: **1905; 1902-08;** company registers as Margarete Steiff GmbH, Margarete Steiff's nephews, Paul, Richard and Franz-Josef are managing directors, 974,000 teddy bears produced: **1907;** conveyor belt system introduced: **c. 1920;** teddy bear "Zotty" placed on market: **1951;** celebrates 50th anniversary with "Jackie" bear: **1953;** teddy bears produced in Dralon: **1971;** returns to classic shape: **1966;** produces first replica, opens museum, publishes account of company's history: **1980;** Steiff club founded: **1992;** "button in the ear" 90th anniversary celebration: **1994;** 150th anniversary of Margarete Steiff: **1997.**
*Founder:* Margarete Steiff.
*Trademark/Identification:* "Button in ear".
*Characteristics:* Probably most sought-after bears; highest quality, appealing tender facial expressions; elongated body features; early bears (prior to 1905) had firm metal rod through body, long arms, curved paws and could stand on all fours; easily identifiable hump.
*Buttons, tags and labels used by Steiff from 1904-Present:* The famous Steiff trademark, a small nickel button embedded in the toy animals left ear was first used in 1904 and officially registered the next year.
Buttons: **1904/05:** Elephant Button. **1904/05:** Blank button (with first stock label); small metal Blank button with two prong attachment. **1905-1948:** Printed (raised) STEIFF button with F underscored on metal button with two-prong attachment. **1948-1950:** Blank blue painted button (grays with age). **C. 1950:** Printed (raised) STEIFF button without F underscored on metal button with two-prong attachment. **1950-c. 1970:** Raised *Steiff* in script on metal button with two prong attachment. **1970-1977:** Incised *Steiff* in script on chrome button, riveted in ear. **C. 1977-1981:** Raised *Steiff* in script on small brass button, riveted in ear. **1980-present:** Brass button (slightly larger in size to earlier buttons) with incised *Steiff* in script; riveted into ear.
Chest Tags: **1926-1928:** White paper circle with metal edge. **1928-1950:** Paper circle with red outer rim, beige center and yellow angular bear's head at bottom. From 1984 reproduced for the "1928-1950: Replica Series." **1950-1972:** Paper circle with red outer rim, beige center and yellow smiling bear's head at bottom. From 1983 reproduced for "1950s-1960s

Replica Editions." **1972-present:** Paper circle, top half yellow, bottom half red. Printed with name of bear or animal and Steiff logo.
Labels: **C. 1908:** White paper (a special paper woven with fibers on all paper labels); S.L. Number indicates the exact look of the animal as to posture covering and height (in centimeters). **C. 1910-1926:** White paper S.L. More information added to label "geschutzt" (protected by law): Germany Importe d'Allemage (made in Germany). **C. 1925-1934/35:** Red stock paper label. **C. 1934-1950:** Yellow stock paper label. **C. 1960-1972:** Yellow coated linen label. Style of information has changed and a place is designated for price. **C. 1977-1980:** Yellow coated linen label. Style of information is the same but a slash is now used instead of comma. Design introduced is still used to present time. Material has changed over the years: **1980-82:** White woven S.L. used for limited editions; **1980-82:** Yellow woven S.L. **1982-87:** White cloth weave S.L. used for limited editions. **1982-87:** Yellow cloth weave S.L. **1986-present:** White printed ribbon S.L. used for limited editions. **1986-present:** Yellow printed ribbon S.L.

Steiff. Rod Bears. 35 PB and 28 PB. Circa 1904. 16in and 20in (41cm-51cm); white mohair and beige mohair; large black shoe-button type eyes; sealing wax nose; f.j. (with metal rods) e.s.; elephant button. Price depends on condition, size and elephant button in ear.
CONDITION: Fair to excellent.
**PRICE:** $10,000-$25,000 each.
*Courtesy Puppenhausmuseum, Basel.*

Steiff. Rod Bear. 28PB. Circa 1904. 16in (41cm); long silky honey-colored mohair; large button eyes; diagonal seam at top of head; f.j.; metal rods connect joints; e.s.; body extremely hard; sealing wax nose; five embroidered claws; septum and mouth are a thin light tan thread; elephant button.
CONDITION: Mint.
**PRICE:** $15,000-$20,000.

Steiff. Bear. Circa 1905. 28in (71cm); white mohair; large black shoe-button eyes; f.j.; e.s.; blank button.
CONDITION: Good.
Sold at Christie's South Kensington 1997 auction for approximately $14,000.
*Courtesy Christie's.*

Steiff. Bear. Circa 1905. 30in (76cm); long wavy cinnamon mohair; large shoe-button eyes; f.j.; e.s.; FF button.
CONDITION: Excellent.
**PRICE:** $16,000-up.
Steiff. Bear. Circa 1905. 9in (23cm); honey-colored mohair; shoe-button eyes; f.j.; e.s.; FF button. The first antique bear in Linda Mullins' collection, given to her by her husband Wally the Christmas of 1974.
CONDITION: Fair.
**PRICE:** $1,200-up.

Steiff. Bear. Circa 1905. 12in (30cm); grey mohair; shoe-button eyes; f.j.; e.s.; Richard Steiff design.
CONDITION: Good.
**PRICE:** $10,000 and up.
*Courtesy Puppenhausmuseum, Basel.*

Steiff. "Center-Seam" in Head Bears. Circa 1905. 20in (51cm); cinnamon and honey colored mohair; large shoe-button type eyes; f.j.; e.s; FF button. Highly sought after center-seam in head bears creates appealingly sweet faces.
CONDITION: Very good.
**PRICE:** $10,000-up each.

Price guide for Steiff's basic teddy bear design produced from 1905-1910 in honey-colored mohair with shoe-button eyes; f.j.; e.s.; <u>FF</u> button.
**PRICES:**

|  | Mint Condition | Good Condition | Fair Condition |
|---|---|---|---|
| 10in (25cm) | $3,000-up | $1,500-up | $750-up |
| 16in (41cm) | $7,500-up | $4,000-up | $1,800-up |
| 20in (51cm) | $10,000-up | $6,000-up | $3,000-up |
| 24in (61cm) | $14,000-up | $10,000-up | $4,500-up |
| 28in (71cm) | $22,000-up | $15,000-up | $6,700-up |

Rare colors and extra appealing facial expressions command higher prices.
*Photograph courtesy Deborah and Donald Ratliff.*

Steiff. Bears. (Front) Circa 1905. 13in (33cm); apricot mohair; blank button. (Right) Circa 1910. 12-½in (32cm); dark golden brown mohair; <u>FF</u> button. (Back) Circa 1910. 13in (33cm); pale blonde mohair; <u>FF</u> button. All bears have shoe-button eyes; f.j.; e.s.
CONDITION: (Front) Excellent. (Right) Good. (Back) Good.
**PRICE:** (Front) Approximately $7,000. (Right) Approximately $1,900. (Back) Approximately $1,500. Sold at Christie's South Kensington 1997 auction for the approximate prices printed.
*Courtesy Christie's.*

Steiff. Bear. Circa 1905. 19in (48cm); cinnamon mohair; shoe-button eyes; f.j.; e.s. Came with three original photographs (one of original owner Maude Eldred Thomas with bear).
CONDITION: Excellent. Sold at Christie's South Kensington 1997 auction for approximately $16,900.
*Courtesy Christie's.*

Steiff. ***Batro***. Bear. Circa 1907-1908. 10in (24cm); beige mohair; shoe-button eyes; f.j.; e.s.; Original clothing; dressed in knitted bathing costume with horizontal stripes.
CONDITION: Excellent.
**PRICE:** $10,000-up.
*Courtesy Puppenhausmuseum, Basel.*

Steiff. Bears on Wheels. Circa 1910. From 36in (91cm) long by 30in (76cm) tall to 24in (61cm) long by 16in (41cm) tall. Various colors and types of mohair; glass and shoe-button eyes; n.j. legs; swivel and non-jointed heads; e.s. mounted on metal wheels; <u>FF</u> printed buttons.
CONDITION: Good to excellent.
**PRICE:** 9in (23cm) high, $700-up; 11in (28cm) high, $900-up; 16in (41cm) high, $1,600-up; 22in (56cm) high, $2,500-up; 30in (76cm) high, $3,500-up. Rare colors may command higher prices.

Steiff. Muzzle Bears. Circa 1910. 8in (20cm)-20in (51cm); white, beige and brown tones of mohair; large button eyes; f.j.; e.s. leather muzzles.
CONDITION: Mint to excellent.
**PRICE:** $7,000-$25,000 each.
*Courtesy Puppenhausmuseum, Basel.*

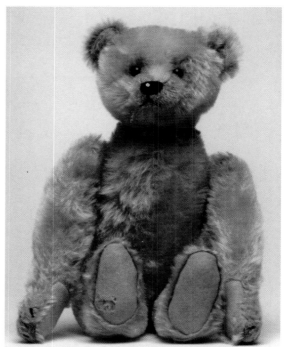

Steiff. "Black" Bears. Circa 1912. 10in (25cm)-16in (41cm); black mohair; glass eyes; f.j.; e.s.; <u>FF</u> button.
CONDITION: Excellent.
**PRICE:** $18,000-$40,000 each.
*Courtesy Puppenhausmuseum, Basel.*

Steiff. Tumbling Bear. Circa 1912. 11in (28cm); beige mohair; shoe-button eyes; f.j.; e.s.; mechanical bear; tumbles when arms are wound.
CONDITION: Good.
**PRICE:** $4,000-$4,700.
*Courtesy Puppenhausmuseum, Basel.*

Steiff. ***Dolly*** Bear. Circa 1912/1913. 12in (31cm); white mohair head; red mohair body; shoe-button eyes; f.j.; e.s.; <u>FF</u> button. Rare color and design.
CONDITION: Very good.
**PRICE:** $20,000-up.
*Courtesy Puppenhausmuseum, Basel.*

Steiff. "Paper" Plush Bear. Circa 1918-1919; 17in (43cm); brownish grey cotton cloth; shoe-button eyes; f.j.; e.s. Very rare.
CONDITION: Excellent.
**PRICE:** $20,000-up.
*Courtesy Puppenhausmuseum, Basel.*

Price guide for Steiff's basic teddy bear design produced from 1910 to 1930 in mohair with glass eyes; f.j.; e.s.; <u>FF</u> button.
**PRICES:**

|            | Mint Condition | Good Condition | Fair Condition |
|------------|----------------|----------------|----------------|
| 10in (25cm) | $1,500-up | $1,000-up | $750-up |
| 16in (41cm) | $4,500-up | $3,000-up | $1,500-up |
| 20in (51cm) | $7,000-up | $5,000-up | $2,500-up |
| 24in (61cm) | $12,000-up | $6,000-up | $4,000-up |
| 28in (71cm) | $15,000-up | $7,500-up | $5,000-up |

Rare colors and extra-appealing facial expressions command higher prices.
*Photograph courtesy Judy and Lee Day.*

Steiff. Bears. (Left) Circa 1920. 8in (20cm); worn beige mohair; shoe-button eyes; f.j.; e.s.; FF button.
CONDITION: Worn.
**PRICE:** $500-$700.
(Right) Circa 1920. 24in (61cm); long white mohair; glass eyes; brown stitched nose, mouth and claws; f.j.; e.s.; FF button.
CONDITION: Excellent.
**PRICE:** $8,000-up.
*Photograph courtesy Horst Poestgens, Auctioneer, Germany.*

(Left) Steiff. Bears. Circa 1920. 10in (25cm); blonde mohair; glass eyes; f.j.; e.s.
CONDITION: Fair.
**PRICE:** $700-$900.
(Right) Circa 1908. 27-½in (70cm); long wavy grayish brown mohair; glass eyes; f.j.; e.s.
CONDITION: Excellent.
**PRICE:** $9,500-up.
*Photograph courtesy of Horst Poestgens, Auctioneer, Germany.*

(Left) Steiff. Bear. Circa 1907. 16in (41cm); cinnamon mohair; shoe-button eyes; f.j.; e.s.; FF button.
CONDITION: Mint.
**PRICE:** $7,000-up.
(Right) Steiff. Bear. Circa 1910. 16in (41cm); cinnamon mohair; glass eyes; f.j.; e.s.; FF Button.
CONDITION: Mint.
**PRICE:** $7,000-up.

Steiff. Bear. *Sotheby*. Circa 1920. 18in (46cm); golden mohair; glass eyes; f.j.; e.s.; FF button.
CONDITION: Mint.
Sold at Christie's South Kensington 1998 auction for approximately $13,300.
*Courtesy Christie's.*

(Left) Steiff. Bear. Circa 1907. 3-1/2in (9cm); gold (worn bare) mohair; black, bead eyes; f.j.; e.s.; FF button.
CONDITION: Worn.
PRICE: $600-$800
(Right) Steiff. Bear Rattle. Circa 1910. 6in (15cm); white mohair; glass eyes; f.j.; e.s.; no paw pads; tiny metal rattle encased in tummy.
CONDITION: Good.
PRICE: $1,500-up.
(Center) Black Forest Bear Inkwell. Circa 1910. 4-1/2in (12cm), carved wood; glass eyes; lift head to disclose glass inkwell.
CONDITION: Excellent.
PRICE: $800-$900.

Steiff. Handpuppet Bears. Circa 1920. (Left) white mohair; (Right) gold mohair; shoe-button eyes; swivel head; jointed arms; e.s. head.
CONDITION: Mint.
PRICE: (Left) $3,500-up, (Right) $2,000-up.
*Courtesy David Douglas.*

Below:
Steiff. "Record" teddy bears. Circa 1920-1930. 5-3/4in-10in (15cm-25cm) tall. Various colors of mohair, f.j. bears with shoe-button and glass eyes, e.s. mounted on metal frames with wooden wheels. All bears have printed Steiff button with FF underscored. Originally introduced in 1912 with a monkey *(Record Peter)*, the popular Record series was produced with a variety of animals and character dolls until 1950.
CONDITION: Excellent.
PRICE: $5,000-$8,000 each. Rare colors command higher prices.
*Private Collection.*

Left:
Steiff. Bear. Circa 1930. 20in (51cm); brown mohair; glass eyes; f.j.; e.s.
CONDITION: Excellent.
**PRICE:** $6,500-up.
Steiff Rooster. Circa 1920. 7in (18cm); beige, yellow/gold and dark blue mohair; shoe-button eyes; n.j.; e.s.
CONDITION: Excellent.
**PRICE:** $800-up.
Steiff Ball. Circa 1950. 10in (25cm); various colors of mohair; s.s.
CONDITION: Excellent.
**PRICE:** $100-$150.
*Photograph courtesy Horst Poestgens, Auctioneer, Germany.*

Right:
Steiff. Mini Clown Bear. Circa 1915. 5in (13cm); light brown mohair (worn bare); shoe-button eyes; f.j.; e.s.; <u>FF</u> button.
CONDITION: Worn.
**PRICE:** $2,000-up.
*Courtesy Puppenhausmuseum, Basel.*

Steiff. Teddy Clowns. Circa 1926. 5in-21in (13cm-52cm); various beige and gold colors of mohair tipped with dark brown; glass eyes; f.j.; e.s.; <u>FF</u> button; original clown hats and ruffs.
CONDITION: Good to Mint.
**PRICE:** $3,000-$30,000 each.
Note center is an extremely rare dual plush *Petsy* musical Teddy Clown (15in (38cm)).
**PRICE:** $26,000-up. Steiff Bears on Wheels. Circa 1910. 12in (31cm) -30in (76cm) tall; brown burlap; large black button eyes; n.j. legs; swivel head; metal wheels; <u>FF</u> button.
CONDITION: Excellent. PRICE: $1,000-$3,500 each.
*Courtesy Puppenhausmuseum, Basel.*

Steiff. *Petsy*. Circa 1928. 19-1/2in (50cm); brown tipped pale gold mohair; "googlie" (glancing to center) eyes; beige stitched (red felt underlined) nose; center seam in head; f.j.; e.s.; extremely rare.
CONDITION: Good.
**PRICE:** $14,000-up.
*Courtesy Puppenhausmuseum, Basel.*

Right:
(Left) Steiff. Bear. (Movable Head Mechanism). Circa 1933. 9in (23cm) tall; dark brown mohair; short beige mohair inset snout; glass eyes; n.j.; e.s.; <u>FF</u> button. Turning tail moves head in circular motion.
CONDITION: Fair.
**PRICE:** $2,500-$3,500.
(Right) Steiff. *Petsy*. Bear. Circa 1928. 20in (51cm); long white mohair tipped with reddish-brown; blue glass eyes; f.j.; s.s.; <u>FF</u> button. Characteristics are: oversized ears fitted with wires; red stitched nose; mouth and claws; blue glass eyes (backed with white milk glass); head seams run down from the center, front, back and cross-wise from ears to back; V-shaped gusset from center of mouth to neck.
CONDITION: Excellent.
**PRICE:** $15,000-up.

Above:
Steiff. *Petsy*. Circa 1928. 13in (34); white mohair; glass eyes; f.j.; e.s.; Prototype; rare.
CONDITION: Mint.
**PRICE:** N.P.A.
*Courtesy Puppenhausmuseum, Basel.*

Right:
Steiff. Polar Bear with Neck Mechanism. Circa 1930. 9in (23cm) high; white mohair; short mohair snout; glass eyes; n.j. legs; turning tail activates head to turn in circular motion; e.s.
CONDITION: Fair.
**PRICE:** $2,500-$3,500.
*Photograph courtesy Horst Poestgens, Auctioneer, Germany*

This group of miniature Steiff Bears depicts the changes in Steiff's miniature bear designs from 1905-1960. All examples are approximately 3-½in (9cm) tall; shades of honey-colored mohair (with the exception of the center bear which is the rare white mohair); tiny black button eyes; f.j.; e.s. Note how the length of the mohair and shape of the faces change over the years. Prices indicated are for bears with Steiff buttons.
CONDITION: Excellent.
**PRICE:** (Left) Circa 1910, $900-up; (Second Left) Circa 1925, $700-up; (Center [White]) Circa 1940, $800-up; (Second Right) Circa 1952, $400-up; (Right) Circa 1960, $300-up.
*Private Collection.*

Steiff. Circus Bear with Neck Mechanism. Circa 1936. Size 12in (30cm); brown mohair; short beige inset snout; glass eyes; "snap jointed" arms and legs; mechanical head (head moves in circular motion when tail is turned); e.s.
CONDITION: Excellent.
**PRICE:** $6,000-$9,000.
*Courtesy Puppenhausmuseum, Basel.*

Steiff. *Teddy Baby*. Circa 1940. 10in(26cm); maize artificial silk plush; glass eyes; f.j.; e.s.; FF button; C.T.
CONDITION: Mint
**PRICE:** $2,000-$2,500.
*Courtesy Puppenhausmuseum, Basel.*

Steiff. *Teddy Babies*. Circa 1930-1940; 4in (10cm) - 24in (61cm) various colors of mohair; short mohair inset snout and tops of feet; glass eyes; f.j.; e.s. open and closed mouth versions; FF Button; C.T.
CONDITION: Mint to Excellent.
**PRICE:** $1,500-$4,500 each.
*Courtesy Puppenhausmuseum, Basel.*

Steiff. ***Breuni***. Circa 1950. 5in (13cm); gold mohair head and legs; cloth body; felt outfit; glass eyes; n.j.; e.s.; R.S.B.; Advertisement for department store Breuninger.
CONDITION: Mint.
**PRICE:** $1,500-$2,000.
*Courtesy Puppenhausmuseum, Basel.*

Steiff. ***Teddyli***. Circa 1950. 9in (22cm); brown mohair; beige inset snout; felt lined open mouth; cloth body; glass eyes; jointed arms; stationary legs; swivel head; felt jacket and skirt; cotton shirt; R.S.B.; cloth tag sewn into side seam reads: "U.S. Zone Germany." Same design produced dressed as a boy.
CONDITION: Excellent.
**PRICE:** $1,500-$2,000.
*Courtesy Puppenhausmuseum, Basel.*

Right:
Steiff. Pandas. Circa 1950 (Left to Right) 15in (38cm); 11in (28cm); 8-1/2in (22cm) 5-½in (14cm); black and white mohair; airbrushed facial features; beige felt-lined open mouth; glass eyes; gray leather-type paw pads; f.j.; e.s.; R.S.B.
CONDITION: Excellent.
**PRICE:** $900-$2,000 each.
Steiff Lobster. ***Crabby***. Circa 1963. 4in (10cm) orange felt airbrushed body features; glass eyes; n.j.; e.s.; R.S.B. C.T.
CONDITION: Mint.
**PRICE:** $300-$400.
Steiff V.W. Transporter. Circa 1960. 8-½in (21cm) long.
CONDITION: Excellent.
**PRICE:** $200-$300.
*Photograph courtesy Horst Poestgens Auctioneer, Germany.*

Steiff. Original Teddy. Circa 1950. Golden-colored mohair; glass eyes; f.j.; e.s.; R.S.B.; C.T.
CONDITION: Mint.
**PRICE:** 3-1/2in (9cm) $400-up; 10in (25cm) $525-up; 16in (41cm) $1,000-up; 26in (66cm) $4,000-up; 30in (76cm) $5,000-up. Rare colors command higher prices.

Steiff. **Zotty** Bear. Circa 1950. Long silky caramel-colored mohair tipped with white; short caramel mohair inset snout; gold mohair chest; pink felt lined open mouth; glass eyes; f.j.; paws turned in downward position; e.s.; R.S.B.; C.T.

| PRICE: | Mint Condition | Good Condition | Worn Condition |
|---|---|---|---|
| 9in (23cm) | $275-up | $175-up | $100-up |
| 14in (36cm) | $450-up | $300-up | $150-up |
| 20in (51cm) | $650-up | $400-up | $200-up |

Note: Rare colors command higher prices.
*Photograph courtesy Helen Sieverling.*

Steiff. **Teddy Babies**. (Left) Circa 1950 8-½in (23cm); (Right) Circa 1930. 15-1/2in (40cm); long brown mohair; short beige mohair inset snout; beige felt-lined open mouth; short beige mohair tops of feet; f.j.; e.s.; red collar and bell. (Left) Steiff Rabbit. Circa 1920. 6-½in (17cm) blonde mohair; glass eyes; n.j. legs; swivel head e.s.; <u>FF</u> button.
CONDITION: Bears Mint. Rabbit Good.
**PRICE:** *Teddy Baby* 8-1/2in (23cm) Approximately $1,745. *Teddy Baby* 15-1/2in (40cm) Approximately $1,850. Rabbit 6-1/2in (17cm) Approximately $175. Sold at Horst Poestgens 1999 Auction, Germany for approximate prices printed.
*Courtesy of Horst Poestgens Auctioneer, Germany.*

Steiff. Musical Bear. Circa 1950. 13-3/4in (35cm); caramel mohair; glass eyes; f.j.; e.s.; squeeze type musical mechanism encased in body.
CONDITION: Excellent.
**PRICE:** $3,000-$4,500.
*Courtesy Puppenhausmuseum, Basel.*

Steiff. *Jackie* Bears. Circa 1953. 6in (15cm) and 10in (25cm); blonde -colored mohair; glass eyes; f.j.; e.s.; R.S.B. Created as Steiff's first jubilee bear. Identifying features are dark shaded area for navel, pink silk stitch horizontally sewn across nose; cub style body. Bears sold with Steiff's 50th Anniversary booklet (Center). Steiff. Bat. *Eric*. Circa 1960. 3in (8cm).
CONDITION: Good.
*Jackie* Bear Price Guide: 7in (18cm) $2,000-up; 10in (25cm) $1,500-up; 14in (36cm) $2,000-up; Bat. *Eric* $250-$350.
*Photograph courtesy Horst Poestgens, Auctioneer, Germany.*

Steiff. Bear. (Movable Head mechanism). 1955. 7in (18cm); beige mohair; glass eyes; jointed arms and legs; neck mechanism (head moves in circular motion when tail is turned); e.s.
CONDITION: Excellent.
**PRICE:** $1,800-up.
*Courtesy Puppenhausmuseum, Basel.*

Steiff. Original teddy bear. Circa 1970. Mohair; short mohair heart-shaped face; glass eyes; f.j.; synthetic paw pads; e.s.; I.B.; C.T.
CONDITION: Excellent.
**PRICE:** 10in (25cm) $75-up, 16in (41cm) $125-up, 26in (66cm) $250-up, 30in (76cm) $475-up. Rare colors command higher prices (such as the cream colored bear pictured).

Steiff. Riding Bear. Circa 1948. 23in (58cm); brown mohair; short beige inset mohair snout; glass eyes; n.j.; e.s.; leather collar; pull growler; red painted metal wheels with white rubber tires; metal frame; <u>FF</u> button.
CONDITION: Excellent.
**PRICE:** $1,500-$1,800. Not pictured. Steiff Riding Bear. Circa 1967. R.S.B., C.T..17in (43cm) $300-up, 20in (50cm) $400-up, 24in (60cm) $650-up.

(Right) Steiff. Polar Bear. Circa 1950. 5-½in (14cm) tall; white mohair; glass eyes; n.j.; e.s.
CONDITION: Excellent.
**PRICE:** $250-$300.
(Center) Steiff. Young Bear. Circa 1950. 6-1/2in (17cm) tall; beige mohair; glass eyes; n.j.; e.s.
CONDITION: Excellent.
**PRICE:** $300-$350.
(Right) Steiff. Young Bear. Circa 1950. 5in (13cm) tall; beige mohair; glass eyes; n.j. legs; swivel head; e.s. R.S.B. button.
CONDITION: Excellent.
**PRICE:** $200-250.

Steiff. Bear. *Zooby*. 11in (28cm); Circa 1964; brown mohair; beige mohair inset snout; dark brown mohair feet; open felt lined mouth; felt claws; plastic eyes; jointed head and arms; stationary legs; R.S.B.
CONDITION: Mint.
**PRICE:** $1,000-$1,500.

Steiff. Koala. Circa 1950. Pale gold mohair; short mohair face; gray felt nose; glass eyes; f.j.; e.s.; R.S.B.
CONDITION: Excellent.
**PRICE:** 5in (13cm) $300-up, 8in (20cm) $450-up, 12in (31cm) $650-up.

(Left) Steiff. Pomeranian Dog on wheels. Circa 1903. 8-1/2in x 9in (22cm x 23cm); white mohair body; white felt face and legs; metal frame and wheels; shoe-button eyes; n.j.; e.s.; "Elephant Button". (Right) Steiff Cat. Circa 1903. 4-1/2in (10cm); gray velvet with black and brown markings; shoe-button eyes; n.j.; e.s.; "Elephant Button."
CONDITION: Excellent.
**PRICE:** $3,000-$4,000 each.
*Courtesy Mimi Hiscox.*

Steiff. Skittles (set of 8). Circa 1905. 8in-10in (20cm-25cm); king bear and 7 animals mounted on wooden bases; shoe-button eyes; n.j.; e.s.; <u>FF</u> button.
CONDITION: Excellent.
Sold at Christie's South Kensington 1998 auction for approximately $5,500 (set).
*Courtesy Christie's.*

Steiff. *Fluffy* Cats. Circa 1930. Sizes range from 3-1/2in –7-½in (9cm-19cm); long silky mohair (three white tipped in lilac, one white tipped in blue); n.j. arms and legs; swivel heads; e.s.; <u>FF</u> button; remnants or red labels; C.T.
CONDITION: Mint.
**PRICE:** $750-$1,200 each.
*Courtesy David Douglas.*

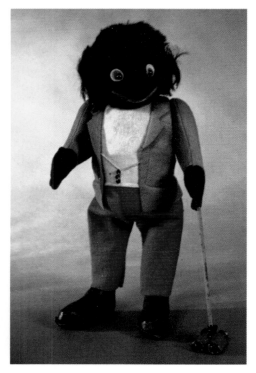

Steiff. Golliwog. Circa 1908. 11in (28cm); black felt head and hands; black mohair hair; shoe-button eyes backed with white and red felt circles; red and white stitched mouth; integral felt clothes; f.j.; e.s. Repaired patch on back.
CONDITION: Very Good.
**PRICE:** $7,500-up.
*Photograph courtesy Horst Poestgens, Auctioneer, Germany.*

(Left to Right) Steiff *Pip*. Circa 1925. 4in (10cm); brown velvet; "googlie" eyes; red felt tongue; n.j. legs; swivel head; e.s.; FF button (remains of red tag). The exaggerated Bulldog caricature *Pip* was inspired by A.B. Payne's comic from the British newspaper the *Daily Mirror*, "Pip, Squeak, and Wilfred." **Chow Chow Brownie**. Circa 1930. 4in (10cm); golden beige mohair; glass eyes; n.j. legs; swivel head; e.s.; FF Button. Reverse of chest tag reads: "Zeppelin mascot." **Mollie** Dog. Circa 1930. 4in (10cm); bright green beige-tipped mohair; glass eyes; n.j. legs; swivel head; e.s.; FF button.
CONDITION: Mint to Excellent.
**PRICE:** $500-$600 each.
*Courtesy Mimi Hiscox.*

Right:
(Left) Steiff Humanized Monkey. Circa 1930. 12in (31cm); brown mohair; beige felt face and ears; glass eyes; f.j.; e.s.; leather gloves an integral part of body; FF button.
CONDITION: Good.
**PRICE:** $1,000-$1,200.
(Right) Steiff. Chimpanzee. Radiator Cap. Circa 1912. 12in (31cm); pale golden beige mohair; beige felt face and paws; glass eyes; f.j.; e.s.; FF button. Part of Steiff's "Automobile Program".
CONDITION: Good.
**PRICE:** $1,500-$2,000.
*Courtesy Mimi Hiscox.*

Left:
Steiff. Doll. **Anton**. Circa 1910. 10in (25cm); felt face, body and clothes; shoe-button eyes; f.j.; e.s.; FF button.
CONDITION: Mint.
**PRICE:** $1,200-$1,500.
*Courtesy Mimi Hiscox.*

Steiff. Animals (Moveable Head mechanism). Head moves in circular motion by turning tail. Circa 1930. (Left to Right) Rabbit. 6in (15cm); beige mohair; glass eyes; n.j. legs; e.s.; FF button.
CONDITION: Good.
**PRICE:** $900-$1,200.
Dogs. *Rattler* (the rat catcher). Schnauzers. 4in/7in (10cm/18cm); brown tipped blonde mohair; glass eyes; n.j. legs; e.s.; FF button; C.T.; tag on tail reads: "Turn here and I will move my head."
CONDITION: Mint.
**PRICE:** $1,200-$1,800 each.
*Courtesy Mimi Hiscox.*

Steiff. *Bully* Dogs. Circa 1950. (Left to Right) 5in –3-1/2in tall) 13cm-9cm); short beige mohair airbrushed in brown tones; beige velvet airbrushed muzzle; glass eyes; n.j. legs; swivel head; R.S.B.; C.T. Dogs are sewn onto pillow. Originally came in wicker basket. Made for F.A.O. SCHWARZ.
CONDITION: Mint.
**PRICE:** $1,000-$1,200 set.
*Private Collection.*

Steiff's realistic cute rabbits from the 1950s-1960s are among the most collectible of their vast range of animals. Steiff Rabbits. Circa 1950s-1960s. Mohair; glass eyes; f.j. and n.j.; e.s.; R.S.B.; C.T.
CONDITION: Mint to Excellent.
**PRICE:** *Niki.* 5-1/2in (14cm) $225-up, 6-1/2in (17cm) $275-up, 8-1/2in (22cm) $300-up, 11in (28cm) $350-up, 13-3/4in (35cm) $500-up. *Manni.* 4in (10cm) $125-up, 8in (20cm) $250-up, 11-3/4in (30cm) $400-up, 15-3/4in (40cm) $650-up, 21-3/4in (55cm) $850-up. *Floppy Hansi.* 6-1/2in (17cm) $50-up, 11in (28cm) $75-up. *Sonny.* 3in (8cm) $100-up, 6in (15cm) $125-up, 7in (18cm) $150-up. *Hoppy.* 3in (8cm) $100-up, 5in (14cm) $125-up, 6-3/4in (17cm) $150-up. *Pummy.* 6in (15cm) $150-up, 10in (25cm) $225-up. *Lulac.* 17in (43cm) $450-up, 23-3/4in (60cm) $750-up. *Lying Rabbit.* 2-1/2in (6cm) $125-up, 3-1/2in (9cm) $140-up, 4in (12cm) $150-up. *Ossi.* 7in (18cm) $ 2 0 0 -up, 9in (23cm) $250-up. *Record Hansi.* (on wooden wheels) 10in (25cm) $700-up.

Steiff. Chimpanzee. *Jocko*. Circa 1950. Brown mohair; beige felt face, paws and feet; airbrushed features; glass eyes; f.j.; e.s.; R.S.B.; C.T.
CONDITION: Mint.
**PRICE:** 4in (10cm) $125-up, 6in (15cm) $150-up, 10in (25cm) $200-up, 13-3/4in (35cm) $250-up, 19-3/4in (50cm) $350-up, 23-1/2in (60cm) $450-up, 31-1/2in (80cm) $600-up. *Record Peter.* (on wooden wheels) 10in (25cm) $500-up.

Steiff. Stagecoach. Circa 1950. 21in (53cm) tall; painted wood; pulled by two Steiff donkeys.
CONDITION: Excellent.
**PRICE:** $2,000-up.
Steiff, Schuco and Hermann animals and dolls decorate the stagecoach. Circa 1950-1980.
CONDITION: Excellent.
**PRICE:** $150-$300 each.

Steiff Animated Display. Circa 1950. 66in (167cm) tall. Steiff *Micki* and *Mecki* and other Steiff animals come to life in an amusing setting; driven by electronic motors.
CONDITION: Good.
**PRICE:** $7,000-up.

Steiff. Studio Animals. Circa 1950. Mohair; glass eyes; f.j. and n.j.; e.s.; R.S.B.; C.T.
CONDITION: Excellent.
**PRICE:** (Sizes are approximate)
*Elephant* 32in (81cm) $1,000-up, 33in (84cm) $1,200-up, 60in (152cm) $3,000-up. *Standing Bear* 66in (167cm) $3,000-up. *Polar Bear* 62in (157cm) $2,000-up. *Panda* 62in (157cm) $1,000-up. *Giraffe* 36in (91cm) $1,200-up, 60in (152cm) $2,000-up, 96in (243cm) $3,500-up. *Lion (sitting)* 30in (76cm) $2,500-up. *Lion (standing)* 40in (101cm) $3,500-up. *Tiger (standing)* 40in (101cm) $3,500-up. *Chimpanzee* 60in (152cm) $2,500-up. *Pony* 39in (99cm) $1,800-up. *Reindeer* 48in (122cm) $2,500-up. *Camel* 40in (101cm) $2,000-up. *Fox. Xorry* 21in (53cm) $1,500-up. *Collie Dog* (laying) 48in (122cm) $2,000-up.

Steiff. First Issue *Jungle Book* Characters. 1968 - 1974. Dralon; plastic eyes; felt and velour features; s.s. and e.s.; Walt Disney copyrights.
CONDITION: Excellent.
(Left to Right) *Baloo*. 16in (41cm). **PRICE:** $800-up. *Baby Hathi*. 8in (20cm). **PRICE:** $275-up. *King Louie*. 10in (25cm). **PRICE:** $375-up. *Shere Khan*. 14in (36cm). **PRICE:** $600-up. Value increases when sold as a set.
*Private collection.*

# Steiff Museum Replicas, Special and Limited Editions

| Item Ear tag# EAN # | Sortiment Book Vol#1 | Vol#2 | Year | Description | Value |
|---|---|---|---|---|---|
| 0153/43 | 393 | **414** | 1980 | **PAPA BEAR** 17in. (43cm) Limited 11,000 (5,000 with a certificate in English) white tag, boxed, replica 1903, 100th Anniversary, first boxed limited edition, worldwide. | $950.00 |
| 0155/38 | 385 | **457** | 1981 | **MAMA AND BABY SET** 15in. (38cm) and 6in. (15cm) Limited 8,000, white tag, boxed, certificate, replica 1903, Steiff's 101st anniversary, the baby does not have an ear tag. U.S.A only. | $600.00 |
| 0223/30 | 386 | **465** | 1982/84 | **BRUNO BEAR** 11-3/4in (30cm) Replica of a teddy bear from the past, U.S.A. only. | $250.00 |
| 0155/26 **404597** 0155/32 **404627** | 384 384 | **465** **465** | 1982/90 1991/99 1982/91 1991/99 | **MARGARET STRONG BEAR GOLD** 10-1/4in (26cm) U.S.A. only.                Current Ear Tag $120.00    Old Ear Tag $145.00 <br>**MARGARET STRONG BEAR GOLD** 12-1/2in (32cm) U.S.A. only. Limited 20,000, white tag, replica 1904, boxed, not issued with a certificate.           Current Ear Tag $150.00    Old Ear Tag $275.00 | |
| 0204/16 | 385 | **457** | 1982/85 | **TEA PARTY SET** 6-1/4in (16cm) each Limited 10,000, boxed, certificate, 102nd Anniversary, four bears, white, dark brown, honey and caramel, Steiff logo tea set, all have the same ear tag number. U.S.A. only. | $550.00 |
| 0203/00 | 385 | **457** | 1982 | **WHITE TEDDY BEAR SERIES** 4-1/4in ( 11cm), 6-1/2in. (18cm), 10-1/4in (26cm), 12-1/2in (32cm) and 16in (41cm) Limited 2,000, white tag, boxed, set of 5 bears, felt paws, U.S.A. only. | $500.00 |
| 0118/25 | 68 | **489** | 1983/87 | **BOXER DOG** 10in (25cm) Limited 2,000, yellow tag, U.S.A. only. | $165.00 |
| 0165/38 **406331** 0165/51 | 393 393 | **424** **424** | 1983/88 1983/88 | **1909 GOLD TEDDY BEAR** 15in (38cm) Yellow tag, worldwide. <br>**1909 GOLD TEDDY BEAR** 20in (51cm) Yellow tag, worldwide. | $325.00 $650.00 |
| 0140/38 | 386 | **465** | 1983 | **KLEIN ARCHIE BEAR** 15in (38cm) Limited 2,500, made for Enchanted Doll House, Vermont, U.S.A. only. | $295.00 |
| 3020/00 | 408 | **489** | 1983/85 | **MANNI RABBIT SET** 4in (10cm), 8in (20cm) and 11-3/4in (30cm) Limited 2,000, white tag, boxed, standing in a begging position, U.S.A. only. | $325.00 |
| 0310/19 | 22 | | 1983/85 | **MANSCHLI or BUDDHA BEAR** 7- 1/4in (19cm) Yellow tag, U.S.A. only. | $300.00 |
| 0155/42 **404832** | 384 | **465** | 1983/90 1991/99 | **MARGARET STRONG BEAR GOLD** 16-1/2in (42cm) U.S.A. only. Yellow tag, replica 1904 bear, U.S.A. only.          Current Ear Tag $220.00    Old Ear Tag $395.00 | |
| 0160/00 | 384 | **457** | 1983 | **MARGARET STRONG CHOCOLATE BROWN SET** 7in (18cm), 10in (26cm), 12-1/2in (32cm) and 16-1/2in (42cm) Limited 2,000, white tag, boxed, U.S.A. only. | $850.00 |
| 0210/22 | 385 | **457** | 1983 | **NIMROD TEDDY ROOSEVELT COMMEMORATIVE SET** 9 in (22cm) each bear Limited 10,000, white tag, boxed, certificate, three bears, white, gold, caramel, dressed, for the 125th birthday of Teddy Roosevelt and 80th birthday of teddy bear, U.S.A. only. | $450.00 |
| 0150/32 | 393 | **414** | 1983/84 | **RICHARD STEIFF BEAR** 12-1/2in (32cm) Limited ed. 20,000, white tag, boxed, not issued with a certificate, replica 1902-1903 for the 80th birthday of the teddy bear, worldwide. | $550.00 |

| Item Ear tag# EAN # | Sortiment Book Vol#1 | Vol#2 | Year | Description | Value |
|---|---|---|---|---|---|
| 0112/17 | 408 | **489** | 1983/87 | **TIGER** 6-1/2in (17cm) Yellow tag, limited 2,000, replica 1953, U.S.A. only. | $200.00 |
| 0112/28 | 408 | **489** | 1983/87 | **TIGER** 11in (28cm) Yellow tag, limited 2,000, replica 1953, U.S.A. only. | $300.00 |
| 0130/17 | 408 | **490** | 1983/84 | **UNICORN** 6-1/2in (17cm) Limited 2,000, white tag, U.S.A. only. | $350.00 |
| 0130/27 | 408 | **490** | 1983/84 | **UNICORN** 10-1/2in (27cm) Limited 2,000, white tag, U.S.A. only. | $295.00 |
| 8495/03 | 464 | | 1984/86 | **BEAR PIN HEAD** Beige 1-1/4in (4cm) | $100.00 |
| 8496/03 | 464 | | 1984/86 | **BEAR PIN HEAD** Caramel 1-1/4in (4cm) | $100.00 |
| 8497/03 | 464 | | 1984/86 | **BEAR PIN HEAD** White 1-1/4in (4cm) | $100.00 |
| 8498/03 | 464 | | 1984/88 | **BEAR PIN HEAD** Chocolate 1-1/4in (4cm) | $100.00 |
| 0162/00 **405808** | 393 | **414** | 1984/87 | **GIENGEN TEDDY SET or Birthplace of the Teddy** 4in (10cm), 13-3/4in (35cm) Limited 16,000, boxed, certificate, mama and baby, worldwide. | $425.00 |
| 0165/28 | 393 | **424** | 1984/86 | **1909 GOLD TEDDY BEAR** 11in (28cm) Yellow tag, worldwide. | $250.00 |
| 0165/60 | 393 | **424** | 1984/86 | **1909 GOLD TEDDY BEAR** 23-1/2in (60cm) Yellow tag, worldwide. | $850.00 |
| 0173/ 25,30,32 | | **458** | 1984 | **GOLDILOCKS AND THE THREE BEARS (large set)** 16in. (41cm.), 12-1/2in (32cm), 11-3/4in (30cm) and 10in (25cm) Made for Reeves International. Limited 2,000, boxed, **large set** Susan Gibson doll and papa, mama and baby bear, U.S.A. only. | $850.00 |
| 0155/00 | 408 | **490** | 1984/86 | **HOPPY RABBIT SET** 3in (8cm), 5-1/2in (14cm) and 6-1/2in (17cm) Limited 2,000, white tag, boxed, running position, U.S.A. only. | $325.00 |
| 0111/21 **402425** | 408 | **428** | 1984/86 | **LION** 8-1/4in (21cm) Limited 2,000, yellow tag, replica 1956, U.S.A. only. | $175.00 |
| 0111/35 **402449** | 408 | **428** | 1984/86 | **LION** 13-3/4in (35cm) Limited 1,000, yellow tag, replica 1956, U.S.A. only. Also 1992 Lion 402463 | $225.00 |
| 0155/37 | 383 | | 1984/89 | **MARGARET STRONG GROOM BEAR** 14-1/2in (37cm) Yellow tag, boxed, U.S.A. only. | $400.00 |
| 0155/36 | 383 | | 1984/89 | **MARGARET STRONG BRIDE BEAR** 14in (36cm) Yellow tag, boxed, U.S.A. only. | $400.00 |
| 0156/00 | 384 | **458** | 1984 | **MARGARET STRONG CINNAMON SET** 7in (18cm), 10-1/4in (26cm), 12-1/2in (32cm) and 16-1/2in (42cm) Limited 2,000, white tag, boxed, certificate, U.S.A. only. | $850.00 |
| 0157/26 | 384 | **466** | 1984/86 | **MARGARET STRONG CREAM BEAR** 10-1/4in (26cm) Yellow Tag, U.S.A. only. | $200.00 |
| 0157/32 | 384 | **466** | 1984/86 | **MARGARET STRONG CREAM BEAR** 12-1/2in (32cm) Yellow tag, U.S.A. only. | $325.00 |
| 0157/42 | 384 | **466** | 1984/86 | **MARGARET STRONG CREAM BEAR** 16-1/2in (42cm) Yellow tag, U.S.A. only. | $450.00 |
| 0155/51 **404863** | 384 | **465** | 1984/90 1991/99 | **MARGARET STRONG GOLD BEAR** 20in (51cm) U.S.A. only.        **Current Ear Tag** $350.00    **Old Ear Tag** $495.00 | |
| 0155/60 **404894** | 384 | | 1984/90 1991 | **MARGARET STRONG GOLD BEAR** 23-3/4in (60cm) U.S.A. only. Yellow tag, replica 1904 bear, currently available.        **Current Ear Tag** $450.00    **Old Ear Tag** $550.00 | |
| 0080/08 **400025** | 408 | **414** | 1984/87 | **MUSEUM FELT ELEPHANT** 3in (8cm) Limited 10,000, boxed, replica 1880, issued with button only. U.S.A. only. | $175.00 |
| 0082/20 **406247** | 393 | | 1984/87 | **MUSEUM ROLY-POLY BEAR** Replica 1894, 8in (20cm) Limited 9,000, boxed, replica 1898. | $250.00 |
| 0151/25 | 387 | **466** | 1984/86 | **MR. CINNAMON BEAR** 10in (25cm) Yellow tag, 1903 replica. U.S.A. only. | $350.00 |
| 0151/32 | 387 | **466** | 1984/85 | **MR. CINNAMON BEAR** 12-1/2in (32cm) Yellow tag, 1903 replica. U.S.A. only. | $450.00 |
| 0151/40 | 387 | **466** | 1984/85 | **MR. CINNAMON BEAR** 15-3/4in (40cm) Yellow tag, 1903 replica. U.S.A. only. | $600.00 |

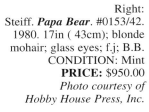

Left:
Steiff. *Manni Rabbit Set*.
#3020/00. 1983-1985. Air-brush
painted mohair; glass eyes; n.j;
arms and legs; B.B.
CONDITION: Mint
Left: 12in (30cm), Center: 4in
(10cm), Right: 8in (20cm).
**PRICE:** $325.00 set.
*Photo courtesy of Hobby House
Press, Inc.*

Right:
Steiff. *Papa Bear*. #0153/42.
1980. 17in ( 43cm); blonde
mohair; glass eyes; f.j; B.B.
CONDITION: Mint
**PRICE:** $950.00
*Photo courtesy of
Hobby House Press, Inc.*

| Item Ear tag# EAN # | Sortiment Book Vol#1 | Vol#2 | Year | Description | Value |
|---|---|---|---|---|---|
| 0151/55 | 387 | **466** | 1984 | **MR. CINNAMON BEAR** 21-1/2in (55cm) Yellow tag, 1903 replica. Germany only. | $1,200.00 |
| 0201/10 | 385 | **466** | 1984/85 | **ORIGINAL TEDDY BEAR** Beige, 4in (10cm) Yellow tag. | $100.00 |
| 0202/10 | 385 | **466** | 1984/85 | **ORIGINAL TEDDY BEAR** Caramel, 4in (10cm) Yellow tag. | $100.00 |
| 0203/10 | 385 | **466** | 1984/85 | **ORIGINAL TEDDY BEAR** White, 4in (10cm) Yellow tag. | $100.00 |
| 0206/10 | 385 | **466** | 1984/85 | **ORIGINAL TEDDY BEAR** Chocolate, 4in (10cm) Yellow tag. | $100.00 |
| 0225/42 | 387 | **468** | 1984/89 | **OPHELIA BEAR** 16-1/2in (42cm) Issued button only, tag on the leg, not issued with a box, U.S.A. only. | $450.00 |
| 0178/29 | 386 | **466** | 1984/85 | **PANDA BEAR** 11-1/41in (29cm) Yellow tag, replica 1938, reissued 1992. | $295.00 |
| 0178/35 | 386 | **466** | 1984/85 | **PANDA BEAR** 13-3/4in (35cm) Yellow tag, replica 1938, reissued 1992. | $400.00 |
| 7635/19 | 382 | **484** | 1984/88 | **SANTA CLAUS DOLL** 7-1/2in (19cm) Also see 1985 Santa # 7635/28. | $175.00 |
| 0175/29 | 386 | **466** | 1984/89 | **TEDDY BABY BROWN** 11-1/4in (29cm) Yellow tag, replica 1930, U.S.A. only. | $250.00 |
| 0175/35 | 386 | **466** | 1984/90 | **TEDDY BABY BROWN** 13-3/4in (35cm) **Also 1991 407758** | $350.00 |
| 0175/42 | 386 | **466** | 1984/89 | **TEDDY BABY BROWN** 16-1/2in (42cm) Yellow tag, replica 1930, U.S.A. only. | $495.00 |
| 0251/34 | 386 | **467** | 1985/87 | **BERLIN BEAR** 13-1/2in (34cm) Yellow tag, boxed, U.S.A. only. | $275.00 |
| 0172/32 407505 | 394 | **414** | 1985/88 | **DICKY BEAR** 12-1/2in (32cm) Limited 20,000, white tag, replica 1930, worldwide. | $350.00 |
| 0172/32 | 390 | **458** | 1985/86 | **DICKY CLOWNS AROUND** 12-1/2in (32cm) Limited 100, yellow tag, very rare, made for Ronald McDonald House, Dicky bear is dressed as Ronald McDonald, U.S.A. only. | $3,000.00 |
| 0167/32 | 387 | | 1985/89 | **1906 GRAY GIENGEN BEAR** 12in (32cm) Yellow tag, replica 1906, light gray. U.S.A. only. | $225.00 |

| Item Ear tag# EAN # | Sortiment Book Vol#1 | Vol#2 | Year | Description | Value |
|---|---|---|---|---|---|
| 0167/42 | 387 | **467** | 1985/89 | **1906 GRAY GIENGEN BEAR** 16in (42cm) Yellow tag, light gray, replica 1906, U.S.A. only. **Also see Gray Giengen Bears 1986 #0167/22 and 0167/52.** | $350.00 |
| 0173/ 22,18,14 | | **458** | 1985 | **GOLDILOCKS and THE THREE BEARS** 8-1/2in (22cm), 7 in (18cm) and 5-1/2in (14cm) Limited 5,000, **small set**, Susan Gibson doll, boxed, three Steiff bears, Papa, Mama, Baby. | $550.00 |
| 0211/26 | 386 | **467** | 1985 | **LUV BEAR-ER** 10-1/4in (26cm) | $175.00 |
| 0211/36 | 386 | **467** | 1985 | **LUV BEAR-ER** 14in (36cm) Yellow tag, dressed in a yellow felt vest with embroidered red heart, difficult to find, U.S.A. only. | $195.00 |
| 0157/51 | 384 | **466** | 1985/86 | **MARGARET STRONG CREAM BEAR** 20in (51cm) Yellow tag, U.S.A. only. | $800.00 |
| 0157/60 | 384 | **466** | 1985/86 | **MARGARET STRONG CREAM BEAR** 23-1/2in (61cm) Yellow tag, U.S.A. only. | $1,300.00 |
| 0155/23 | 383 | | 1985/87 | **MARGARET STRONG RING BEAR-ER** 9in (23cm) Yellow tag, boxed, U.S.A. only. | $250.00 |
| 0155/22 | 383 | | 1985/87 | **MARGARET STRONG FLOWER BEAR-ER** 8-1/2in (22cm) Yellow tag, boxed, U.S.A. only. | $250.00 |
| 0158/25 | 384 | **458** | 1985/88 | **MARGARET STRONG WHITE LEATHER PAW BEAR** 10in (25cm) Limited 3,000, white tag, U.S.A. only. | $300.00 |
| 0158/31 | 384 | **458** | 1985/88 | **MARGARET STRONG WHITE LEATHER PAW BEAR** 12in (31cm) Limited 2,500, white tag, U.S.A. only. | $400.00 |
| 0158/41 | 384 | **458** | 1985/88 | **MARGARET STRONG WHITE LEATHER PAW BEAR** 16in (41cm) Limited 2,000, white tag, U.S.A. only. **Also see 1986 for largest size made 0158/50** | $600.00 $2,000.00 |
| 0277/28 | N/A | | 1985 | **MARSHALL FIELD'S HANS (BOY)** 11in (28cm) Limited 5,000, white tag, boxed, dressed in lederhose. Special for Marshall Fields Store, U.S.A. only. | $250.00 |
| 0278/28 | N/A | | 1985 | **MARSHALL FIELD'S HELGA (GIRL)** 11in (28cm) Limited 5,000 white tag, boxed, special for Marshall Fields Store. U.S.A. only. | $300.00 |
| 0085/12 **400377** | 393 | **414** | 1985/87 | **MUSEUM BEAR ON WHEELS** 4-1/2in (12cm) Limited 12,000, boxed, replica 1905, issued button only. | $200.00 |
| 0150/17 | 409 | **428** | 1985/87 | **MUSEUM PENGUIN** 6-1/2in (17cm) Limited 8,000, boxed, replica 1928, issued button only. | $200.00 |
| 0134/22 | 408 | **428** | 1985 | **NIKI RABBIT** 8-1/2in (22cm) Yellow tag, replica 1952. Limited 3,500. | $225.00 |
| 0134/28 | 408 | **428** | 1985 | **NIKI RABBIT** 11in (28cm) Yellow tag, replica 1952. Limited 2,500 **Also see 1992 Niki #4021159.** | $275.00 |
| 0207/10 | 385 | | 1985/86 | **ORIGINAL TEDDY BEAR** Gray 4in (10cm) Yellow tag. | $100.00 |
| 0208/10 | 385 | | 1985/86 | **ORIGINAL TEDDY BEAR** Black 4in (10cm) Yellow tag. | $100.00 |
| 0245/40 | 22 | | 1985/88 | **PASSPORT BEAR** 15-1/4in (41cm) Yellow tag, includes a passport booklet in a vinyl holder around its neck, worldwide. | $325.00 |
| 7635/28 | 382 | | 1985/88 | **SANTA CLAUS DOLL** 11in (28cm) Limited 1,200, replica 1950. | $195.00 |
| 0176/29 | 386 | **467** | 1985/86 | **TAN TEDDY BABY** 11-1/4in (29cm) U.S.A. only. | $300.00 |
| 0176/35 | 386 | **467** | 1985/86 | **TAN TEDDY BABY** 13-3/4in (35cm) U.S.A. only. | $395.00 |
| 0176/42 | 386 | **467** | 1985/86 | **TAN TEDDY BABY** 16-1/2in (42cm) U.S.A. only. | $495.00 |
| 4006 | | **490** | 1986 | **ALICE AND HER FRIENDS** Limited 3,000 sets. Many sets are broken up and the animals were sold separately. | $300.00 |
| 0146/13 | | **490** | 1986 | **ALICE CAT** 5in (13cm) | $95.00 |
| 0148/13 | | **490** | 1986 | **ALICE MOUSE** 5in (13cm) | $75.00 |

| Item Ear tag# EAN # | Sortiment Book Vol#1 | Vol#2 | Year | Description | Value |
|---|---|---|---|---|---|
| 0147/20 | | **490** | 1986 | **ALICE RABBIT** 8in (20cm) | $100.00 |
| 8494/03 | 387 | | 1986/88 | **BEAR PIN HEAD** Gold 1-1/4in (4cm) | $100.00 |
| 0100/86 | 378 | **479** | 1986/88 | **CALLIOPE AND ELEPHANT** Limited 5,000, white tag, boxed and certificate. Elephant only #0135/22. | $1,200.00 |
| 0168/22 0168/42 0168/32 | 387 387 | **468** **468** | 1986/88 1986/88 1988 | **1906 GOLD GIENGEN BEAR** 8-1/2in (22cm) Yellow tag, U.S.A. only. **1906 GOLD GIENGEN BEAR** 16-1/2in (42cm) Yellow tag, U.S.A. only. **1906 GOLD GIENGEN BEAR** 12in (32cm) Yellow tag, worldwide. | $250.00 $350.00 $500.00 |
| 0167/22 0167/52 | 387 387 | **467** **467** | 1986/90 1986/89 | **1906 GRAY GIENGEN BEAR** 8-1/2in (22cm) Yellow tag, light gray, replica 1906. **1906 GRAY GIENGEN BEAR** 20-1/2in (52cm) Yellow tag, light gray, replica 1906. U.S.A.only. **Also see Gray Giengen Bears 1986 # 0167/32 and #0167/42.** | $175.00 $450.00 |
| 0190/25 **408502** | 394 | **415** | 1986/87 | **JACKIE BEAR** 10in (25cm) Limited 10,000, white tag, boxed, certificate, worldwide. | $250.00 |
| 0155/15 | 383 | **486** | 1986/87 | **MARGARET STRONG CHRISTENING BEAR** 6in (15cm) Yellow tag, boxed, U.S.A. only. | $250.00 |
| 0155/38 | 382 | **484** | 1986/89 | **MARGARET STRONG SANTA BEAR** 15in (38cm) Yellow tag, boxed, dressed in traditional U.S. Santa's outfit. Replica 1904. **Also see 1987 St. Nickolas # 0156/38 U.S.A. only.** | $400.00 |
| 0155/34 0155/35 | 383 383 | **486** **486** | 1986 1986 | **MARGARET STRONG VICTORIAN GIRL BEAR** 13-1/2in (34cm) **MARGARET STRONG VICTORIAN BOY BEAR** 13-3/4in (35cm) Yellow tag, boxed, certificate, replica 1904, U.S.A. only. **Also see 1987 Victorian Lady # 0156/36 and Victorian Man #0156/37.** | $400.00 $400.00 |
| 0158/50 | 384 | **458** | 1986 | **MARGARET STRONG WHITE LEATHER PAW BEAR** 19-1/2in (50cm) Limited 750, white tag, U.S.A. only. | $2,000.00 |
| 0101/14 **400957** 0104/10 **401237** | 409 409 | **428** **428** | 1986/87 1986/88 | **MUSEUM BULLY DOG** 5-1/2in (14cm) Limited 6,000, boxed, replica 1927, issued button only. **MUSEUM TABBY CAT** 4in (10cm) Limited 6,000, boxed, replica 1928, issued button only. | $250.00 $250.00 |
| 0165/38 | N/A | | 1986 | **RINGMASTER BEAR** 15in (38cm) Limited 255, yellow tag, 1909 gold bear. Special for a store in Southern California signing session for Hans Otto Steiff. The outfit was made by Vera Oliver Fuchs. Red jacket, white bib, black top hat, special printed tag on arm, reading "Steiff Ringmaster Admit One" with "Ltd. Edition #listed." | $600.00 |
| 0210/10 0213/10 0214/10 | 385 385 385 | | 1986 1986 1986 | **ORIGINAL TEDDY BEAR** Light Gold 4in (10cm) Yellow tag. Germany only. **ORIGINAL TEDDY BEAR** Cinnamon 4in (10cm) Yellow tag. **ORIGINAL TEDDY BEAR** Gold 4in (10cm) Yellow tag. Both the charcoal and cinnamon were issued with the same numbers. | $100.00 $100.00 $100.00 |
| 0270/28 0271/28 | 363 363 | **361** **361** | 1986/88 1986/88 | **TEDDY BRIDE BEAR** 11in (28cm) **TEDDY GROOM BEAR** 11in (28cm) Open edition, yellow tag, boxed. | $250.00 $250.00 $250.00 |
| 0170/32 **407253** | 393 | **414** | 1986/87 | **TEDDY CLOWN BEAR** 12-1/2in (32cm) Limited 10,000, white tag, replica 1926, boxed, certificate, U.S.A. only. | $450.00 |
| 0275/28 0276/28 **010170** | 363 363 | **361** **361** | 1986 1986/89 | **TEDDY "DIRNDL" GIRL BEAR** 11in (28cm) Yellow tag, boxed, worldwide. **TEDDY "LEDERHOSE" BOY BEAR** 11in (28cm) Yellow tag, boxed, worldwide. | $250.00 $250.00 |

| Item Ear tag# EAN # | Sortiment Book Vol#1 | Vol#2 | Year | Description | Value |
|---|---|---|---|---|---|
| 0280/28 010200 | 363 | **361** | 1986/89 | **TEDDY SAILOR BOY BEAR** 11in (28cm) Open edition, yellow tag, boxed. | $250.00 |
| 0281/28 010224 | 363 | **361** | 1986/89 | **TEDDY SAILOR GIRL BEAR** 11in (28cm) Open edition, yellow tag, boxed. | $250.00 |
| 0255/35 | 387 | **468** | 1987/89 | **CLIFFORD BERRYMAN BEAR** 13-3/4in (35cm) Yellow tag, Linda Mullins' special piece, difficult to find, U.S.A. only. | $400.00 |
| 0164/32 | 378 | | 1987/89 | **CIRCUS DOLLY GREEN BEAR** 12-1/2in (32cm) | $350.00 |
| 0164/34 | 378 | **480** | 1987/89 | **CIRCUS DOLLY VIOLET BEAR** 13-1/4in (34cm) Limited 2,000, white tag, replica 1913, U.S.A. only. | $350.00 |
| 0164/30 | 378 | **480** | 1987 | **CIRCUS DOLLY MISTAKE PALE YELLOW BEAR** 11-3/4in (30cm) Limited 480, white tag, replica 1913, U.S.A. only. | $650.00 |
| 0164/31 | 378 | **480** | 1987/89 | **CIRCUS DOLLY YELLOW BEAR** 12in (31cm) | $350.00 |
| 0162/33 | 389 | **471** | 1987 | **F.A.O. SCHWARZ 1ST 1906 CHOCOLATE BEAR** 13in (33cm) Limited 1,000, white tag, 125th Anniversary, boxed, certificate. | $395.00 |
| 9102/50 412400 | 412 | **509** | 1987/90 | **GENTLEMAN IN MORNING COAT** 19-1/2in (50cm) | $350.00 |
| 9112/45 412509 | 412 | **509** | 1987/90 | **PEASANT MAN** 17-1/2in (45cm) | $375.00 |
| 9110/43 412202 | 412 | **509** | 1987/90 | **PEASANT LADY** 17in (43cm) | $375.00 |
| 9100/45 412301 | 412 | **509** | 1987/90 | **BETTY TENNIS LADY** 17-1/2in (45cm) Limited 2,000, white tag, boxed, certificate, replica 1913, special two buttons one brass and one silver raised script, worldwide. | $350.00 |
| 0201/14 | 389 | **469** | 1987 | **HANS HELPER BEAR** 5-1/2in (14cm) Limited 200, yellow tag, dressed for Steiff Festival Hobby Center Toy Store, Toledo, Ohio. | $350.00 |
| 0100/87 | 378 | **479** | 1987/88 | **LION WAGON** Limited 5,000, boxed, certificate. Lion only. 6in (15cm) #0136/15 | $350.00 |
| 7101 | N/A | | 1987 | **LITTLE RED RIDING HOOD and WOLF SET** | $195.00 |
| 0156/38 | 382 | | 1987/89 | **MARGARET STRONG ST. NICHOLAS BEAR** 15in (38cm) Yellow tag, boxed, dressed in traditional Victorian Santa's outfit, replica 1904, U.S.A. only. | $450.00 |
| 0156/36 | 383 | **486** | 1987/89 | **MARGARET STRONG VICTORIAN LADY BEAR** 14in (36cm) | $400.00 |
| 0156/37 | 383 | **486** | 1987/89 | **MARGARET STRONG VICTORIAN MAN BEAR** 14-1/2in (37cm) Yellow tag, boxed, replica 1904, U.S.A. only. **Also see 1986 Victorian Girl # 0155/34 and Victorian Boy # 0155/35** | $400.00 |
| 4006 | N/A | | 1987 | **MARY and HER LAMB SET** | $175.00 |
| No # | | **469** | 1987 | **MR. SANTA or NICKLAUS BEAR** Limited 300, yellow tag, this dressed Mr. Santa was also offered at the first year of the Steiff Festival in Toledo, Ohio, for Hobby Center Toys, U.S.A. only. | $450.00 |
| No # | | **469** | 1987 | **MRS. SANTA BEAR** Limited 150, yellow tag, first year, special dressed piece for the Steiff Festival in Toledo, Ohio, for Hobby Center Toy Store, by Beth and Ben Savino, U.S.A. only. | $450.00 |
| 0090/11 400568 | 394 | **415** | 1987/88 | **MUSEUM POLAR BEAR** 4-1/4in (11cm) Limited 3,000, boxed, replica 1909, issued button only. | $375.00 |

Steiff. *Margaret Woodbury Strong Gold Bear*.
#0155/60. 1984. 23-3/4in (60cm); gold mohair;
felt pads; glass eyes; f.j; B.B.
CONDITION: Mint
**PRICE:** $550.00.
*Photo courtesy of Hobby House Press, Inc.*

| Item Ear tag# EAN # | Sortiment Book Vol#1 | Vol#2 | Year | Description | Value |
|---|---|---|---|---|---|
| 4007 | N/A | | 1987 | **ROSE RED and SNOW WHITE DOLL and BEAR SET** Bear only. | $300.00 $250.00 |
| 0284/28 **010279** | 363 | | 1987 | **TEDDY FARMER BOY BEAR**  11in (28cm) Yellow tag, boxed, dressed Petsy bears, U.S.A. only. | $250.00 |
| 0163/19 | 380 | **480** | 1987 | **TEDDY CLOWN JR. or CLOWN TEDDY**  7in (19cm) Limited 5,000 total, 2,000 white tag and 3,000 yellow tag, gold mohair, checked outfit. | $250.00 |
| 0283/28 **010255** | 363 | | 1987 | **TEDDY BLACK FOREST GIRL BEAR**  11in (28cm) Yellow tag, boxed, dressed Petsy bears, U.S.A. only. | $250.00 |
| 0171/41 **407208** | 394 | **415** | 1987/89 | **TEDDY ROSE**  16in (41cm) Limited 10,000, boxed, certificate, replica 1925, 1987 U.S.A. only, 1988 worldwide. | $700.00 |
| 0227/33 | 387 | **468** | 1987/89 | **SCHNUFFY BEAR REPLICA 1907**  13in (33cm) Issued button only,  U.S.A. only. | $450.00 |
| 0166/29 | 399 | **453** | 1987 | **WILLIAM SHAKESPEARE BEAR**  11-1/2in (29cm) Limited 2,000, white tag, 1909 style, blond mohair, U. K. only. | $275.00 |
| 0225/27 | 387 | **468** | 1988/90 | **BABY OPHELIA BEAR**  10-1/2in (27cm) Issued button only, U.S.A. only. | $325.00 |
| 0173/40 **406003** | 395 | **415** | 1988/89 | **BLACK BEAR REPLICA 1907**  15-3/4in (40cm) Limited 4,000, white tag, boxed, certificate, (short smooth mohair fur, leather nose). U.S.A. only. | $650.00 |
| 0166/25 **406201** 000355 | 394 | **424** **424** | 1988/90 1991/92 1993/99 | **1909 BLOND TEDDY**  10in (25cm)  Yellow tag, worldwide. **1909 BLOND TEDDY**  10in (25cm)   Yellow tag, worldwide. **1909 BLOND TEDDY**  10in (25cm)   Yellow tag, worldwide. | $115.00 $115.00 $115.00 |
| 0166/35 **406225** | 394 | **424** | 1988/90 1991/92 | **1909 BLOND TEDDY**  13-3/4in (35cm) Yellow tag, worldwide. **1909 BLOND TEDDY**  13-3/4in (35cm)  Yellow tag, worldwide. | $155.00 $155.00 |

| Item Ear tag# EAN # | Sortiment Book Vol#1 | Vol#2 | Year | Description | Value |
|---|---|---|---|---|---|
| 000379 | | 424 | 1993/99 | **1909 BLOND TEDDY** 13-3/4in (35cm) Yellow tag, worldwide. | $155.00 |
| 0166/43 | 394 | | 1988/90 | **1909 BLOND TEDDY** 17in (43cm) Yellow tag, worldwide. | $240.00 |
| **406256** | | 424 | 1991/92 | **1909 BLOND TEDDY** 17in (43cm) Yellow tag, worldwide. | $240.00 |
| **000393** | | 424 | 1993/99 | **1909 BLOND TEDDY** 17in (43cm) Yellow tag, worldwide. | $240.00 |
| 0156/34 | 388 | **468** | 1988/89 | **CAPTAIN STRONG BEAR** 13-1/4in (34cm) Yellow tag, boxed, dressed, Margaret Strong replica 1904, U.S.A. only. | $350.00 |
| 0120/19 | 379 | **481** | 1988/89 | **CIRCUS BEAR BANDMASTER** 7in (19cm) | $225.00 |
| 0122/19 | 379 | **481** | 1988/89 | **CIRCUS CAT BANDSMAN** 7in (19cm) | $200.00 |
| 0124/19 | 379 | **481** | 1988/89 | **CIRCUS CROCODILE BANDSMAN** 7in (19cm) | $200.00 |
| 0121/19 | 379 | **481** | 1988/89 | **CIRCUS DOG BANDSMAN** 7in (19cm) | |
| 0123/19 | 379 | **481** | 1988/89 | **CIRCUS LION BANDSMAN** 7in (19cm) Limited 5,000, boxed, white tag, U.S.A. only. | $200.00 |
| 9130/43 **412189** | 412 | **509** | 1988/90 | **COLORO-CLOWN DOLL** 18in (43cm) Limited 3,000, replica 1911, boxed, certificate. | $495.00 |
| 0243/32 | 389 | **475** | 1988 | **DISNEY WORLD 1ST CONVENTION BEAR ANTIQUE GOLD** 12in (32cm) Limited 1,000, white tag, Margaret Strong Bear, suede paws, for Disney World Epcot Center. U.S.A. only. | $1,800.00 |
| | | | | **Also made a special 7 foot (213cm) size called Hans Willie.** | $25,000.00 |
| 0163/34 **650388** | 389 | **471** | 1988/89 | **F.A.O. SCHWARZ 1909 WHITE TEDDY BEAR** 13in (34cm) Limited 2,000, white tag, boxed, exclusively for F.A.O. Schwarz Toy Store. | $450.00 |
| 0100/88 | 378 | | 1988/89 | **GIRAFFE WAGON** Limited 5,000, boxed and certificate. Giraffe only. 11in (28cm) # 0137/28 | $375.00 |
| 0163/26 **650291** | 399 | **449** | 1988 | **HAMLEY'S BEAR** 10-1/4in (26cm) Limited 2,000, white tag, boxed, for Hamley's Department Store, U.K. only. | $325.00 |
| 0190/35 **408526** | 394 | **415** | 1988/89 | **JACKIE BEAR** 13-3/4in (35cm) Limited 4,000, white tag, boxed, certificate, worldwide. | $450.00 |
| 0155/22 | 382 | | 1988 | **MARGARET STRONG SANTA'S ELF BEAR** 8-1/2in (22cm) Yellow tag, not boxed, U.S.A. only. | $275.00 |
| 0126/20 **401350** | 409 | **429** | 1988/89 | **MUSEUM DONKEY** 8 in (20cm) Limited 4,000, white tag, boxed, replica 1931. | $200.00 |
| 0081/14 **400186** | 409 | **428** | 1988/89 | **MUSEUM FELT DUCK** 5-1/2in (14cm) Limited 4,000, boxed, issued button only, replica 1892. | $195.00 |
| 0095/17 **400605** | 409 | **428** | 1988 | **MUSEUM HOLLANDER RABBIT** 6-3/4in (17cm) Limited 4,000, boxed, replica 1911, 7-way jointed, issued button only. | $250.00 |
| 0125/24 **401404** | 409 | **429** | 1988/89 | **MUSEUM JUMBO ELEPHANT** 9-1/2in (23cm) Limited 4,000, white tag, boxed, replica 1932. | $225.00 |
| 0132/24 **400858** | 394 | **415** | 1988/89 | **MUSEUM WIWAG - BEAR PULL TOY** 9-1/2in (24cm) Limited 4,000, white tag, boxed, replica 1924 worldwide. | $350.00 |
| 0174/46 | 395 | **415** | 1988/90 | **MUZZLE BEAR 1908 WHITE** 18in (43cm) Limited 5,000, U.S.A. only. | $475.00 |
| 0218/14 | 389 | **469** | 1988 | **PANDA BEAR** 5in (14cm) Limited 1,000, Made for The Toy Store's Festival of Steiff, first piece issued as a factory special, previous years were yellow tag bear dressed by the Toy Store, U.S.A. only. | $450.00 |
| 0177/00 | | **434** | 1988 | **PAUL WOLFF TEDDY BABY and WOLF SET #1** 11in (28cm) Limited 1,000, white tag, boxed, 85th year anniversary of doing business with Steiff Co. | $1,000.00 |
| 0115/18 | 387 | **459** | 1988/89 | **ROLY POLY BEAR** 7in (18cm) Limited 3,000, white tag, replica 1908, U.S.A. only. | $395.00 |

| Item<br>Ear tag#<br>EAN # | Sortiment Book | | Year | Description | Value |
|---|---|---|---|---|---|
| | Vol#1 | Vol#2 | | | |
| 0116/28 | 408 | | 1988/89 | **ROLY POLY CLOWN** 11in (28cm)<br>Limited 3,000, white tag, replica 1909, U.S.A. only. | $375.00 |
| 0131/00<br><br>0131/25<br>0131/23<br>0131/24 | 385 | **459** | 1988 | **RUB-A-DUB-DUB THREE BEARS IN A TUB**<br>Limited 2,000, boxed, all in a wooden tub, U.S.A. only.<br>**BUTCHER** 10in (25cm)<br>**BAKER** 10in (25cm)<br>**CANDLE-STICK MAKER** 9-1/4in (24cm) | $550.00 |
| 0177/00 | 395 | | 1988 | **TEDDY BABY AND WOLF SET** 11in (28cm)<br>Limited 1,000, boxed, certificate, 85th anniversary of Paul Wolff's Toy Store, Germany only. | $950.00 |
| 0130/28 | 388 | **459** | 1989/90 | **BEAR ON ALL FOURS** 11in (28cm)<br>Limited 3,000, boxed, certificate, replica 1931, head rotates with tail movement. | $550.00 |
| 0174/61<br>**406104** | 399 | **447** | 1989 | **1907 BRITISH COLLECTOR'S BLOND TEDDY** 23-1/2in (61cm)<br>Limited 2,000, white tag, box and certificate, U.K. only. | $1,300.00 |
| | | | | *BUTTON IN THE EAR BOOK* **LIMITED EDITION**<br>Limited 1,500, hard bound book with slipcover, "Teddy Bears Picnic"<br>record, signed hand numbered.<br>*BUTTON IN THE EAR BOOK* **REGULAR EDITION**<br>Same book as above without the signature, slipcover or the record. | $275.00<br><br><br>$150.00 |
| 0293/32<br>**011931** | 390 | **459** | 1989 | **CALIFORNIA MUSICAL "HONEY" BEAR** 12-1/2in (32cm)<br>Limited 2,000, made for Lucettes, U.S.A. only. | $300.00 |
| 0175/19<br><br>0143/19<br>0145/19<br>0146/19<br>0147/12<br>**650444** | 380<br><br>380<br>380<br>381<br>380 | **482**<br><br>**482**<br>**482**<br>**482**<br>**482** | 1989<br><br>1989<br>1989/90<br>1989/90<br>1989/91 | **CIRCUS TEDDY BABY RINGMASTER BEAR** 7-1/4 in (19cm)<br>Limited 7,000.<br>**CIRCUS CHIMP ON UNICYCLE** 7-1/4 in (19cm)<br>**CIRCUS ELEPHANT BALLOON SELLER** 7-1/4 in (19cm)<br>**CIRCUS HIPPO FAT LADY** 7-1/4 in (19cm)<br>**CIRCUS SEAL WITH BALL** 4-1/2 in (12cm)<br>Limited 5,000, white tag, all are boxed. | $250.00<br><br>$275.00<br>$275.00<br>$275.00<br>$225.00 |
| 0244/35<br>**011443** | 390 | **475** | 1989 | **DISNEY WORLD 2ND CONVENTION WHITE PETSY BEAR** 13-3/4in (35cm)<br>Limited 1,000, white tag.<br>Also made a special 5 foot size with suede paws, made for Disney<br>World Epcot Center. | $1,000.00<br><br>$10,500.00 |
| 0285/29<br>**010309** | 390 | **471** | 1989 | **F.A.O. SCHWARZ GOLDEN GATE BEAR** 11-1/4in (29cm)<br>Limited 2,000, white tag, grand opening of San Francisco's F.A.O. Schwarz Toy Store,<br>boxed, certificate, U.S.A. only. | $550.00 |
| 0168/28<br>**650284** | 399 | **450** | 1989 | **HAMLEY'S 1906 REPLICA BEAR** 11-1/4in (29cm)<br>Limited 2,000, white tag, replica 1906, made for Hamley's department store, U.K. only. | $375.00 |
| 0291/26<br>**011917** | 399 | **451** | 1989/90 | **HARRODS WHITE MUSICAL BEAR REPLICA 1909** 10-1/4in (26cm)<br>Limited 2,000, white tag, boxed, certificate, "Brahms Lullaby," U.K. only. | $650.00 |
| 0190/17<br>**408496** | 394 | **415** | 1989/90 | **JACKIE BEAR** 6-1/2in (17cm)<br>Limited 12,000, white tag, replica 1953, boxed, certificate, worldwide. | $250.00 |
| 0152/25<br>**011412** | 389 | **469** | 1989 | **MR. VANILLA BEAR** 10in (25cm)<br>Limited 1,000, white tag, The Toy Store's Steiff Festival in Toledo, Ohio,<br>long white mohair. | $850.00 |
| 0135/20<br>**401602** | 395 | **415** | 1989/90 | **MUSEUM BABY BEAR PULL TOY** 8in (20cm)<br>Limited 4,000, boxed, white tag, replica 1939 prototype, worldwide. | $350.00 |

| Item<br>Ear tag#<br>EAN # | Sortiment Book<br>Vol#1 | Vol#2 | Year | Description | Value |
|---|---|---|---|---|---|
| 0093/12<br>**400582** | 409 | **429** | 1989/90<br>1991/92 | **MUSEUM FOX** 4-1/2 in (12cm)<br>Limited 4,000, boxed, replica 1910, issued button only. | $200.00 |
| 0091/14<br>**400551** | 409 | **429** | 1989/90<br>1991/92 | **MUSEUM PIG** 5-1/2 in (14cm)<br>Limited 4,000, boxed, replica 1909, issued button only. | $200.00 |
| 0174/60 | 395 | **415** | 1989/90 | **MUZZLE BEAR WHITE** 23-1/2in (61cm)<br>Limited 2,650, worldwide, replica 1908, boxed, certificate. | $695.00 |
| 0180/50<br>**407307** | 388 | **459** | 1989/91 | **PETSY BEAR BI-COLOR** 19-1/2in (50cm)<br>Limited 5,000, white tag, blue eyes, boxed, certificate, replica 1927, U.S.A. only. | $700.00 |
| 0181/35<br>**407376** | 395 | **416** | 1989/90 | **PETSY BEAR BRASS COLOR** 14in (36cm)<br>Limited 5,000, white tag, boxed, certificate, replica 1927, worldwide. | $325.00 |
| 0118/00 | 382 | **484** | 1989/91 | **REINDEER and SANTA SLEIGH SET** 17in (43cm)<br>Limited 6,000, white tag, boxed, reindeer replica 1956 and Santa 1906.<br>**Also see 1990 2nd year Reindeer 660115 - 0118/17** | $495.00 |
| 0158/17<br>**406607** | 395 | **416** | 1989/91 | **SNAP-A-PART BEAR** 6-1/2in (17cm)<br>Limited 5,000, white tag, boxed, certificate, replica 1908, highly sought after, worldwide. | $350.00 |
| 0163/20 | 380 | **481** | 1989 | **TEDDY CLOWN JR. or CLOWN TEDDY**<br>Limited 5,000, white tag, white mohair, striped outfit, U.S.A. only. | $250.00 |
| 0100/89 | 378 | **480** | 1989 | **TIGER WAGON**<br>Limited 5,000, white tag, boxed, certificate. Tiger only 4in (10cm) #0139/10 | $400.00 |
| 0167/23 | 390 | **459** | 1989 | **UFDC BLACK 1989 CONVENTION BEAR** 9in (23cm)<br>Limited 360, white tag, celebrates 4th birthday of U.F.D.C. | $395.00 |
| 0208/15<br>**009624** | 389 | **459** | 1989 | **WISHING BEAR** 6in (15cm)<br>Limited 1,000, made to celebrate Diamond Jubilee for Meyer's Department store, U.S.A. only. | $195.00 |
| 0184/35<br>**406195** | 400 | | 1990 | **ALFONZO TEDDY BEAR** 13-3/4in (35cm)<br>Limited 5,000, white tag, boxed, certificate, red mohair, made for Teddy Bears of Witney, U.K. only. | $850.00 |
| 0169/65<br>**407329** | 396 | **416** | 1990 | **BI-COLORED 1926 "HAPPY" BEAR** 25-1/2in (65cm)<br>Limited 5,000, white tag, boxed, certificate, worldwide. | $1,000.00 |
| 0174/33<br>**406096** | 399 | **447** | 1990 | **1906 BRITISH COLLECTOR'S TEDDY** 13in (33cm)<br>Limited 3,000, white tag, box and certificate, U.K. only. | $425.00 |
| 0149/19<br>**650475** | 381 | **483** | 1990/91 | **CIRCUS FIRE EATER DRAGON** 7-1/4in (19cm)<br>Limited 5,000, white tag, boxed. | $250.00 |
| 0144/19<br>**650482** | 381 | **482** | 1990/91 | **CIRCUS GORILLA STRONGMAN** 7-1/4in (19cm)<br>Limited 5,000, white tag, boxed. | $250.00 |
| 0177/19 | 381 | **483** | 1990 | **CIRCUS TEDDY BABY FOOD VENDOR** 7-1/4in (19cm)<br>Limited 5,000, white tag, boxed. | $275.00 |
| 0100/90 | 378 | **480** | 1990 | **DICKY BEAR WAGON**<br>Limited 5,000, white tag, **2 Bears 650505-0172/16 and 650512-0172/17.** | $450.00 |
| 0245/32<br>**011429** | 391 | **476** | 1990 | **DISNEY WORLD 3RD CONVENTION CHARCOAL GRAY BEAR**<br>12-1/2in (32cm) Limited 1,000. | $750.00 |
| 0245/60 | | | 1990 | 23-1/2in (60cm) Limited 10. | $6,000.00 |
| 0245/80 | | | 1990 | 31-1/2in (80 cm) Limited 1. | $8,000.00 |
| 0245/99 | | | 1990 | 39in (99 cm) Limited 1.<br>White tag, suede paws, issued with convention pin made for Disney World Epcot Center. | $9,500.00 |

Steiff. *1909 Gold Teddy*. #0165/51. 1983-1988.
20in (51cm); gold mohair; felt pads; glass eyes;
f.j. B.B.
CONDITION: Mint
**PRICE:** $650.00.
*Photo courtesy of Hobby House Press, Inc.*

| Item<br>Ear tag#<br>EAN # | Sortiment Book<br><br>Vol#1 | Vol#2 | Year | Description | Value |
|---|---|---|---|---|---|
| 1232/25<br>**652059** | 390 | **472** | 1990 | **F.A.O. SCHWARZ BLACK BEAR CUB** 10in (25cm)<br>Limited 2,000, white tag, boxed, certificate, 1st issue for the North American<br>Wildlife Series, U.S.A. only. | $325.00 |
| 0181/36<br>**650277** | 400 | **450** | 1990 | **HAMLEY'S BEAR OLIVER** 14in (36cm)<br>Limited 2,000, white tag, boxed, certificate, made for Hamley's Store, U.K. only. | $450.00 |
| 0151/27<br>**650369** | 400 | **451** | 1990 | **HARRODS REPLICA 1904/05 MUSICAL BEAR** 10-1/2in (27cm)<br>Limited 2,000, white tag, plays "Mozart's Lullaby," cinnamon mohair, U.K. only. | $550.00 |
| 0159/26<br>**650376** | 391 | **460** | 1990 | **"J.P." BLACK BEAR** 10-1/4in (26cm)<br>Limited 1,000, white tag, made for Mary D's Dolls and Bears and Such, U.S.A. only. | $200.00 |
| 0050/28<br>**401701** | 410 | **429** | 1990<br>1991 | **MUSEUM DINOSAUR** 11in (28cm)<br>Limited 4,000, white tag, boxed, replica 1959, issued button only. | $275.00 |
| 0180/14 | 410 | **429** | 1990 | **MUSEUM DRINKING CAT** 5-1/4in (14cm)<br>Limited 4,000, boxed, replica 1933, issued button only. | $265.00 |
| 0055/00<br>**401800** | 410 | **429** | 1990<br>1991 | **MUSEUM ERIC THE BAT SET** 4-1/2in (12cm) and 6-1/2in (17cm)<br>Limited 4,000, white tag, boxed, replica 1960, issued button only. | $300.00 |
| 0116/25<br>**400698** | 395 | **416** | 1990 | **MUSEUM RECORD TEDDY** 10in (25cm)<br>Limited 4,000, white tag, boxed, replica 1913, worldwide. | $450.00 |
| 0174/35<br>**406126** | 395 | **415** | 1990 | **MUZZLE BEAR WHITE** 13-3/4in (35cm)<br>Limited 6,000, white tag, white mohair, leather muzzle, boxed, certificate. | $450.00 |
| 0211/10 | 385 | | 1990 | **ORIGINAL TEDDY BEAR** Rose 4in (10cm) Yellow tag. | $100.00 |
| 0117/18<br>**660155** | 382 | **484** | 1990<br>1991 | **REINDEER REPLICA 1956** 8in (20cm)<br>Limited 4,000, white tag. **Also see 1989 Reindeer Sleigh Set #660101-0118/00.** | $250.00 |
| 0179/19<br>**650260** | 390 | **470** | 1990 | **TEDDY BABY ROSE** 7-1/4in (19cm)<br>Limited 1,000, white tag, certificate, The Toy Store's Steiff Festival, Toledo, Ohio, U.S.A. only. | $475.00 |
| 0188/25<br>**408854** | 396 | **416** | 1990/91 | **TEDDY NECK MECHANISM REPLICA 1955** 10in (25cm)<br>Limited 4,000, white tag, boxed, certificate, worldwide. | $300.00 |

| Item<br>Ear tag#<br>EAN # | Sortiment<br>Book<br>Vol#1 | Vol#2 | Year | Description | Value |
|---|---|---|---|---|---|
| 0171/25<br>**407154** | 394 | **415** | 1990 | **TEDDY ROSE**  10in (25cm)<br>Limited 8,000, boxed, certificate, replica 1925, worldwide. | $395.00 |
| 0164/29<br>**406553** | 396 | **416** | 1990/91 | **SOMERSAULT BEAR**  11-1/4in (29cm)<br>Limited 5,000, white tag, boxed, certificate, replica 1909, worldwide. | $450.00 |
| 0260/25<br>**650352** | 391 | **460** | 1990 | **SOUTHERN CHARM or JACKIE BEAR ROSE**  10in (25cm)<br>Limited 1,000, white tag, made for My Doll House. | $375.00 |
| **655364** | N/A | | 1990 | **WERTHEIM BERLINER MILIEU**<br>Limited 1,500, white tag, white mohair, blue jacket, black pants and German<br>helmet, Germany only. | N.P.A. |
| 0150/50<br>**404108** | 396 | **417** | 1991 | **BARLE 35 PB BEAR**  19-1/2in (50cm)<br>Limited 6,000, white tag, replica 1904, string fastened disk joints, replica<br>sealing wax nose, boxed, certificate, worldwide. | $850.00 |
| 0169/40<br>**407215** | 396 | **416** | 1991 | **BI-COLOR PETSY "HAPPY" BEAR**  15-1/2in (40cm)<br>Limited 6,000, white tag, boxed, certificate, small size, worldwide. | $500.00 |
| 0173/48<br>**406829** | 400 | **448** | 1991 | **BLACK 1912 BRITISH  COLLECTOR'S TEDDY BEAR**  19in (48cm)<br>Limited 3,000, white tag, boxed, certificate, replica 1912, long black mohair, U.K. only. | $600.00 |
| **650550**<br><br>0145/00 | 381 | **483** | 1991 | **CIRCUS BEARBACK RIDER SET**  8in (18cm) Horse<br>6in (15cm) Bears<br>Limited 5,000, white tag, boxed, U.S.A. only. | $550.00 |
| **650536**<br>0148/19 | 381 | **483** | 1991 | **CIRCUS KANGAROO JUGGLER**  8in (19cm)<br>Limited 5,000, white tag, boxed, U.S.A. only. | $225.00 |
| **650543**<br>0138/19 | 381 | **483** | 1991 | **CIRCUS TIGER JUMPING THROUGH HOOP**  8in (19cm)<br>Limited 5,000, white tag, boxed, U.S.A. only. | $225.00 |
| **650529**<br>0178/19 | 381 | **483** | 1991 | **CIRCUS TEDDY BABY TICKET SELLER**  8in (19cm)<br>Limited 5,000, white tag, boxed, U.S.A. only. | $275.00 |
| 0172/19<br>0172/18 | 391 | **470** | 1991 | **DICKY ROSE and MAUVE BEAR SET**  7-1/4in (19cm)<br>Limited 2,000, white tag, bears for the Toy Store Steiff Festival, Toledo, Ohio.<br>**011962/0172/19 Mauve   011955/0172/18 Rose** | $400.00 |
| 0246/32<br>**011269** | 391 | **476** | 1991 | **DISNEY WORLD 4TH CONVENTION MICKEY MOUSE BEAR**<br>12-1/2in (32cm) Limited 1,500, white tag. | $1,300.00 |
| 0246/60<br>**011276** | | **476** | 1991 | 23-1/2in (60cm) Limited 20, white tag. | $6,000.00 |
| 0246/80<br>011283 | | **476** | 1991 | 31-1/2in (80cm) Limited 1. | $8,000.00 |
| 0246/99<br>**011290** | | **476** | 1991 | 39in (99cm) Limited 1.<br>Black mohair bear wearing a  Mickey mask, made for Disney World<br>Epcot Center, U.S.A. only. | $10,500.00 |
| 0294/42<br>**011924** | 400 | **451** | 1991 | **HARRODS MUSICAL BEAR**  16-1/2in (42cm)<br>Limited 2,000, white tag, boxed, certificate, gold mohair, plays "Fuer Elise"<br>by Beethoven, made for Harrods, U.K. only. | $525.00 |
| 401732 | 410 | **430** | 1991/92 | **MUSEUM SPIDER SET**  9in (23cm) and 5in (13cm.)<br>Limited 4,000, white tag, boxed, replica 1960. | $345.00 |
| 0051/20<br>**401718** | 410 | **430** | 1991/92 | **MUSEUM TYRANNOSAURUS**  8in (20cm)<br>Limited 4,000, white tag, boxed, replica 1959. | $300.00 |
| 0173/35<br>**406119** | 395 | **460** | 1991 | **MUZZLE BEAR BROWN**  13-3/4in (35cm)<br>Limited 5,000, white tag, boxed, certificate, replica 1908. | $450.00 |

| Item<br>Ear tag#<br>EAN # | Sortiment Book<br>Vol#1 | Vol#2 | Year | Description | Value |
|---|---|---|---|---|---|
| 0212/10<br>030567 | 385 | | 1991 | **ORIGINAL TEDDY BEAR**  Charcoal 4in (10cm)<br>Yellow tag. | $100.00 |
| RL0010 | | **487** | 1991 | **RALPH LAUREN PREPPY BEAR**  13-3/4in (35cm)<br>Not a limited edition, Polo bear dressed by Ralph Lauren, in gray flannel<br>trousers, blue crew neck wool sweater, blue oxford button down shirt, black<br>watch tie, woven leather belt. | $600.00 |
| 0098/20<br>400704 | 395 | 416 | 1991/92 | **RECORD TEDDY ROSE**  8in (20cm)<br>Limited 4,000, white tag, boxed, replica 1913. | $395.00 |
| 0174/34<br>406034 | 400 | 491 | 1991 | **1907 REPLICA (JAPAN 1ST BEAR)**  13-1/4in (34cm)<br>Limited 5,000, white tag, light brown mohair, Japan and Vienna only. | $400.00 |
| 407758 | 386 | | 1991 | **TEDDY BABY BROWN**  13-3/4in (35cm) | $395.00 |
| 408113<br>0178/15 | 388 | 460 | 1991 | **TEDDY BABY-MAIZE (YELLOW)**  6in (15cm) | $225.00 |
| 408144<br>0178/32 | 388 | 460 | 1991 | **TEDDY BABY-MAIZE (YELLOW)**  12-1/2in (32cm)<br>Limited 5,000, white tag, replica 1931, unique closed mouth, U.S.A. only. | $295.00 |
| 0220/36<br>010354 | 39 | | 1991/94 | **TEDDY - BLOND**  14in (36cm) Yellow tag. | $200.00 |
| 0220/43<br>010408 | 39 | | 1991/94 | **TEDDY - BLOND**  17in (43cm) Yellow tag. | $250.00 |
| 0220/55<br>010453 | 39 | | 1991/94 | **TEDDY - BLOND**  21-1/2in (55cm) Yellow tag. | $400.00 |
| 0223/36<br>010859 | 39 | | 1991/94 | **TEDDY - TAFFY**  14in (36cm) Yellow tag. | $250.00 |
| 0223/43<br>010903 | 39 | | 1991/94 | **TEDDY - TAFFY**  17in (43cm) Yellow tag. | $300.00 |
| 0223/55<br>010958 | 39 | | 1991/94 | **TEDDY - TAFFY**  21-1/2in (55cm) Yellow tag. | $425.00 |
| 011382<br>**011382** | 391 | 460 | 1991 | **TEDDY'S, CHARCOAL TEDDY BABY**  7-1/4in (19cm)<br>Limited 1,000, white tag, made for Teddy's Toy Store, U.S.A. only. | $300.00 |
| 8530/43 | 414 | | 1991 | **TEDDY WATCH DISPLAY WITH 13 WATCHES**  17in (43cm)<br>Limited 2,000, white tag, replica 1930s, display 13 watches, cream color<br>bear, closed mouth.<br>**TEDDY BABY**  sold separately.<br>**WRIST WATCHES**  sold separately. | $900.00<br><br><br>$595.00<br>$75.00 |
| 038006<br><br>038006<br><br>038303 | 407<br><br><br><br>407 | 506<br><br><br><br>506 | 1992/97<br><br><br><br>1992/95 | **ARK BAMBOO and NOAH AND HIS WIFE BEARS**<br>59in (100cm) and 11-3/4in (30cm)<br>**ARK WOODEN and NOAH AND HIS WIFE BEARS**<br>59in (100cm) and 11-3/4in (30cm)<br>Limited 8,000, available in bamboo or wood, also includes 2 dressed bears.<br>**ARK ELEPHANT SET**  Boat 11-3/4in (30cm)<br>Elephants 6 and 6-1/2in (15 and 17cm) Limited 8,000, 2 elephants, includes small bamboo boat. | $650.00<br><br>$650.00<br><br><br>$325.00 |
| 406805 | 396 | 417 | 1992 | **BLACK BEAR**  15-3/4in (40cm)<br>Limited 7,000, white tag, boxed, certificate, replica 1912, distressed mohair fur. | $400.00 |
| 406645 | 400 | 448 | 1992 | **BRITISH  COLLECTOR'S WHITE TEDDY BEAR**  16in (42cm)<br>Limited 3,000, white tag, boxed, certificate, replica 1911, U.K. only. | $450.00 |
| 029073 | 404 | 497 | 1992/97 | **CINNAMON BEAR**  6-1/4in (16cm) Yellow tag. | $150.00 |
| 011986 | 392 | 476 | 1992 | **DISNEYLAND 1ST CONVENTION GRAY BEAR**<br>12-1/2in (32cm), Limited 2,000. | $495.00 |

| Item Ear tag# EAN # | Sortiment Book Vol#1 | Vol#2 | Year | Description | Value |
|---|---|---|---|---|---|
| **011993** | | | 1992 | 23-1/2in ( 60cm) Limited 20. | $4,200.00 |
| **012006** | | | 1992 | 31-1/2in (80cm) Limited 1. | N.P.A. |
| | | | | Light gray mohair, white tag, leather paws, with red printed ribbon, U.S.A. only. | |
| | | | | **DISNEY WORLD 5TH CONVENTION MINNIE MOUSE BEAR** | |
| **011863** | 391 | **476** | 1992 | 12-1/2in (30cm) Limited 1,500. | $900.00 |
| **011870** | | | 1992 | 23-1/2in (60cm) Limited 20. | $6,000.00 |
| **011832** | | | 1992 | 31-1/2in (80cm) Limited 1. | N.P.A. |
| **011849** | | | 1992 | 39in (99cm) Limited 1. | N.P.A. |
| | | | | Black mohair, white chest, wearing a mask, Disney World Epcot Center. U.S.A. only. | |
| **011948** | 400 | **450** | 1992 | **HAMLEY'S "TOBIAS" BEAR**  15in (38cm) Limited 2,000, white tag, boxed, certificate, made for Hamley's, U.K. only. | $425.00 |
| **011894** | 400 | **451** | 1992 | **HARRODS MUSICAL CLOWN BEAR**  14in (36cm) Limited 2,000, white tag, boxed, certificate, 1926 replica, plays "The Entertainer," U.K. only. | $550.00 |
| **402463** | 408 | **428** | 1992/98 | **LION**  19-1/2in (50cm) Limited 4,000. | $525.00 |
| **402357** | 410 | **430** | 1992/97 | **LYING LEOPARD**  11in (28cm) Limited 4,000, white tag, replica 1953. | $275.00 |
| **402463** | 408 | | 1992/95 | **LYING LEO LION**  18-1/2in (50cm) Limited 4,000, white tag, replica 1956. | $600.00 |
| **402043** | 410 | **430** | 1992 | **MUSEUM RATTLER TERRIER**  6-1/2in (17cm) Limited 4,000, white tag, boxed, replica 1930. | $250.00 |
| **400872** | 410 | **430** | 1992 | **MUSEUM WIWAG with MONKEY AND BEAR**  10in (24cm) Limited 4,000, white tag, boxed, replica 1924. | $275.00 |
| **011184** | 40 | | 1992/93 | **MUSICAL TEDDY**  15-1/4in (39cm) Yellow tag, dusty pink mohair, music box plays "Teddy  Bear Picnic". | $350.00 |
| **011214** | 40 | | 1992/93 | **MUSICAL TEDDY**  15-1/4in (39cm) Yellow tag, red-blond mohair, music box plays " Love Story". | $350.00 |
| **402159** | 408 | **428** | 1992/98 | **NIKI RABBIT**  13-3/4in (35cm) Limited 5,000, white tag. | $295.00 |
| **406744** | 388 | **460** | 1992 | **OTTO STEIFF TEDDY BEAR**  15-3/4in (40cm) Limited 5,000, white tag, boxed, certificate, replica 1912,  signed Otto Steiff on one foot and U.S. flag on other, made for the occasion of establishing the new Steiff Company, U.S.A. only. | $450.00 |
| **408304** | 396 | **424** | 1992/98 | **PANDA  BEAR**  11-1/4in (29cm)  Yellow tag, replica 1938. | $250.00 |
| **408311** | 396 | **424** | 1992/98 | **PANDA  BEAR**  12-3/4in (35cm)  Yellow tag, replica 1938. | $300.00 |
| **029424** | 404 | **498** | 1992/99 | **PETSY BRASS**  6in (16cm) Yellow tag. | $150.00 |
| **029479** | 404 | **498** | 1992/97 | **PETSY OLD-GOLD**  6in (16cm) Yellow tag. | $150.00 |
| **029523** | 404 | **498** | 1992/95 | **PETSY PALE GOLD**  6in (16cm) Yellow tag. | $150.00 |
| **RL0020** **406225** | N/A | **486** | 1992 | **RALPH LAUREN  AMERICAN FLAG BEAR**  13in (35cm) Limited 3,500, Ralph Lauren blue jeans, American Flag sweater, shirt, T-shirt, leather belt. | $550.00 |
| **RL0030** **650598** | N/A | **486** | 1992 | **RALPH LAUREN CHAIRMAN OF THE BOARD #1**  18in (43cm) Limited 1,000, dressed pinstripe suit, white shirt, tie, crocodile belt with silver buckle. | $800.00 |
| **402043** | 410 | | 1992 | **RATTLER  REPLICA 1930 DOG**  6-1/2in (17cm) Limited 4,000, white tag, replica 1930's. | $400.00 |
| **029172** | 404 | **497** | 1992/97 | **RICHARD BEAR**   6in (16cm) Yellow tag. | $150.00 |

Steiff. *Margaret Strong Replica 1904.* Cream Bears. 1984 - 1986. 10in (26cm), 13in (32cm), 16in (42cm); cream mohair; plastic eyes; f.j. s.s.; B.B.; yellow label. CONDITION: Mint.
**PRICE:**
10in (26cm)  $200.
13in (32cm)  $325.
16in (42cm)  $450.
*Photograph courtesy Steiff.*

| Item Ear tag# EAN # | Sortiment Book Vol#1 | Vol#2 | Year | Description | Value |
|---|---|---|---|---|---|
| 420016 | 414 | **511** | 1992/93 | **STEIFF  EURO. CLUB TEDDY BABY BLUE**  11in (28cm) Limited 7,959, white tag, boxed, made for members of Steiff, Europe only. | $850.00 |
| 011979 | 391 | **470** | 1992 | **"TEDDILE" TEDDY BEAR**  7in (19cm) Limited 1,500, white tag, peach mohair, for Toy Store's Steiff Festival, U.S.A. only. | $450.00 |
| 407833 407857 | 396 424 | | 1992/96 1992/93 | **TEDDY BABY TAN**  11-1/4in (29cm)  Worldwide. **TEDDY BABY TAN**  13-3/4in (35cm)  Worldwide. Yellow tag, replica 1930, the 2 teddy babies that were reissued in 1992 have the <u>new</u> <u>yellow</u> tag. | $200.00 $250.00 |
| 029677 029622 029721 | 404 404 | 498 | 1992/98 1992/98 1992/98 | **TEDDY BABY MAIZE**  6in (16cm) Yellow tag. **TEDDY BABY WHITE**  6in (16cm) Yellow tag. **TEDDY BABY BROWN**  6in (16cm) Yellow tag. | $150.00 $150.00 $150.00 |
| 011054 011108 011153 | 39 39 39 | | 1992/93 1992/93 1992/93 | **TEDDY - BROWN**  14in (36cm) **TEDDY - BROWN**  17in (43cm) **TEDDY - BROWN**  21-1/2in (55cm) Yellow tag. | $300.00 $400.00 $500.00 |
| 606304 | 414 | 506 | 1992 | **TEDDY WATCH DISPLAY WITH 13 WATCHES**  17in (43cm) Limited 4,000, white tag, replica 1930's, gray color bear with closed mouth, worldwide. **TEDDY BABY**  sold separately. **WRIST WATCHES**  sold separately. | $1,250.00 $575.00 $75.00 |
| 407550 407574 | 394 394 | 417 | 1992/93 1992 | **WHITE  DICKY BEAR**  10in (25cm) Limited 9,000. **WHITE  DICKY BEAR**  13-3/4in (35cm) Limited 7,000, white tag, boxed, certificate, replica 1930, worldwide. | $250.00 $295.00 |
| 650307 | 401 | **453** | 1992 | **WILLIAM SHAKESPEARE BEAR**  11-1/4in (29cm) Limited  amount unknown, white tag, replica 1909, light gold with leather paws, U.K only. | $350.00 |
| 407482 | 396 | **417** | 1992/94 | **YELLOW MUSICAL BEAR**  15-3/4in (40cm) Limited 8,000, white tag, boxed, certificate, replica 1928, has squeeze music box that plays "You Are My Sunshine," worldwide. | $400.00 |

| Item Ear tag# EAN # | Sortiment Book Vol#1 | Vol#2 | Year | Description | Value |
|---|---|---|---|---|---|
| 650574 | 388 | 460 | 1993/94 | **ALICE BEAR**  15-3/4in (40cm) <br> Limited  5,000, white tag, boxed, certificate, replica 1903, embroidered paws <br> 1903 on right and 1993 on left, named for President Roosevelt's daughter Alice, <br> U.S.A. only. | $450.00 |
| 999765 | 392 | 461 | 1993 | **AMELIA**  13-3/4in (35cm) <br> Limited 650, white tag, special piece for I. Magnum Department stores, <br> dressed in flying suit. | $900.00 |
| 999765 | | | 1993 | **AMELIA**  Limited 350, white tag, bear with a ruffled collar only, U.S.A. only. | $695.00 |
| 038327 | 407 | 507 | 1993/96 | **ARK  BEAR SET**  4-1/2in (12cm) <br> Limited 8,000, 2 - bears, 038341. | $295.00 |
| 038341 | 407 | 507 | 1993/95 | **ARK  GIRAFFE SET WITH RAMP** <br> Limited 8,000, one male 8in (20cm) and one female 7in (18cm). | $295.00 |
| 404207 | 396 | 417 | 1993/94 | **BARLE PAB 35 REPLICA  1905**  15-3/4in (50cm) <br> Limited  6,000, white tag, cardboard disc jointed, replica sealing wax nose, <br> kapok filled, boxed, certificate, worldwide. | $400.00 |
| 010057 | 24 | | 1993/94 | **BERLIN BEAR**  11-1/4in (29cm) <br> Yellow tag, boxed, open mouth. | $275.00 |
| 027505 | 24 | | 1993/94 | **BILLY MUSICAL BEAR**  10in (25cm) <br> Yellow tag, boxed, blond mohair, guitar, music box  plays "Yellow Rose of <br> Texas," worldwide. | $225.00 |
| 029202 | 405 | 498 | 1993/95 | **BLACK BEAR**  6-1/2in (16cm) Yellow tag. | $150.00 |
| 027529 | 24 | | 1993/95 | **BOBBY MUSICAL BEAR**  10in (25cm) <br> Yellow tag, boxed, black mohair, with guitar, music box plays "Sweet Georgia <br> Brown," worldwide. | $225.00 |
| 406065 | 401 | | 1993 | **BRITISH COLLECTOR'S TEDDY  DARK BROWN**  23-1/2in (60cm) <br> Limited 3,000, boxed, certificate, U.K. only. | $850.00 |
| 000256 | 397 | 425 | 1993/99 | **CLASSIC 1906 TEDDY BEAR REPLICA**  20in (51cm) <br> Yellow tag, replica 1906, worldwide. | $350.00 |
| 000355 <br> 000379 <br> 000393 | 394 <br> 394 <br> 394 | | 1993/95 <br> 1993/95 <br> 1993/95 | **CLASSIC 1909 BEAR**  10in (25cm) <br> **CLASSIC 1909 BEAR**  14in (35cm) <br> **CLASSIC 1909 BEAR**  17in (43cm) <br> Yellow tag, replica 1909, blond mohair, worldwide. | $165.00 <br> $215.00 <br> $265.00 |
| 000423 <br> 000447 <br> 000461 | 397 <br> 397 <br> 397 | <br> <br> 424 | 1993/99 <br> 1993/99 <br> 1993/99 | **CLASSIC 1909 BEAR**  10in ( 25cm) <br> **CLASSIC 1909 BEAR**  13-3/4in (35cm) <br> **CLASSIC 1909 BEAR**  17in (43cm) <br> Yellow tag, replica 1909, dark brown mohair, worldwide. | $165.00 <br> $215.00 <br> $265.00 |
| 650703 | N/A | | 1993 | **CLASSIC 1920 BEAR**  16-1/2in (42cm) <br> Limited 250, made with a scarf for Kober, Vienna. | $265.00 |
| 000751 | 398 | 425 | 1993/99 | **CLASSIC 1920 BEAR**  16-1/2in (42cm) <br> Yellow tag, replica 1920, light brown mohair, worldwide. | $265.00 |
| 000850 | 398 | 425 | 1993/99 | **CLASSIC 1920 BEAR**  16-1/2in (42cm) <br> Yellow tag, replica 1920, dark brown mohair, worldwide. | $265.00 |

| Item<br>Ear tag#<br>EAN # | Sortiment<br>Book<br>Vol#1 | Vol#2 | Year | Description | Value |
|---|---|---|---|---|---|
| 651205<br>651212<br>651229 | 392 | 476 | 1993<br>1993<br>1993 | **DISNEY WORLD CONVENTION DONALD DUCK BEAR**<br>11-3/4in (30cm) Limited 1,500.<br>Limited 25.<br>Limited 2<br>White tag, white mohair, dressed in blue suit and hat, made for Disney World<br>Epcot Center U.S.A. only. | $850.00<br>$3,500.00<br>N.P.A. |
| 651526<br>651540 | 392 | 476 | 1993 | **DISNEYLAND 2ND CONVENTION GOLD BEAR**<br>11-3/4in (30cm) Limited 1,500.<br>23-1/2in (60 cm) Limited 5.<br>White tag, light gold mohair, smaller size plays one tune "When You Wish<br>Upon a Star," and the larger plays two tunes "When You Wish Upon A Star"<br>and "It's A Small World," U.S.A. only. | $475.00<br>$4,200.00 |
| 650888 | 401 | 435 | 1993 | **ERWIN TEDDY BEAR** 17in (43cm)<br>Limited 7,777, boxed, certificate, for Germany's Children's Cancer Aid, worldwide. | $550.00 |
| 652080 | 392 | 472 | 1993 | **F.A.O. SCHWARZ MUSICAL TEDDY 33** 13in (33cm)<br>Limited 2,000, white tag, gold mohair, boxed, certificate, plays "Welcome to<br>our World of Toys," U.S.A only. | $425.00 |
| 70316<br>704191<br>704074<br>704193 | <br>349<br>349<br>349 | | 1993/95<br>1993/95<br>1993/95<br>1993/95 | **GOLDILOCKS BEARS SET with STEIFF DOLL** 19-1/2in (50cm)<br>Papa bear.<br>Mama bear.<br>Baby bear.<br>Limited 1,500, white tag, boxed set, worldwide. | <br>$375.00<br>$375.00<br>$275.00 |
| 650680 | 401 | 452 | 1993 | **HARRODS 1926 VICTORIAN MUSICAL BEAR** 16-1/2in (42cm)<br>Limited 2,000, white tag, boxed, certificate, replica 1926, wearing a vest,<br>plays "The Thieving Magpie," made for Harrods, U.K. only. | $495.00 |
| 999789 | 401 | | 1993 | **KARLE BREUNINGER 1909 STUTGART BEAR** 11-3/4in (30cm)<br>Limited 200, yellow tag, yellow and black ribbon bow. | $250.00 |
| 408458 | 397 | 418 | 1993 | **MUSICAL TEDDY REPLICA 1951** 13-3/4in (35cm)<br>Limited 7,000, white tag, boxed, certificate, red felt circle on chest when<br>depressed it plays German lullaby, worldwide. | $375.00 |
| 000201 | 397 | 425 | 1993/99 | **MR. CINNAMON CLASSIC TEDDY BEAR** 12-3/4in (55cm)<br>Yellow tag, replica 1903. | $375.00 |
| 400759 | 410 | | 1993 | **MUSEUM JOCKO RECORD PETER** 10in (25cm)<br>Limited 4,000, white tag, boxed, replica 1921, worldwide. | $335.00 |
| 400919 | 397 | 418 | 1993/95 | **MUSEUM CLOCKWORK UR-TEDDY BEAR** 8in (20cm)<br>Limited 4,000, white tag, boxed, replica 1926, worldwide. | $325.00 |
| 401367 | 411 | 430 | 1993 | **MUSEUM ST. BERNARD** 11in (28cm)<br>Limited 4,000, white tag, boxed, replica 1931. | $365.00 |
| 401213 | 411 | 430 | 1993 | **MUSEUM JOCKO CHIMPANZEE** 15-3/4in (40cm)<br>Limited 4,000, white tag, boxed, replica 1928. | $330.00 |
| 029189<br>029196 | 405<br>40 | <br>498 | 1993/94<br>1993/95 | **MUZZLE BEAR DARK BROWN** 6in (16cm) Yellow tag.<br>**MUZZLE BEAR LIGHT BROWN** 6in (16cm) Yellow tag. | $150.00<br>$150.00 |
| 651847 | 392 | 470 | 1993 | **"PETSILE"** 7-1/4in (19cm)<br>Limited 1,5000, white tag, brass mohair, for The Toy Store's Steiff Festival Toledo, Ohio. | $450.00 |
| RL0050<br>027079 | | 486 | 1993 | **RALPH LAUREN CHAIRMAN OF THE BOARD #2** 17in (43cm)<br>Limited 1,500, glen plaid suit, dress shirt, tie, pocket square, boutonniere. | $800.00 |

| Item Ear tag# EAN # | Sortiment Book Vol#1 | Vol#2 | Year | Description | Value |
|---|---|---|---|---|---|
| RL0060 027093 | | 486 | 1993 | **RALPH LAUREN PRODUCER BEAR** 17in (43cm) Limited 1,500, gray stripe wool suit, belt, silver watch chain, black cashmere turtleneck sweater, pocket square, sunglasses. | $800.00 |
| RL0040 027055 | | 487 | 1993 | **RALPH LAUREN RANCH BEAR** 13-3/4in (35cm) Limited 3,500, Ralph Lauren blue jeans, jean jacket, plaid flannel shirt, bandana, T-shirt, long-horn buckle belt. | $495.00 |
| RL0070 027086 | | 487 | 1993 | **RALPH LAUREN VARSITY BEAR** 13-3/4in (35cm) Limited 3,500, Ralph Lauren blue jeans, USA sweatshirt. | $495.00 |
| 406010 | 397 | 418 | 1993 | **1907 REPLICA DARK BROWN TEDDY** 27-1/2in (70cm) Limited 5,000, white tag, boxed, certificate, replica 1907, worldwide. | $950.00 |
| 420801 | 415 | 512 | 1993 | **STEIFF CLUB TEDDY SAM** 11in (28cm) Limited 4,000, white tag, boxed, no certificate, Premiere Edition Steiff Club, U.S.A. only. | $650.00 |
| 420023 | 415 | 511 | 1993 | **STEIFF CLUB TEDDY CLOWN 1928** 11in (28cm) Limited 11,020, white tag, boxed, certificate, member of the Steiff Club, worldwide. | $495.00 |
| 029721 | 404 | | 1993/94 | **TEDDY BABY BROWN** 6in (16cm) Yellow tag. | $150.00 |
| 407512 | 397 | 417 | 1993 | **TEDDY BABY GIRL (MAID) DRESSED** 10in (25cm) | $300.00 |
| 407529 | | 417 | | **TEDDY BABY BOY DRESSED** 10in (25cm) Limited 7,000 white tag, boxed, replica 1930s, dressed, blond mohair, worldwide. | $300.00 |
| 029226 | 405 | 498 | 1993/99 | **TEDDY BEAR RED** 6-1/2in (16cm) Yellow tag. | $150.00 |
| 606502 | 414 | 506 | 1993 | **TEDDY BEAR WITH 13 PENDANT WATCHES** 17in (43cm) Limited 3,000, brown teddy bear, worldwide. **TEDDY BEAR** sold separately. **NECKLACE WATCHES** sold separately. | $1,250.00 $575.00 $75.00 |
| 029394 | 404 | | 1993/95 | **TEDDY CLOWN ROSE** 6-1/2in (16cm) Yellow tag. | $150.00 |
| 029400 | 404 | | 1993/95 | **TEDDY CLOWN WHITE** 6-1/2in (16cm) Yellow tag. | $150.00 |
| 029387 | 404 | | 1993/95 | **TEDDY CLOWN YELLOW** 6-1/2in (16cm) Yellow tag. | $150.00 |
| 650710 | N/A | | 1993 | **TEDDY BEAR DARK BROWN "KARAWANKEN"** 10in (25cm) Limited 250, wearing a scarf, made for Austria. | N.P.A. |
| 650727 650581 | N/A | | 1993 | **TEDDY BEAR BLOND "SALZBURG"** 10in (25cm) Limited 250, Classic 1909 bear, scarf, Austria, also produced for Ralph Lauren. | N.P.A. |
| 029905 | 404 | 498 | 1993/96 | **TEDDY PANDA** 6-1/2in (16cm) Yellow tag. | $150.00 |
| 650855 | 401 | 435 | 1993 | **TEDDY TED** 17in (42cm) Limited 3,333, yellow tag, for German store Idee and Spiel, Germany only. | $250.00 |
| 038440 | | 507 | 1994/96 | **ARK LION SET** Limited 8,000, one lion 4-1/2in (12cm) and one lioness 4in (10cm) | $230.00 |
| 038464 | | 507 | 1994/95 | **ARK GORILLA SET** Limited 8,000, one male 7in (18cm) and one female 7in (18cm) | $315.00 |
| 655104 | N/A | 436 | 1994 | **ALSTERHAUS MICHAEL DER HANSEAT 42** 16-1/2in (42cm) Limited 300, white tag, Michael Der Hanseat 42, dressed as a merchant from the middle ages, black velvet coat and tam, gold medallion and chain, Germany only. | $495.00 |
| 029097 | 405 | 499 | 1994/97 | **BARLE PAB** 6-1/2in (16cm) Yellow tag. | $150.00 |
| 406072 | 402 | 448 | 1994 | **BRITISH COLLECTOR'S TEDDY BEAR 1908 BLOND** 15-3/4in (40cm) Limited 3,000, boxed, certificate, curly blond mohair, U.K. only. | $400.00 |
| 000737 | 398 | 425 | 1994/99 | **CLASSIC 1920 BEAR** 13-3/4in (35cm) Yellow tag, replica 1920, light brown mohair, worldwide. | $215.00 |

Steiff. *Teddy Baby, Replica 1930*.
#0175/42. 1984-1990. 16-1/2in (42cm);
brown mohair; felt pads; glass eyes; f.j;
B.B.
CONDITION: Mint
**PRICE:** $495.00.
*Photo courtesy of Hobby House Press,
Inc.*

| Item Ear tag# EAN # | Sortiment Book Vol#1 | Vol#2 | Year | Description | Value |
|---|---|---|---|---|---|
| 000836 | 398 | 425 | 1994/99 | **CLASSIC 1920 BEAR**  13-3/4in (35cm) | $215.00 |
| 000829 | 398 | 425 | 1994/99 | **CLASSIC 1920 BEAR**  10in (25cm) | $165.00 |
| | | | | Yellow tag, replica 1920, dark brown mohair, worldwide. | |
| 000911 | 398 | 425 | 1994/97 | **CLASSIC PETSY 1927 BEAR**  11in (28cm) | $195.00 |
| 000935 | 398 | 425 | 1994/97 | **CLASSIC PETSY 1927 BEAR**  13-3/4in (35cm) | $225.00 |
| | | | | Yellow tag, replica 1927, worldwide. | |
| 029783 | 405 | 498 | 1994/95 | **DICKY BEAR 1930**  6-1/2in (16cm) Yellow tag. | $150.00 |
| 029789 | 405 | 49 | 1994/95 | **DICKY  BEAR BLOND**  6-1/2in (16cm) Yellow tag. | $150.00 |
| | | | | **DISNEY WORLD 7TH CONVENTION POOH BEAR** | |
| 651243 | 388 | 477 | 1994 | 11-3/4in (30cm) Limited 2,500, white tag. | $1,300.00 |
| 651250 | | | 1994 | 24in (60cm) Limited 25, white tag. | $10,000.00 |
| 651270 | | | 1994 | Limited  5. | N.P.A. |
| | | | | "Winnie the Pooh" bear dressed in a sweater with convention pin, Disney World Epcot Center. | |
| 650925 | 402 | 435 | 1994 | **1909 "EDDI" TEDDY BEAR**  10-1/2in (27cm) Limited  2,000, bright gold mohair, cotton bag, embroidered paw, Spiel and Spass, Germany only. | $400.00 |
| 412011 | 413 | 510 | 1994 | **GUSTO DOLL**  12in (31cm) Limited 1,000, replica 1911, white tag, boxed. | $395.00 |
| 652813 | 402 | 450 | 1994 | **HAMLEY'S CHARLOTTE 1909**  13-3/4in (35cm) Limited 2,000, white tag, white mohair, suede paws, dark purple ribbon, boxed certificate. | $425.00 |

| Item Ear tag# EAN # | Sortiment Book | | Year | Description | Value |
|---|---|---|---|---|---|
| | Vol#1 | Vol#2 | | | |
| 029929 | 405 | 499 | 1994/99 | **JACKIE BEAR** 6-1/2in (16cm) Yellow tag. | $150.00 |
| 650789 | 388 | 461 | 1994/95 | **LOUIS BEAR 1904** 17-1/2 in (44cm) Limited 3,500, white tag, boxed, with St. Louis World's Fair grand prize medal, U.S.A. only. | $395.00 |
| 653131 | | 452 | 1994 | **HARRODS MUSICAL BEAR** Limited 2,000, white tag, white mohair, black cape. | $525.00 |
| 400810 | 41 | 431 | 1994 | **MUSEUM SIAMY SIAMESE CAT** 8-1/2in (22cm) Limited 4,000, boxed, replica 1930, worldwide. | $275.00 |
| 401534 | 397 | 418 | 1994/95 | **MUSEUM CIRCUS BEAR WITH SNAP JOINTS** 12-1/2in (32cm) Limited 4,000, white tag, boxed, certificate, replica 1935, worldwide. | $375.00 |
| RL0080 650598 | | 488 | 1994 | **RALPH LAUREN MARTINI BEAR** 17in (43cm) Limited 500, dressed in a black wool tux with tails, white broadcloth button-down shirt with white pique bow tie and vest, linen pocket square. | $850.00 |
| RL0090 027116 | | 488 | 1994 | **RALPH LAUREN WELLINGTON BEAR** 13-3/4in (35cm) Limited 1,070, dressed in green wool jacket and trousers, wool sweater and cotton T-shirt. | $450.00 |
| RL0100 650581 | | 487 | 1994 | **RALPH LAUREN RUSSIA BEAR** 13-3/4in (35cm) Limited 1,100, female bear dressed in red velvet jacket, beret and muff made of faux curly lamb, and red garnet earring. | $450.00 |
| 405891 | 398 | 418 | 1994/95 | **1906 REPLICA TEDDY BEAR** 17in (43cm) Limited 5,000, boxed, certificate, replica 1906, worldwide. | $350.00 |
| 655067 | N/A | 436 | 1994 | **SEEBAR KARSTADT of HAMBURG** Limited 450, white tag, caramel bear, captain's outfit, sweater, cap, metal ship's telegraph, Germany only. | $895.00 |
| 650918 | 402 | 435 | 1994 | **SPIELZEUGRING BEAR 25TH YEAR** 7-1/4in (19cm) Limited 3,000, cinnamon mohair 1960s style, a sash and green ribbons, cotton bag, worldwide. | $375.00 |
| 420047 | 415 | 512 | 1994/95 | **STEIFF CLUB 1908 BLUE 35 BEAR (ELLIOT)** 13-3/4in (35cm) Limited 14,910, white tag, made for Steiff Club members. $35.00 club membership fee. | $550.00 |
| 029271 | 405 | | 1994/95 | **TEDDY 1926 BI-COLOR** 6-1/2in (16cm) Yellow tag. | $150.00 |
| 029974 | 404 | | 1994/95 | **TEDDY BEAR** 6-1/2in (16cm) Yellow tag. | $150.00 |
| 407192 | 398 | 418 | 1994 | **TEDDY ROSE** 19in (48cm) Limited 7,000, white tag, boxed, certificate, replica 1927, kapok filled, worldwide. | $495.00 |
| 650802 | | 484 | 1994 | **TINSEL XMAS ORNAMENT** 4in (10cm) Limited 2,500, white bear dressed in a red sweater and cap, boxed and certificate, U.S.A. only. | $395.00 |
| 651854 | 392 | 470 | 1994 | **T.R. SAFARI TEDDY BEAR** 7-1/4in (19cm) Limited 1,500, white tag, made for The Toy Store and Steiff Festival, Toledo, Ohio. | $550.00 |
| 411601 | 412 | 509 | 1994 | **UNCLE SAM DOLL** 19-1/2in (50cm) Limited 1,000, white tag, replica 1904, boxed, certificate. | $300.00 |
| 650901 | 402 | 435 | 1994 | **VEDES TEDDY BEAR BLOND** 15-3/4in (40cm) Limited 6,000, boxed, made for Vedes, special for 90th birthday of the teddy bear, wearing a sash, Germany only. | $395.00 |
| 406041 | 398 | 418 | 1994 | **1908 WHITE TEDDY BEAR** 25-1/2in (65cm) Limited 7,000, boxed, certificate, replica 1908, curly white mohair, worldwide. | $850.00 |

| Item Ear tag# EAN # | Sortiment Book Vol#1 | Vol#2 | Year | Description | Value |
|---|---|---|---|---|---|
| 655111 | N/A | 437 | 1995 | **"ANTON" STEIGER-BAR** 13-3/4in (35cm)<br>Limited 490, white tag, caramel mohair, miners outfit, white pants, blue towel, brass lantern, leather apron and hat "Steiger Anton exclusive fur Lutfenau, Dortmund auflage 490 struck, Germany only. | $600.00 |
| 038488 | 407 | 507 | 1995/97 | **ARK TIGER SET**<br>Limited 8,000, one male and one female 4-1/2in (12cm) and 4in (10cm) | $265.00 |
| 038501 | 407 | 507 | 1995/96 | **ARK LLAMA SET**<br>Limited 8,000, one male and one female 6-1/4in (16cm) | $225.00 |
| 653773 | 403 | 453 | 1995 | **BABY ALFONZO** 9-1/4in (24cm)<br>Limited 5,000, white tag, smaller version of Alfonzo, red mohair dressed in Cossack outfit, boxed, certificate, Teddy Bears of Witney, U.K. only. | $395.00 |
| 654404 | N/A | 448 | 1995 | **BRITISH COLLECTORS TEDDY BEAR** 13-3/4in (35cm)<br>Limited 3,000, white tag, brown-tipped mohair, clipped muzzle, boxed, certificate, U.K. only. | $300.00 |
| 655050 | N/A | 437 | 1995 | **BUDDENBROOK BAR** 13in (33cm)<br>Limited 2,000, looks like a Sam bear, white tag, gold curly mohair, white ruffled collar, black hat, trimmed in ribbons, holds a red book, made for a Morgenroth, Luebeckstore, Germany. | $375.00 |
| 650840 | | 492 | 1995 | **"CHOOKY" THE HOLLYWOOD BEAR (JAPAN)** 13-3/4in (35cm)<br>Limited 2,000, white tag, cinnamon mohair, embroidered paws, boxed, certificate, Japan only. | $575.00 |
| 036064 | 398 | 425 | 1995 | **1938 CLASSIC BEAR ON WHEELS** 11-3/4in (30cm) Yellow tag. | $275.00 |
| 036354 | 411 | | 1995 | **1927 CLASSIC MOLLY DOG** 10in (25cm) Yellow tag. | $275.00 |
| 036200 | 411 | | 1995 | **1928 CLASSIC TABBY CAT** 8in (20cm) Yellow tag. | $275.00 |
| 000966 | 398 | 425 | 1995/97 | **CLASSIC 1928 PETSY BEAR** 13-3/4in (35cm) | $240.00 |
| 000980 | 398 | 425 | 1995/99 | **CLASSIC 1928 PETSY BEAR** 17in (43cm)<br>Yellow tag, replica 1928, gold-tipped fur, kapok stuffing, worldwide. | $300.00 |
| 650833 | | 485 | 1995 | **COAL XMAS ORNAMENT** 4in (10cm)<br>Limited 3,500, yellow tag, certificate, charcoal bear, red felt stocking, white embroidered. red satin cuff. | $175.00 |
| 405259 | 392 | 474 | 1995 | **COLLECTORS UNITED 1ST BEAR SMALL** 10-1/4in (26cm)<br>Limited 650, white tag, blond mohair, for the Collector United Gathering, dressed in a white sweater with C.U. on the pocket, holding a green flag, white ribbon with printed C.U. and 95. | $350.00 |
| 405279 | | 474 | 1995 | **COLLECTORS UNITED 1ST BEAR LARGE** 20in (50cm)<br>Limited 165, white tag, same as above item. | $1,200.00 |
| 650819 | 388 | 461 | 1995 | **COMPASS ROSE** 17-1/2in (44cm)<br>Limited 3,500, white tag, wearing a mariner's compass, boxed, certificate, U.S.A. only. | $395.00 |
| 029776 | 405 | 499 | 1995/96 | **DICKY BEAR WHITE** 6-1/2in (16cm) Yellow tag. | $150.00 |
| 651274<br>651281 | | 477 | 1995 | **DISNEY WORLD 8TH CONVENTION BALOO BEAR**<br>11in (28cm) Limited 2,500, white tag.<br>24in (60cm) Limited 25, white tag.<br>31-1/2in (80cm) Limited 5, white tag.<br>Made for Disney World Epcot Center. | $525.00<br>$4,000.00<br>N.P.A. |
| 999086 | N/A | | 1995 | **GIENGEN UNICORN**<br>Limited 3,000, white tag, city of Giengen, Germany, rearing, yellow mohair with white felt horn. | $425.00 |

| Item<br>Ear tag#<br>EAN # | Sortiment Book<br>Vol#1 | Vol#2 | Year | Description | Value |
|---|---|---|---|---|---|
| 651861<br>J04104<br>J04082 | | 470 | 1995 | **GOLLI G and TEDDY B** 9in (24cm) and 4in (10cm)<br>Limited 1,500, white tag, special for the Toy Store, Toledo, Ohio, dressed in red pants, blue jacket, white vest, holding a tan teddy bear, boxed and certificate. | $600.00 |
| 653148 | N/A | 452 | 1995 | **HARRODS CENTENARY MUSICAL BEAR** 17-1/4in (44cm)<br>Limited 2,000, white tag, olive green, necktie, plays "Anniversary Waltz," U.K. only. | $475.00 |
| 999079 | 403 | 456 | 1995 | **HERCULE BEAR** 11in (28cm)<br>Limited 3,000, white tag, cream mohair, gold medallion "Amade" children's charity, Monaco only. | $400.00 |
| 650857 | 403 | 454 | 1995 | **HOLLAND 1ST TEDDY BEAR ORANGE** 15-3/4in (40cm)<br>Limited 1,500, white tag, orange mohair, special for Holland to commemorate the 50th anniversary of the liberation of Holland, boxed, certificate, Holland only. | $595.00 |
| 655241 | N/A | | 1995 | **IASERNER GUSTAV BEAR BLOND 36** 14in (36cm)<br>Limited 1,500, white tag, light gold mohair, black jacket, hat, iron worker outfit, Germany only. | $425.00 |
| 999062 | N/A | | 1995 | **JOHANNES POSTMAN BEAR** 12-1/2in (32cm)<br>Limited 1,500, white tag, gold mohair, 1918 blue Postman's outfit, hat, leather mail bag, holding a letter, for Post Museum Shop, boxed, certificate, Germany only. | $550.00 |
| 655166 | N/A | 437 | 1995 | **KUDDEL DER LUTTFIHER FISHER BEAR** 16-1/2in (42cm)<br>Limited 400, white tag, navy pants, blue and white shirt, red scarf, blue hat, made for Alsterhaus, Germany only. | N.P.A. |
| 657931 | N/A | 455 | 1995 | **LAFAYETTE 1ST BEAR** 16-1/2in (42cm)<br>Limited 1,500, white tag, no chest tag, red curly mohair, black velvet pads, Galleries Lafayette embroidered in red floss on right foot, France only. | $600.00 |
| 401190 | 411 | 431 | 1995/96 | **MUSEUM 1926 PIG** 13-3/4in (35cm)<br>Limited 3,000, white tag, boxed, replica 1926, worldwide. | $390.00 |
| 408335 | 399 | 419 | 1995 | **1951 PANDA BEAR** 19-3/4in (50cm)<br>Limited 3,000, white tag, boxed, certificate, replica 1951, worldwide. | $600.00 |
| 029561 | 405 | | 1995/99 | **PETSY BEAR** 6-1/2in (16cm) Yellow tag. | $150.00 |
| 655098 | | | 1995 | **POLAR BEAR and WOLF SET** 12-1/2in (32cm) and 6-1/2in (16cm)<br>Limited 2,000, white tag. | $475.00 |
| 665028 | N/A | | 1995 | **Q.V.C. 1906 ROUGH RIDER BEAR** 11-3/4in (30cm)<br>Limited 7,000, white tag, light brown Petsy bear, boots, scarf and gun made U.S.A. only. | $375.00 |
| 027008 | | 488 | 1995 | **RALPH LAUREN NAUTICAL BEAR**<br>Limited 1,500, rain coat over black seaman's outfit and black knit cap. | $550.00 |
| 027147 | | 488 | 1995 | **RALPH LAUREN ROMANTIC GIRL** 13in (35cm)<br>Limited 1,500, angora sweater, white ruffled blouse, leather fringed kilt, green beret, black tights. | $550.00 |
| 406058 | 398 | 419 | 1995 | **1909 REPLICA CREAM BEAR** 25-1/2in (65cm)<br>Limited 5,000, boxed, certificate, replica 1909, worldwide. | $875.00 |
| 420054 | | 512 | 1995/96 | **STEIFF CLUB BABY BEAR 1946** 13in (33cm)<br>Limited 10,880 to Steiff Club members. $40.00 yearly membership fee. | $450.00 |
| 420061 | | 513 | 1995/96 | **STEIFF CLUB CAMEL ON WHEELS 1930** 13-3/4in (35cm)<br>Limited 1,770 to Steiff Club members. $40.00 yearly membership fee. | $795.00 |
| 650864 | | 492 | 1995 | **TARRO BEAR (JAPAN)** 11in (28cm)<br>Limited 2,000, white tag, wearing a blue hat and ribbon, Japan only. | $650.00 |

Steiff. *1938 Panda Replica*. #0178/35.
1984-1986. 14in (35cm); black and white
mohair; felt pads; glass eyes; f.j; B.B.
CONDITION: Mint
**PRICE:** $400.00.
*Photo courtesy of Hobby House Press, Inc.*

| Item Ear tag# EAN # | Sortiment Book Vol#1 | Vol#2 | Year | Description | Value |
|---|---|---|---|---|---|
| **408175** | 399 | **419** | 1995 | **1929 TEDDY BABY WITH TEETH**  13-3/4in (35cm) <br> Limited 3,000, white tag, boxed, certificate, replica 1929, worldwide. | $375.00 |
| **650871** | N/A | **445** | 1995 | **TEDDY BAR AUSTRIA BOY**  12-1/2in (32cm) <br> Limited 1,500, white tag, blond mohair, leather lederhosen, boxed, certificate, Europe only. | $350.00 |
| **650871** | 403 | | 1995 | **TEDDY BAR CARAMEL 40/Australian Boy**  12-1/2in (32cm) <br> Limited 1,500, white tag, caramel mohair, lederhosen and felt hat, boxed, certificate, <br> Europe only. | $450.00 |
| **008016** | 40 | | 1995 | **TEDDY BEAR PALE BLOND**  15in (38cm) Yellow tag. | $275.00 |
| **008078** | 40 | | 1995 | **TEDDY BEAR PALE BLOND**  18in (46cm) Yellow tag. | |
| **008504** | 40 | | 1995 | **TEDDY BEAR RED BROWN**  15in (38cm) Yellow tag. | $275.00 |
| **008542** | 40 | | 1995 | **TEDDY BEAR RED BROWN**  18in (46cm) Yellow tag. | $400.00 |
| No Ean # | | | 1995 | **TEDDY BAR TOTAL**  12-1/2in (32cm) <br> Limited 40, white tag, caramel, German Convention. | $1,400.00 |
| _____ | N/A | | 1995 | **U.F.D.C. CONVENTION BEAR**  10-1/4in (26cm) <br> Limited 350, light brown mohair,  wearing a sash "Remember The Ladies". | $350.00 |
| **652509** | | **492** | 1995 | **VICTORIA TEDDY (JAPAN)**  16in (40cm) <br> Limited 500, white tag, light brown with blue ribbon, Japan only. | $495.00 |
| **999208** | 403 | | 1995 | **ZEITSCHRIFT  SPIELZEUGMARKTR  TEDDY**  4-1/2in (12cm) <br> Limited 170, white tag. | N.P.A. |
| **029950** | 404 | | 1995/99 | **ZOTTY 1951 BEAR**  6-1/2in (16cm) Yellow tag. | $150.00 |

| Item Ear tag# EAN # | Sortiment Book Vol#1 | Vol#2 | Year | Description | Value |
|---|---|---|---|---|---|
| 038525 | 507 | | 1996/97 | **ARK DONKEY SET** 6-1/4in (16cm) Limited 8,000, white tag, one brown and one gray. | $275.00 |
| 038549 | 507 | | 1996/97 | **ARK CAMEL SET** 6-1/4in (16cm) Limited 8,000, white tag, one light sand and one cinnamon. | $275.00 |
| 659874 | 493 | | 1996 | **ASIAN HAPPINESS TEDDY** 15-3/4in (40cm) Limited 3,000, yellow mohair, certificate is in both Chinese and English translation, Asia only. | $400.00 |
| 659850 | 446 | | 1996 | **AUSTRIA BEAR GIRL** 12-1/2in (32cm) Limited 1,500, white tag, blond mohair, traditional print jumper with white blouse, Austria only. | $400.00 |
| 655258 | N/A | | 1996 | **BAREN AUSLESE CONVENTION BEAR** Limited edition, white tag, tan and black vest, blue ribbon across the chest, with 19-20 OKT1996 Stiehl Bacharach printed on the ribbon, (see next item). | $395.00 |
| 655258 | N/A | | 1996 | **FACTORY TOUR BEARS FOR ONE WORLD** 14-1/2in (37cm) Limited 3,000, white tag, white bear with blue banner across the chest. | $395.00 |
| 652516 | 492 | | 1996 | **BABY MASAKO (JAPAN)** 8-1/2in (23cm) Limited 3,000, pink mohair, smaller size. **(Also see 1994 Masako)** Japan only. | N.P.A. |
| 665127 | 462 | | 1996 | **BOATSWAIN BEAR** 4in (10cm) Limited 3,500, white tag, blue bear with hand knitted wool sweater and cap in a flat bottom. | $195.00 |
| 665110 | 461 | | 1996 | **BOGGY CREEK BOB** 11in (28cm) Limited 3,000, shirt, tan shorts and hat, mascot for children's camp of life threatening diseases, 10% of sales will go to the camp. | $295.00 |
| 654411 | 448 | | 1996 | **BRITISH COLLECTORS TEDDY BEAR** 17in (43cm) Limited 3,000, blond mohair wearing a vest. | N.P.A. |
| 665141 | 462 | | 1996 | **BUCCANEER BEAR** 13-1/2in (35cm) Limited 500, blond mohair, white satin shirt, black cape, brown pants and hat, belt and sword, U.S.A. only. | N.P.A. |
| 665789 | 478 | | 1996 | **BUGS BUNNY** 12-1/2in (32cm) Limited 2,500, made for the Warner Bros. Co. | $450.00 |
| 4008427 | 420 | | 1996 | **1951 CARAMEL TEDDY BEAR** 19-1/2in (50cm) Limited 5,000, white tag, worldwide. | $575.00 |
| 665134 | 462 | | 1996 | **CASEY BEAR** 13in (33cm) Limited 500, white tag, 1920s style bear, railroad engineer's outfit cap, red shirt and scarf, overalls, mock watch and a small toy railcar, made for Campbell's Collectibles, U.S.A. only. | $500.00 |
| 027550 | 426 | | 1996/97 | **CLASSIC 1907 TEDDY WHITE** 10-1/2in (26cm) | $250.00 |
| 027567 | 426 | | 1996/97 | **CLASSIC 1907 TEDDY WHITE** 13in (33cm) | $295.00 |
| 027673 | 426 | | 1996/97 | **CLASSIC 1907 TEDDY CINNAMON** 15-3/4in (40cm) | $375.00 |
| 659867 | 492 | | 1996 | **"CLASSY" (JAPAN)** 10-1/2in (26cm) Limited 3,000, special chest tag, red-blond mohair, no growler, third piece, Japan only. | $400.00 |
| 665073 | 474 | | 1996 | **COLLECTORS UNITED OLYMPIAN 2ND** 9in (23cm) Limited 650, white tag, dressed in a Olympic outfit. | $225.00 |
| 665080 | 474 | | 1996 | **COLLECTORS UNITED OLYMPIAN 2ND** 20in (50cm) Limited 165, white tag, (see above item). | N.P.A. |

| Item<br>Ear tag#<br>EAN # | Sortiment Book | | Year | Description | Value |
|---|---|---|---|---|---|
| | Vol#1 | Vol#2 | | | |
| 651311 | | 477 | 1996<br>1996 | **DISNEY WORLD 9TH CONVENTION GEPPETTO and PINOCCHIO BEARS**<br>13-3/4in (35cm) Limited 1,500, white tag.<br>24in (60cm) Limited 25, white tag.<br>31-1/2in (80cm) Limited 5, white tag.<br>Geppetto is a mohair bear with a traditional wooden Pinocchio, Disney World<br>Epcot Center. | $650.00<br>N.P.A.<br>N.P.A. |
| 655241 | N/A | | 1996 | **"EISERNER GUSTAR"**<br>Limited 1,500, for a shopping center in Berlin, Germany, sail boat, box and certificate. | $425.00 |
| | N/A | | 1996 | **ENZO BEAR** 14-1/2in (37cm)<br>Limited 3,000, could be purchased at the Steiff Factory, replica for a 1950s bear wearing<br>a sash. | N.P.A. |
| 652158 | | 473 | 1996 | **F.A.O. SCHWARZ TOY SOLDIER BEAR** 13-3/4in (35cm)<br>Limited 2,000, white tag, plays store theme "Welcome to Our World of Toys". | $450.00 |
| 655210 | | 439 | 1996 | **"FINKENWERDER FISHERWOMAN BEAR** 16-1/2in (42cm)<br>Limited 1,500, Alsterhaus store, Germany only. | $400.00 |
| | N/A | | 1996 | **FISHERWOMAN BEAR**<br>Limited 500, white tag, Alsterhaus store, Germany only. | $600.00 |
| 651342 | 477 | | 1996 | **FISHERMAN BEAR** 12-1/2in (32cm)<br>Limited 1,500, made for Disney World Epcot Center. | $325.00 |
| 665059 | | 461 | 1996 | **FOREVER FRIENDS** 9in (23cm)<br>Limited 4,000, white tag, set of two bears, icy blue mohair and gray mohair, U.S.A. only. | $350.00 |
| 411687 | N/A | | 1996 | **GRANDPA FOXY DOLL** 13-3/4in (35cm)<br>Limited 1,200, worldwide. | $450.00 |
| 652820 | | 450 | 1996 | **HAMLEY'S CHESTER BEAR** 12-1/2in (32cm)<br>Limited 2,000, white tag, apricot distressed mohair, leather paws, boxed and certificate. | $395.00 |
| 659843 | N/A | | 1996 | **HOLLAND'S 1ST DELFTEER BEAR** 13in (33cm)<br>Limited 1,500, white tag, curly deft blue mohair body, white mohair head, white leatherette<br>pads and lace collar, blue and white bear picture tag, boxed and certificate, Holland only. | $350.00 |
| 653162 | | 452 | 1996 | **HARRODS BEAR** 17-1/4in (44cm)<br>Limited 2,000, white tag, gold mohair, green scarf and glasses, play's "Toy" by Haydn.<br>U.K only. | $400.00 |
| | N/A | | 1996 | **HIMBEEREN** 16-1/2in (42cm)<br>Limited 2,000, berry-colored distressed mohair, made for a French department store. | N.P.A. |
| 411984 | N/A | | 1996 | **HUNGARIAN WITH HORSE 1912 REPLICA** 17in (43cm) and 11in (28cm)<br>Limited 1,200. | $850.00 |
| 655180 | N/A | | 1996 | **IRON GUSTAV "HAUPTMANN KOPENICK BEAR"** 13-3/4in (35cm)<br>Limited 250, blond distressed mohair, long uniform coat, belt, buckle and cap, Germany only. | $900.00 |
| 655272 | N/A | | 1996 | **KAPITAN OF THE S.S. PASSAT** 13-3/4in (35cm)<br>Limited 1,500, white tag, uniform with gold braid and buttons, shirt, tie, hat visor, carries<br>a life preserver. | $450.00 |
| 657948 | | 455 | 1996 | **LAFAYETTE 2ND BEAR** 11-3/4in (30cm)<br>Limited 1,500, white tag, 100th birthday Galleries Lafayette, France only. | N.P.A. |

| Item<br>Ear tag#<br>EAN # | Sortiment<br>Book<br>Vol#1  Vol#2 | Year | Description | Value |
|---|---|---|---|---|
| 650970 | 438 | 1996 | **LIEBHABAR (LOVE BEAR)** 12-1/2in (32cm)<br>Limited 2,500, curly blond mohair, tuxedo, shirt, trousers, cape and a red rose<br>Idee and Spiel. | $350.00 |
| 659898 | 446 | 1996 | **MILLENNIO AUSTRIA'S BEAR**<br>Limited 1,500,white mohair, red ribbon, red embroidered German coat of arms on the paw. | $350.00 |
| 651878 | 471 | 1996 | **MOLLY GOLLI AND PEG** 8-1/2in (22cm) and 4in (10cm)<br>Limited 2,500, white tag, blue shirt, red vest, white blouse, holding a peg doll,<br>boxed and certificate, made for Toy Store's Steiff festival. | $450.00 |
| 400896 | N/A | 1996/98 | **MUSEUM MONKEY URFIPS 1926** 7in (18cm)<br>Limited 3,000, white tag, boxed. | $400.00 |
| 411908 | N/A | 1996 | **MUSICIAN BROWN 1911 (DOLL)** 17in (43cm)<br>Limited 1,200, worldwide | $650.00 |
| 650963 | 439 | 1996 | **NIKOLAS-BAR or SANTA BEAR** 12-1/2in (32cm)<br>Limited 2,000, white tag, blond mohair, traditional U.S. Santa's outfit, Spielzeugring,<br>Germany only. | $300.00 |
| 665066 | 485 | 1996 | **PERCUSSION CHRISTMAS ORNAMENT** 4in (10cm)<br>Limited 3,500, gold mohair, red and white knitted drum, red knitted hat trimmed with<br>gold braid and beads. | $175.00 |
| 998959 | N/A | 1996 | **POSTMAN BEAR #2** 13-3/4in (35cm)<br>Limited 2,000, white tag, wearing a 1820s Postman's outfit with cape and cap, Germany only. | $400.00 |
| 012907<br>012921 | N/A<br>N/A | 1996<br>1996 | **PETSY DARK BLUE** 11in ( 28cm)<br>**PETSY DARK BLUE** 11-3/4in (35cm.)<br>Yellow tag, dark blue acrylic fur with gold thread. | $125.00<br>$165.00 |
| 665028 | 475 | 1996 | **QVC ROUGH RIDER EVENT BEAR** 11in (28cm)<br>Limited 1,906, white tag, hat, boots and scarf with medallion. | $250.00 |
| 407468 | 419 | 1996 | **RECORD PETSY 1928** 10in (25cm)<br>Limited 4,000, white tag, worldwide. | $425.00 |
| 027154 | 488 | 1996 | **RALPH LAUREN COLLEGIATE BEAR** 13-3/4in (35cm)<br>Limited 1,000, letterman sweater over button-down shirt and tan overcoat. | $800.00 |
| 027004 | 488 | 1996 | **RALPH LAUREN RACEY BEAR** 13-3/4in (35cm)<br>Limited 800, pants, white shirt, beret, sunglasses and handbag. | $800.00 |
| _____ | N/A | 1996 | **ROBERT and PINKY** 13-3/4in (35cm)<br>Limited 250 of 1,500, Robert is a caramel bear, Pinky is a pink dinosaur, boxed and<br>certificate, Liechtenstein only. | $355.00 |
| 655203 | 438 | 1996 | **ROBIN HOOD BEAR** 16-1/2in (42cm)<br>Limited 1,500, white tag, made for Karstadt Department store, Germany only. | $525.00 |
| 488061 | N/A | 1996 | **SALAMANDER TRAIN SET**<br>Limited 1,000, train car and Steiff salamander, boxed. | $130.00 |
| 655296 | 443 | 1996 | **SANTA BEAR CHRISTMAS ORNAMENT** 4in (10cm)<br>Limited 5,000, white tag, beige bear in a red and white knitted Santa's outfit, Europe only. | $175.00 |
| 408243 | 419 | 1996 | **SNAP-DICKY BEAR** 12-1/2in (32cm)<br>Limited 5,000, white tag, worldwide. | $525.00 |

Steiff. ***Black Bear, 1907 Replica***.
#0173/40. 1988-1989. 16in (40cm); black
mohair; tan pads; glass eyes; f.j.; B.B.
CONDITION: Mint
**PRICE:** $650.00.
*Photo courtesy of Hobby House Press, Inc.*

| Item<br>Ear tag#<br>EAN # | Sortiment<br>Book<br>Vol#1 | Vol#2 | Year | Description | Value |
|---|---|---|---|---|---|
| **665172** | | 490 | 1996 | **SNOWMAN "1ST WINTER" SEASON** 14 in (36cm)<br>Limited 5,000, first in a series of 4 seasons, white mohair, black hat and broom, carrot<br>nose with black buttons, U.S.A. only. | $295.00 |
| **420078** | | 512 | 1996/97 | **STEIFF CLUB DICKY BEAR 1935**<br>Limited 7,965, Steiff Club members. Yearly membership fee of $40.00. | N.P.A. |
| **420085** | | 513 | 1996/97 | **STEIFF CLUB WHITE POODLE DOG** 11in (28cm)<br>Limited 3,545, Steiff club member. Yearly membership fee of $40.00. | $350.00 |
| **610172** | N/A | | 1996 | **STEIFF SORTIMENT 1947-1995 BOOK** by Günther Pfeiffer. | $150.00 |
| **652547** | | 492 | 1996 | **SUGAR (JAPAN)** 10in (25cm)<br>Limited 3,000, white curly mohair, Japan only. | N.P.A. |
| **655265** | N/A | | 1996 | **TEDDY BAR TOTAL PEACH**<br>Limited 500, white tag, special peach mohair, with a embroidered badge on the chest. | $500.00 |
| **655227** | | 438 | 1996 | **"THEO" BEAR** 17in (43cm)<br>Limited 1,946, brass-colored bear with his name embroidered on one foot and the years<br>1946-1996 on the other, department store Kaufhaus-Horten, Germany only. | $375.00 |
| **665042** | | 462 | 1996 | **UFDC CONVENTION BEAR "BEAUTIFUL CHILDREN"** 12 in (31cm)<br>Limited 365, white tag, gold mohair, white banner "Beautiful Children Steiff UFDC 1996." | $400.00 |
| **654411** | N/A | | 1996 | **1906 U.K. BEAR REPLICA** 17in (43cm)<br>Limited 3,000, certificate, boxed, blond long pile mohair with a growler, wears a<br>tweed vest. | $400.00 |
| **407123** | N/A | | 1996 | **WHITE 1921 TEDDY BEAR** 15-3/4in (40cm)<br>Limited 4,000, white tag, worldwide. | $475.00 |

| Item<br>Ear tag#<br>EAN # | Sortiment<br>Book<br>Vol#1 Vol#2 | Year | Description | Value |
|---|---|---|---|---|
| 665158 | 461 | 1996 | **WIGGINS BEAR** 12-1/2in (32cm)<br>Limited 500, brownish 1920s Margaret Strong style bear, made for Teddy Bear Museum of Naples, Florida wearing a striped swimsuit, U.S.A. only. | $350.00 |
| 655289 | 438 | 1996 | **WILLI DER STAHKOCHER #2 or WILLIE STEEL WORKER**<br>13-3/4in (35cm) Limited 1,500, cinnamon, hat, leather and wooden shovel with iron scoop, printed on the leather apron "Stahkocher Willi Exkluseb Fur Lutgenau" Dortmund, Germany only. | $ 450.00 |
| _____ | N/A | 1996 | **WILLIAM SHAKESPEAR BEAR** 10-1/4in (26cm)<br>Limited 2,000, white tag, dark yellow mohair, leather paws, England only. | N.P.A. |
| _____ | N/A | 1996 | **ZIEGLER "FEUERWEHABAR" FIREMAN BEAR** 14in (34cm)<br>Limited 3,000, blond mohair, fireman's outfit, for the Ziegler Fire Engine Co., Germany only. | $375.00 |
| 029967 | 499 | 1996/99 | **ZOTTY BEAR - WHITE** 6-1/4in (16cm) Yellow tag. | $175.00 |
| 038563<br>038587 | 508<br>N/A | 1997<br>1997 | **ARK DOVE SET** 4in (10cm)<br>Limited 8,000, white tag, one gray and one white.<br>**ARK NOAH'S CHILDREN SET** 6in (15cm)<br>Limited 8,000, white tag, #J06021 caramel bear and #J06020 Blond Bear dressed. | $190.00 |
| 659911 | 446 | 1997 | **AUSTRIAN CHILDREN BOY and GIRL SET** 10in (25cm.)<br>Limited 1,847, dressed Brown and Blond bears. | $350.00 |
| 655364 | 439 | 1997 | **BERLIN SCHUTZMAN POLICEMAN BEAR** 12-1/2in (32cm)<br>Limited 1,500, white tag. | $400.00 |
| 655333 | 444 | 1997 | **BLACKEY GIENGEN FESTIVAL BEAR** 11in (28cm)<br>Limited 3,000, white tag, Teddy Baby, black mohair, Germany only. | $900.00 |
| 665400 | 463 | 1997 | **BRIDE BEAR** 10in (25cm)<br>Limited 365, white tag, white mohair, white suede paws, white sash "To Have and To Hold Steiff UFDC 1997" and a pink flower and bead headdress. | $400.00 |
| 654497 | 449 | 1997 | **BRITISH COLLECTOR'S SET of 5 BEARS** 6-1/4in (16cm) each.<br>Limited 1,847, white tag, Blond, Black, White, Dark Brown mohair. | N.P.A. |
| 659942 | 456 | 1997 | **BRUEGHEL BEAR or GOLDEN BROWN 42** 16-1/2in (42cm)<br>Limited 1,847, white tag, Belgium's First Bear, Flemish Painter Bear, boxed and certificate. | $345.00 |
| 665189 | N/A | 1997 | **BUGS BUNNY** 12in (31cm)<br>Limited 2,500, for the Warner Bros. Co. gray mohair, holding a carrot, black embroidered bag with Warner Bros. and Steiff logos, U.S.A. only. | $495.00 |
| 659904 | 494 | 1997 | **CAPTAIN JAMES BEAR** 15in (38cm)<br>Limited 1,500, white tag, pale curly mohair, pewter medallion and a map of Australia and New Zealand. | $550.00 |
| 670169 | 441 | 1997 | **CARNIVAL GIRL BEAR MARIECHEN** 13-3/4in (35cm)<br>Limited 2,000, white tag. | $300.00 |
| 665387 | 474 | 1997 | **COLLECTORS UNITED 3RD BEAR** 10-1/4in (26cm)<br>Limited 650, white tag, C.U. Convention, white mohair with a black top hat and cane, U.S.A. only. | $225.00 |
| 665394 | 474 | 1997 | **COLLECTORS UNITED BEAR** 20-1/2in (52cm)<br>Limited 140, white tag, C.U. Convention, white mohair with a black top hat and cane. | $750.00 |

| Item<br>Ear tag#<br>EAN # | Sortiment<br>Book<br>Vol#1 | Vol#2 | Year | Description | Value |
|---|---|---|---|---|---|
| 651359 | N/A | | 1997<br>1997<br>1997 | **DISNEY WORLD 10TH CONVENTION "ZEHN"**<br>11in (28cm) Limited 2,000.<br>24in (60cm) Limited 25.<br>31-1/2in (80cm) Limited 5.<br>White tag, peach mohair, Disney World Epcot Center, U.S.A. only. | $350.00<br>$3,500.00<br>$6,000.00 |
| 665417 | | 485 | 1997 | **EVERGREEN TREE BEAR U.S. CHRISTMAS ORNAMENT** 5in (12cm)<br>Limited 4,000, white tag, U.S.A. only. | $125.00 |
| 652172 | | 473 | 1997 | **FAO SCWARZ AUGUSTUS ROMAN EMPEROR BEAR** 8-1/2in (22cm)<br>Limited white tag, cream nimrod style bear, white toga, red cap, wearing a laurel<br>crown. Special for the grand opening of the Las Vegas store. | $325.00 |
| 400926 | | 420 | 1997 | **GALLOP TEDDY 1926** 4-1/2in (12cm)<br>Limited 2,500, white tag, two small bears on a metal pull toy frame. | $400.00 |
| 670138 | | 443 | 1997 | **CHRISTMAS TREE BEAR GOLDEN BROWN 10**<br>Limited 5,000, white tag, cream mohair bear, sitting in a red and black felt boot<br>with fur trim, Europe only. | $250.00 |
| 652837 | | 450 | 1997 | **HAMLEY'S WINSTON BEAR** 15in (38cm)<br>Limited 1,500, white tag, boxed and certificate, U.K. only. | N.P.A. |
| 652615 | | 494 | 1997 | **HARMONY BEAR (ASIA)**<br>Limited 1,997, brown tipped fur, made for Hong Kong and China. | N.P.A |
| 670107 | | 440 | 1997 | **HEIDESCHAFER "VINCENT" SHEPHERD BEAR** 13-3/4in (35cm)<br>Limited 2,000, white tag, boxed and certificate, 1950s style, black pants, red vest and<br>blue cape. | $425.00 |
| 653780 | | 454 | 1997 | **HENDERSON** 22in (56cm)<br>Limited 2,000, made for Teddy Bears of Witney, U.K. only. | $499.00 |
| 659935 | | 455 | 1997<br><br>1997/99 | **HOLLAND'S 2ND TULIP BEAR** 13-1/2in (35cm)<br>Limited 1,847 bright green mohair, boxed, certificate.<br>**HOLLAND'S TEDDY BEAR** 6-1/4in (16cm)<br>Yellow tag, salmon-pink mohair. | $400.00<br><br>N.P.A. |
| 400285 | | 445 | 1997 | **JUBILEE ASSORTMENT ANIMAL SET**<br>Limited 1,847, white tag, set of 6 animals made for the 150th anniversary of<br>Margaret Steiff. | $650.00 |
| 670152 | | 441 | 1997 | **JUBILEE GEINGEN BEAR** 16in (40cm)<br>Limited 3,999, white tag. | $950.00 |
| 670220 | | 441 | 1997<br><br>1997 | **JUBILEE GEINGEN BEAR** 11-3/4in (30cm)<br>Limited 300, white tag.<br>**JUBILEE GEINGEN (AUCTION BEAR)** 21-1/2in (55cm)<br>Limited 15, white tag, auctioned for charity. | $1200.00<br><br>$1200.00 |
| 670190<br>670206<br>670183 | | 441<br>441<br>441 | 1997<br>1997<br>1997 | **150th JUBILEE BEAR** 11in (28cm) Light Blond.<br>**150th JUBILEE BEAR** 11in (28cm) Dark Brown.<br>**150th JUBILEE BEAR** 11in (28cm) White. | $190.00<br>$190.00<br>$190.00 |
| 660030 | N/A | | 1997 | **JOHANN STRAUSS BEAR**<br>Limited 1,847, white tag, light gray mohair, signed Johann Shafer. | $395.00 |
| 657986 | | 456 | 1997 | **LAFAYETTE 3RD BEAR** 13in (34cm)<br>Limited 1,500, white tag, white mohair. | N.P.A. |
| 652622 | | 493 | 1997 | **LITTLE SANTA BEAR (JAPAN)** 8in (20cm)<br>Limited 2,500, white tag, boxed and certificate, Japan only. | $350.00 |

| Item Ear tag# EAN # | Sortiment Book Vol#1 | Vol#2 | Year | Description | Value |
|---|---|---|---|---|---|
| 655357 | | 440 | 1997 | **MAID MARIAN BEAR** 17-1/2in (44cm) Limited 1,500, white tag, pink taffeta dress and hat. | $400.00 |
| 657962 | | 457 | 1997 | **MICKEY MOUSE (BELGIUM)** 15-1/4in (39cm) Limited 2,000, white tag, gray mohair, dressed in plaid wool pants, certificate and boxed, first Mickey since 1934, especially made for Cadeau Reve Store. | $ 600.00 |
| 99900 | N/A | | 1997 | **MILCH BAR (MILK BEAR)** Limited 1,500, special advertising bear for a Milk Co., 1950s replica. | $450.00 |
| 998744 | N/A | | 1997 | **MORITZE THE POSTMAN BEAR** 12-1/2in (32cm) Limited 2,000, boxed and certificate, Germany only. | $395.00 |
| 651885 | | 471 | 1997/99 | **MR. CHOCOLATE** 10in (25cm) Limited 2,000, The Toy Store, same pattern as Mr. Vanilla, brown leather paws, issued with a pin in a small gold foil box, U.S.A. only. | $300.00 |
| 411915 | N/A | | 1997 | **MUSICIAN 1911** 17in (43cm) Limited 1,200, white tag, felt doll. | $700.00 |
| 654480 | | 449 | 1997 | **BRITISH COLLLECTOR'S BEAR** 15in (38cm) Limited 3,000, white tag, pink moair, boxed, certificate, U.K. only. | $375.00 |
| 655371 | 439 | | 1997 | **PIRATE BEAR** 15in (38cm) Limited 1,500, carries his own treasure chest. | $350.00 |
| 652561 | | 493 | 1997 | **PROSPERITY BEAR** 13-3/4in (35cm) Limited 1,847, white, boxed, Asia only. | $425.00 |
| 665363 | | 475 | 1997 | **QVC DELIGHTED BEAR** 9-1/2 in (24cm) Limited 7,500, white tag, gold mohair, ceramic chest medallion. | $315.00 |
| 665097 | | 475 | 1997 | **QVC CLIFFORD BERRYMAN BEAR** Limited 7,000, white tag, brown, medallion around neck. | $395.00 |
| 652578 | | 494 | 1997 | **RAFFLES BEAR** 17in (43cm) Limited 1,847, white tag, long cinnamon mohair, with a hand painted silk scarf, Singapore only. | $625.00 |
| 665219 | | 463 | 1997 | **REGGIE BEAR** 13in (32cm) Limited 3,250, white tag, khaki safari outfit and bush hat with Ghurk back pack. | $460.00 |
| 665219L | | 463 | 1997 | **REGGIE BEAR WITH SAFARI SET** Limited 250 set, includes backpack and book, U.S.A. only. | $990.00 |
| US012 | | 463 | 1997 | **SAFARI BOOK ONLY** U.S.A. only. | $25.00 |
| 665431 | | 489 | 1997 | **RALPH LAUREN SAFARI GIRL BEAR** 13-3/4in (35cm) Limited 1,000, yellow tag, scarf dress and head covering with brass earrings and armbands. | $850.00 |
| 665424 | | 489 | 1997 | **RALPH LAUREN RACER BOY BEAR** 13-3/4in (35cm) Limited 1,000, yellow tag, black outfit with yellow and black jacket and bill cap. | $800.00 |
| 652530 | | 494 | 1997 | **ROMANTIC RED BEAR** 13-3/4in (35cm) Limited 2,000, white tag, cherry red mohair, commemorating Hong Kong's 99 years of British rule, Hong Kong only. | $450.00 |
| 652196 | N/A | | 1997 | **SLEEPY BEAR KEEPSAKE** 13in (33cm) Limited 1,500 white tag, gold bear dressed in red knit pajamas suit. | $195.00 |
| 665226 | | 463 | 1997 | **SPECIAL DELIVERY BEAR** 6-1/4in (16cm) Limited 3,500, white tag, brown bear with a red metal truck, U.S.A. only. | $550.00 |

Steiff. *Eric Bat Set, Replica 1960*. #0055/00. 1990. 16-1/2in (42cm); brown and white mohair; tan felt; glass eyes; B.B. CONDITION: Mint **PRICE:** $300.00 set. *Photo courtesy of Hobby House Press, Inc.*

| Item Ear tag# EAN # | Sortiment Book Vol#1 | Vol#2 | Year | Description | Value |
|---|---|---|---|---|---|
| 665271 | N/A | | 1997 | **SPROUT BEAR SPRING 2ND SEASON** 12in (31cm) <br> Limited 5,000, white tag, green body, yellow face, tulip hat, 2nd seasons series, U.S.A. only. | $275.00 |
| 420115 | | 513 | 1997/98 | **STEIFF CLUB ELEPHANT ON WHEELS** 8-1/2in (22cm) <br> Limited 3,236, Steiff Club members only. | $450.00 |
| 420108 | | 512 | 1997/98 | **STEIFF CLUB PICKNIK BEAR** 17in (43cm) <br> Limited 9,888, Steiff Club members only, curly mohair, Porcelain chest tag, basket and green/blue checked picnic cloth, bottle and 2 plates, boxed and certificate. | $350.00 |
| 665295 | | 490 | 1997/98 | **"PUMPKIN PATCH" FALL 4TH SEASON** 12-1/2in (31cm) <br> Limited 5,000, white tag, pumpkin suit, 4th in the seasons series, U.S.A. only. | $325.00 |
| 665288 | | 490 | 1997/98 | **SUNBEAM BEAR SUMMER 3RD SEASON** 9-3/4in (24cm) <br> Limited 5,000, white tag, blue body and yellow face sitting on a cloud, 3rd in the seasons series, U.S.A. only. | $290.00 |
| 665202 | N/A | | 1997 | **TEDDY BAR 22 STEIFF FESTIVAL BEAR** <br> Limited 100, Special pink mohair bear with a white lace collar and elephant pin, also a birthday cake for Margaret Steiff's 150th birthday celebration, U.S.A. only. | $295.00 |
| 404306 | | 420 | 1997 | **TEDDY BEAR 1905** 19-1/2in (50cm) <br> Limited 6,000, white tag, red-brown mohair. | $700.00 |
| 408434 | | 420 | 1997 | **TEDDY BEAR 1951 BLOND** 19-1/2in (50cm) <br> Limited 4,000, white tag, blond mohair. | $600.00 |
| 404306 | | | 1997/98 | **TEDDY GIRL 1905** 19-1/2in (50cm) <br> Limited 6,000, white tag, Teddy Girl is a replica of the Teddy Girl that sold for $177,000.00 at the London auction. 1998 Teddy Boy #404320 is a partner to the girl bear. | $1225.00 |
| 408328 | | 420 | 1997 | **TEDDY VISCOSE BEAR 1948** 10in (25cm) <br> Limited 5,000, white tag, blond viscose woven fur. | $275.00 |

| Item Ear tag# EAN # | Sortiment Book Vol#1 | Sortiment Book Vol#2 | Year | Description | Value |
|---|---|---|---|---|---|
| 412080 | N/A | | 1997 | **TRAINER and ELEPHANT 1911** 17in (43cm) Limited 1,200, white tag, felt doll and mohair elephant. | $950.00 |
| 651007 | | 439 | 1997 | **WIZARD BEAR or ZAUBARER BEAR** 13in (32cm) Limited 2,000, white tag, gray mohair, cape, hat and wand, Germany only. | $300.00 |
| 651069 | | 441 | 1998 | **ACCORDIAN BEAR TEDDY BEAR** 11-3/4in (30cm) Limited 1,500, white tag, gold mohair, dressed in a blue jacket and hat, holding a red accordion, made for Splelzeugring store. | $550.00 |
| 658037 | | 457 | 1998 | **BELGIUM'S BEACH BEAR** 11in (28cm) Limited 1,500, white tag, blue mohair, blue felt paw pads and one is embroidered with 3 interlaced initials BBB, Belgium only. | $275.00 |
| 659928 | | 447 | 1998 | **BERNER BEAR** 13in (32cm) Limited 1,847, cinnamon, jacket, embroidered paw pads, Switzerland only. | $425.00 |
| 659973 | | 449 | 1998 | **BRITISH COLLECTOR'S RED BEAR** 15-3/4in (40cm) Limited 3,000, white tag, red mohair, boxed and certificate, U.K. only. | $395.00 |
| 657955 | | 455 | 1998 | **BOMMEL BEAR HOLLAND** 15-3/4in (40cm) Limited 3,000, white tag, Holland only. | $300.00 |
| 005015 | N/A | | 1998 | **CLASSIC APRICOT TEDDY** 11in (28cm) | $200.00 |
| 005022 | N/A | | 1998 | **CLASSIC APRICOT TEDDY** 15-3/4in (40cm) | $275.00 |
| 000492 | N/A | | 1998/99 | **CLASSIC 1909 BRASS BEAR** 10in (25cm) | $130.00 |
| 000317 | N/A | | 1998 | **CLASSIC 1909 BRASS BEAR** 13-3/4in (35cm) | $170.00 |
| 005077 | N/A | | 1998 | **CLASSIC CINNAMON TEDDY** 11in (28cm) | $200.00 |
| 005121 | N/A | | 1998 | **CLASSIC CINNAMON TEDDY** 15-3/4in (40cm) | $275.00 |
| 005305 | N/A | | 1998 | **CLASSIC GREEN TEDDY** 11in (28cm) | $200.00 |
| 005312 | N/A | | 1998 | **CLASSIC GREEN TEDDY** 15-3/4in (40cm) | $275.00 |
| 005206 | N/A | | 1998 | **CLASSIC GOLD BLOND TEDDY** 11in (28cm) | $200.00 |
| 005213 | N/A | | 1998 | **CLASSIC GOLD BLOND TEDDY** 15-3/4in (40cm) | $275.00 |
| 005060 | N/A | | 1998 | **CLASSIC LIGHT BLUE TEDDY** 11in (28cm) | $200.00 |
| 000300 | | 427 | 1998/99 | **CLASSIC 1907 MOSS GREEN BEAR** 10in (25cm) | $200.00 |
| 000317 | | 427 | 1998/99 | **CLASSIC 1907 MOSS GREEN BEAR** 13-3/4in (35cm) | $225.00 |
| 000171 | | 427 | 1998/99 | **CLASSIC 1903 MR. CINNAMON** 8-1/2in (22cm) | $150.00 |
| 000188 | | 427 | 1998/99 | **CLASSIC 1903 MR. CINNAMON** 11-3/4in (30cm) | $200.00 |
| 005152 | N/A | | 1998 | **CLASSIC RED TEDDY** 11in (28cm) | $200.00 |
| 005169 | N/A | | 1998 | **CLASSIC RED TEDDY** 15-3/4in (40cm) | $275.00 |
| 000263 | | 427 | 1998 | **CLASSIC 1907 ROSE BEAR** 10in (25cm) | $200.00 |
| 000270 | | 427 | 1998 | **CLASSIC 1907 ROSE BEAR** 13-3/4in (35cm) | $225.00 |
| 005206 | N/A | | 1998 | **CLASSIC SILVER GRAY TEDDY** 11in (28cm) | $200.00 |
| 005213 | N/A | | 1998 | **CLASSIC SILVER GRAY TEDDY** 15-3/4in (40cm) | $275.00 |
| 037023 | | 508 | 1998/99 | **CLASSIC MOLE** 10in (25cm) Limited 4,000, white tag, from *"Wind in the Willows,"* black mohair, jointed, dressed in a jacket, pants, white shirt and scarf. | $325.00 |
| 037016 | | 508 | 1998/99 | **CLASSIC TOAD** 10in (25cm) Limited 4,000, white tag, from *"Wind in the Willows,"* green mohair, jointed, dressed in a jacket, pants, white shirt, red vest, and tie. | $325.00 |

| Item Ear tag# EAN # | Sortiment Book Vol#1 | Sortiment Book Vol#2 | Year | Description | Value |
|---|---|---|---|---|---|
| 029608 | | 501 | 1998/99 | **COMPASS ROSE** 6-1/4in (16cm) Yellow tag. | $135.00 |
| 652165 | | 473 | 1998/99 | **CURIOUS GEORGE** 13in (33cm) Limited 2,000, white tag, F.A.O. Schwarz exclusive. | $325.00 |
| 665646 | | 474 | 1998 | **COLLECTORS UNITED "HAWAIIAN GIRL BEAR"** 10-1/4in (26cm) Limited 550, white tag. | $350.00 |
| 665653 | | 474 | 1998 | **COLLECTORS UNITED "HAWAIIAN GIRL BEAR"** 16-1/2in (42cm) Limited 165, white tag. | $650.00 |
| 651427 | | 478 | 1998 | **DISNEY'S SNOWMAN ORNAMENT** Limited 500, white tag, red hat, first Christmas Disney Collectible Convention. | $225.00 |
| 651380 651397 651403 | | 477 477 477 | 1998 1998 1998 | **DISNEY WORLD 11TH CONVENTION SEABAR** 12-1/2in (32cm) Limited 2,000. 23-1/2in 60cm Limited 25. 31-1/2in (80cm) Limited 5. White tag, lavendar mohair, ceramic medallion made for Disney World Epcot Center, U.S.A. only. | $350.00 |
| 028564 | N/A | | 1998 | **DOCTOR BEAR** 13-3/4in (35cm) Yellow tag. | $270.00 |
| 998713 | | 447 | 1998 | **DOLLHOUSE LOGO BEAR BASEL MUSEUM** 10in (25cm) Limited 1,500, white tag, blond mohair, Switzerland's Basel museum. | N.P.A. |
| 996733 | N/A | | 1998 | **DUTCHER FUSSBALL-SUND** Limited Edition, white tag, gold curly fur, black pants, Dutcher Fussball-sund printed on a white shirt. | $250.00 |
| 670329 | | 443 | 1998 | **EURO. CHRISTMAS TREE ORNAMENT BEAR (WHITE 12)** 4-1/2in (12cm) Limited 5,000, white tag white mohair bear, Christmas tree is the same as the American with a cream bear version, European market. | $195.00 |
| 652165 | | 473 | 1998/99 | **F.A.O. SCHWARZ CURIOUS GEORGE** Limited 2,000, white tag. U.S.A. only. | |
| 200493 | | 473 | 1998/99 | **F.A.O. SCHWARZ KING KONG and MADAME ALEXANDER DOLL** Limited 500, white tag. U.S.A. only | $850.00 |
| 652219 | | 473 | 1998 | **F.A.O. SCHWARZ POLAR BEAR ORNAMENT** 5in (12cm) Limited 2,000, white tag. | $225.00 |
| 652141 | | 473 | 1998 | **F.A.O. SCHWARZ RUDOLPH** 9-1/2in (24cm) Limited 2,000, white tag, made from the classic 1939 Robert L. May style, F.A.O. Schwarz exclusive certificate. | $275.00 |
| 659959 | | 455 | 1998 | **GOUDA BEAR (HOLLAND'S 4TH)** 11-3/4in (30cm) Limited 1847, white tag, yellow mohair, holding a cheese tin, boxed and certificate. | $300.00 |
| 66009 | | 456 | 1998 | **GRAND CRU BEAR VINTAGE (FRANCE)** 13in (34cm) Limited 1,500 white tag, boxed, certificate, bordeaux color, gold thread nose, wine tasting plate on red, white and blue ribbon. | N.P.A |
| 652844 | | 451 | 1998 | **HAMLEY'S DOMINIC BEAR** 11in (28cm) Limited 1,500 white tag, black bear, U.K. only. | $250.00 |
| 653186 | | 453 | 1998 | **HARRODS GAVOTTE D. POET BEAR** 13in (34cm) Limited 2,000, caramel mohair, white ruffled collar and holding a feather quill. | N.P.A. |
| 653780 | N/A | | 1998 | **HENDERSON** 21-1/2in (55cm) Limited 2,000, white tag, curled gold mohair, center seam, replica Lieutenant-Colonel Robert Henders from the Royal Scots Regiments bear, boxed and certificate, £10 will be donated to the Good Bears Of The World Charity. | $525.00 |

| Item Ear tag# EAN # | Sortiment Book Vol#1 | Vol#2 | Year | Description | Value |
|---|---|---|---|---|---|
| 652776 | | 495 | 1998 | **LITTLE SANTA BEAR (JAPAN)** 8-1/2in (23cm)<br>Limited 2,500, white tag, wearing a hooded cape, Japan only. | N.P.A. |
| 651076 | N/A | | 1998 | **IDEE SPIEL SCHABARNACK** 10-1/4in (26cm)<br>Limited 1,500, white tag, gold bear, yellow and blue jester outfit, Idee Spiel, Germany only. | $255.00 |
| 670152<br>670220 | 441<br>441<br>441 | | 1997<br>1997<br>1997 | **JUBILEE BEAR** 15-5/8in (40cm) Limited 3,999.<br>**JUBILEE BEAR** 11-5/8in (30cm) Limited 300.<br>**JUBILEE BEAR** 21-1/2in (55cm) Limited 15. Auctioned for Charity only.<br>White tag, porcelin medallion, to celebrate 150th birthday of Margaret Steiff. | $950.00<br>$1,200.00<br>N.P.A. |
| 658044 | | 456 | 1998 | **LAFAYETE GALLERIES EIFFEL TOWER BEAR** 13in (34cm)<br>Limited 1,500, white tag, blue mohair with gold ribbon and holding a metal Eiffel tower. | $525.00 |
| 665479 | N/A | | 1998 | **LAVENDER BLUE BEAR** 16-1/2in (42cm)<br>Limited 3,500, white tag, U.S.A. only. | $350.00 |
| 028571 | N/A | | 1998 | **LAWYER BEAR** 13-3/4in (35cm) Yellow tag. | $270.00 |
| 665165 | N/A | | 1998 | **LITTLE BEAR JACKIE** 7in (19cm)<br>Limited 2,500, white tag, small Jackie bear, "The Loving Doll" set, with T-shirt and bear. | $250.00 |
| 652769 | | 495 | 1998 | **MICKEY AND MINNIE DELUXE SET (JAPAN)** 11in (28cm)<br>Limited 3,000, white tag, pie eyed set of Mickey, traditional red pants and Minnie in a blue skirt with white polka dots and red and yellow hat, Japan only. | $850.00 |
| 651410 | | 478 | 1998 | **MICKEY MOUSE CHRISTMAS ORNAMENT** 5-1/2in (14cm)<br>Limited 1,928, white tag, Mickey's 70th birthday, for Disney's catalog, fully jointed, mohair. | $250.00 |
| 652721 | | 495 | 1998 | **MIFUYU (JAPAN)** 11in (28cm)<br>Limited 3000, white tag, special ribbon printed one side "Japan Teddy 1998 Mifuyu," and the other Margaret Steiff GmbH, left paw is embroidered, Japan only. | $295.00 |
| 655425 | N/A | | 1998 | **MORGANPOST or MORNING POST BEAR** 12-1/2in (32cm)<br>Limited 1,500, white tag, blond mohair, gray jacket with green trim and hat, darker gray pants. | $425.00 |
| 670114 | N/A | | 1998 | **M.S. STEIFF BEAR**<br>Limited 2,000, white tag, gold mohair, navy blue sweater, blue wool pants and hat, smoking pipe. | $395.00 |
| 652592 | | 494 | 1998 | **NAGANO JAPAN BEAR** 11-3/4in (30cm)<br>Limited 2,500, white tag, light gray with white jacket, made for 1998 Winter Olympics. | $850.00 |
| 401312 | N/A | | 1998 | **ORANG-UTAN MIMOCCULO** 10in (25cm)<br>Limited 3,000, white tag, rust brown mohair, turntable eyes, worldwide. | $625.00 |
| 996757 | N/A | | 1998 | **PAMPER'S 25TH ANNIVERSARY BEAR (plush)** 11in (28cm) | $99.00 |
| 406614 | | 421 | 1998 | **PANTOM (PUPPET) BEAR** 13-3/4in (35cm)<br>Limited 4,000, white tag, brown mohair, on a wooden puppet mechanism, worldwide. | $950.00 |
| 000379 | N/A | 489 | 1998 | **RALPH LAUREN HIGHLANDER BEAR**<br>Limited 500. **As of December 1999 this is the last bear in the series.** | $1,000.00 |
| 651380 | N/A | | 1998 | **SEA BAR**<br>Limited 2,000, white tag. | $350.00 |
| 652714 | | 495 | 1998 | **SNOOPY (JAPAN)** 10-1/4in (26cm)<br>Limited1,500, white tag, white and black mohair, Japan only. | $695.00 |

| Item<br>Ear tag#<br>EAN # | Sortiment Book<br>Vol#1 | Sortiment Book<br>Vol#2 | Year | Description | Value |
|---|---|---|---|---|---|
| 665592 | | 485 | 1998 | **SNOWMAN CHRISTMAS ORNAMENT** 5in (13cm)<br>Limited 5,000, white tag, U.S.A. only. | $100.00 |
| 652783 | | 495 | 1998 | **SOCCER BEAR (JAPAN)** 13-3/4in (35cm)<br>Limited 2,000, white tag, gray mohair T-shirt and pants, paw pad has France 98,<br>made for Soccer Worlds Championship held in France, Japan only. | N.P.A. |
| 657962 | N/A | | 1998 | **STEIFF BEAR AND HUMMEL FIGURINE**<br>Limited year's production, Christmas Hummel figurine and gold mohair bear with<br>ceramic medallion. | $475.00 |
| 420146 | | 514 | 1998/99 | **STEIFF CLUB HORSE ON WHEELS 1929** (6th year) 13-3/4in (35cm)<br>Limited 2,020, Steiff Club members. Yearly fee of $40.00. | $475.00 |
| 420139 | | 513 | 1998/99 | **STEIFF CLUB FIRST GRADER BEAR** 11-3/4in (30cm)<br>Limited 8,730, Steiff Club members. Yearly fee of $40.00, green bear. | $400.00 |
| 665196 | | 512 | 1998/99 | **STEIFF CLUB TEDDI SAMMI** 9in (22cm) | $350.00 |
| 658051 | N/A | | 1998 | **STEIFF CLUB STORE SERNEELS** 17in (43cm)<br>Limited 50, white tag, long curly golden mohair, one paw has the logo of the Belgium<br>Chamber of Commerce, each bear is dressed by Hermes, Louis Vuttion, Delvaux, Ferrari,<br>Bally, Godiva etc. Proceeds will be donated to the Children's Hospital Reine Fabiola. | **Auction Price** |
| 665370 | | 463 | 1998 | **STRONG TWINS** 6-1/2in (18cm)<br>Limited 5,000, white tag, light gold mohair, unique-only foot pads, U.S.A. only. | $275.00 |
| 665448 | | 478 | 1998 | **SYLVESTER and TWEETY WARNER BROS #2**<br>12-1/2in (32cm) and 5-1/2in (14cm)<br>Limited 2,500, white tag, made for Warner Bros. Stores. | N.P.A. |
| 039010 | | 501 | 1998/99 | **SX 1909 BRASS TEDDY** 2-1/4in (6cm) | $115.00 |
| 039027 | | 501 | 1998/99 | **SX 1909 DARK BROWN TEDDY** 2-1/4in (6cm) | $115.00 |
| 039034 | | 501 | 1998/99 | **SX 1909 WHITE TEDDY** 2-1/4in (6cm) | $115.00 |
| 039119 | | 501 | 1998/99 | **SX 1909 LIGHT BLOND TEDDY** 2-1/4in (6cm) | $115.00 |
| 039126 | | 501 | 1998/99 | **SX 1921 OFF-WHITE TEDDY** 2-1/4in (6cm) | $115.00 |
| 039133 | | 501 | 1998/99 | **SX 1921 DARK BROWN TEDDY** 2-1/4in (6cm) | $115.00 |
| 039218 | | 502 | 1998/99 | **SX 1930 BLOND TEDDY** 2-1/4in (6cm) | $115.00 |
| 039225 | | 502 | 1998/99 | **SX 1930 TEDDY BABY MAIZE** 2-1/4in (6cm) | $120.00 |
| 039232 | | 502 | 1998/99 | **SX 1921 TEDDY BABY BROWN** 2-1/4in (6cm) | $120.00 |
| 039317 | | 502 | 1998/99 | **SX 1951 BLOND TEDDY** 2-1/4in (6cm) | $115.00 |
| 039324 | | 502 | 1998/99 | **SX 1951 CARAMEL TEDDY** 2-1/4in (6cm) | $115.00 |
| 039331 | | 502 | 1998/99 | **SX 1951 DARK BROWN TEDDY** 2-1/4in (6cm) | $115.00 |
| 039515 | N/A | | 1998 | **12 BEARS WITH DISPLAY RACK** | $1,495.00 |
| 039522 | N/A | | 1998 | **DISPLAY RACK ONLY** | N.P.A. |
| 652646 | | 496 | 1998 | **TAWIAN STEIFF SPECIAL** 11in (28cm)<br>Limited 1,500, white tag, green-tipped mohair, green ribbon, left paw is embroidered<br>Teddy. Chinese gift box and collectible tea pot with a Chinese Classic written by a<br>famous tea expert from the Tang Dynasty (A.D. 618-907), Taiwan only. | $395.00 |
| 652738 | | 495 | 1998 | **TAKARA 10TH ANNIVERSARY BEAR** 8in (21cm)<br>Limited 1,500, white tag. | $425.00 |
| 670268 | | 443 | 1998 | **TEDDYBAR NIKOLAUS** 12-1/2in (32cm)<br>Limited 3,000, white tag, hooded Santa coat. | $375.00 |
| 670299 | | 421 | 1998 | **TITANIC POLAR BEAR**<br>Limited 5,000, white tag, white mohair wearing a blue ribbon with a ceramic disk. | $400.00 |
| 665615 | | 463 | 1998 | **T. ROOSEVELT AND CUB** 13in (33cm) and 7in (18cm)<br>Limited 4,000, white tag, light gold fur, Safari outfit with a gun, with small Berryman<br>bear, U.S.A. only. | $500.00 |

| Item Ear tag# EAN # | Sortiment Book Vol#1 | Vol#2 | Year | Description | Value |
|---|---|---|---|---|---|
| 655258 | N/A | | 1998 | **T.R. GOES WEST** 10-1/2in (27cm) Limited 300, white tag, certificate. | $325.00 |
| 670275 | | 421 | 1998 | **TEDDY B (BOY)** 12-1/2in (32cm) Limited to year of issue, white tag, brown mohair, white sweater with Teddy B on the front. | $300.00 |
| 670282 | | 421 | 1998 | **TEDDY G (GIRL)** 12-1/2in (32cm) Limited to year of issue, white tag, white mohair, blue sweater with Teddy G on the front. | $300.00 |
| 029578 | | 500 | 1998 | **TEDDY 1905 BEAR** 6-1/4in (16cm) Yellow tag, red-brown. | $125.00 |
| 406508 | | 421 | 1998 | **TEDDY 1909 BEAR** 13-3/4in (35cm) Limited 7,000, white tag, dark blue mohair, jointed, worldwide. | $400.00 |
| 029585 | | 500 | 1998/99 | **TEDDY 1920 BEAR** 6-1/4in (16cm) Yellow tag, blond. | $125.00 |
| 029592 | | 500 | 1998/99 | **TEDDY BEAR BEIGE** 6-1/4in (16cm) Yellow tag, beige. US SPECIAL YEAR 1983. | $120.00 |
| 404320 | | 420 | 1998 | **TEDDY BOY 1905** 19-1/2in (50cm) Limited 6,000, white tag ,light blond mohair, jointed, worldwide. | $625.00 |
| 404320 boy 404        pair | | | 1998 | **TEDDY GIRL** 19-1/2in (50cm) Limited 6,000, white tag, Teddy Girl is a replica of the  Teddy Girl that sold for $177,000.00 at the London auction. Also see 1997 Teddy Girl #404306 partner to the boy bear. | $1225.00 |
| 665509 | | 463 | 1998 | **THE  LAST  MOHICAN  BEAR**   8in (20cm) Limited 3,000, white tag, light gold mohair, leather pants, bow and arrows sitting in a wooden canoe. | $275.00 |
| 665462 | | 475 | 1998 | **QVC TEDDY'S  BEAR** 11-3/4in (30cm) Limited 7,500, made for the 140th birthday of Theodore Roosevelt. | N.P.A. |
| 655340 | | 444 | 1998 | **WHITEY GEINGEN  FESTIVAL  BEAR** 11in (28cm) Limited 3,000, white tag, Teddy Baby, white mohair, Germany only. | $550.00 |
| 998645 | N/A | | 1998 | **YAYA BIRD**  6-1/2in (17cm standing) Limited 1,500, white tag, German mountain bike project, blue fur body and jointed yellow fur head, blue felt wings, red felt feathers and legs, gray felt beak, Germany and Switzerland only. | $195.00 |
| 652790 | | 494 | 1998 | **YUKATA (JAPAN)** Limited 1,500, white tag, dressed in a traditional blue and white Kimono with a red sash, made for the Japan Teddy Bear Association, Japan only. | $350.00 |
| 665882 | | 485 | 1999 | **ALL  WRAPPED  UP CHRISTMAS  ORNAMENT** 4in (10cm) Limited 5,000, white tag, #6 in series, U.S.A. only. | $110.00 |
| 651908 | | 471 | 1999 | **ANNO TOY STORE'S FESTIVAL BEAR** 13-1/2in (34cm) Limited 1,500, white tag, honey mohair, green eyes, special bronze medallion, black velvet presentation bag and certificate. | $250.00 |
| 665547 | | 469 | 1999 | **BIRTHDAY  BEAR** 13-3/4in (35cm) Open edition, U.S.A. only. | $300.00 |
| 660047 | | 449 | 1999 | **BRITISH COLLECTOR'S LILAC TEDDY BEAR** 14in (36cm) Limited 3,000, white tag, lilac long mohair. | N.P.A. |
| 654695 | | 449 | 1999 | **BRITISH COLLECTOR'S SET OF 5 BEARS** 6-1/4in (16cm) each. Limited 1,847, white tag, blond, brown-tipped, gold, rose, burgandy mohair, in a wooden box. | N.P.A. |

| Item Ear tag# EAN # | Sortiment Book Vol#1 | Vol#2 | Year | Description | Value |
|---|---|---|---|---|---|
| 665455 | | 479 | 1999 | **BUGS BUNNY (WARNER BROS.)** 6in (15cm) Limited 2,500, holding a hand blown Christopher Radko glass ornament, made for the Warners Bros. Co., U.S.A. only. | N.P.A. |
| 670176 | | 423 | 1999 | **CELEBRATION BEAR and BOOK "TEDDYBAR mit KNOPF im OHR"** 8-1/2in (22cm) Limited to 4,000 total (1,000 German and 3,000 English), blond bear. | N.P.A. |
| 665905 | | 465 | 1999 | **CHERISHED TEDDY ENESCO'S DAISY** 13in (33cm) Limited 5,000, white tag, large hat, Cherished Teddy on paw. | $295.00 |
| 037030 | | 508 | 1999 | **CLASSIC BADGER** Limited 4,000, white tag, blue coat gold vest, white shirt and light blue tie. | |
| 067047 | | 508 | 1999 | **CLASSIC RATTY** Limited 4,000, white tag, white outfit with red and white scarf. | |
| 670336 | | 433 | 1999 | **COKE POLAR BEAR** 15-3/4in (40cm) Limited 1,000, white tag, boxed. | $375.00 |
| 665202 | | 474 | 1999 | **COLLECTORS UNITED BEAR** 8-1/2in (22cm) Limited 400, pink mohair with a Arabian hat, veil and necklace. | N.P.A. |
| 665844 | | 464 | 1999 | **DEW DROP ROSE BEAR** 11-3/4in (30cm) Limited 3,500, white tag, U.S.A. only. | $325.00 |
| 651472 | | 433 | 1999 | **DISNEY STEAMBOAT WILLIE** 14in (36cm) Limited 10,000, white tag. | $375.00 |
| 651489 | | 423 | 1999 | **DISNEY WINNIE the POOH** 11in (28cm) Limited 10,000, white tag. | $250.00 |
| 651434 | | 478 | 1999 1999 1999 | **DISNEY WORLD 12TH CONVENTION DAWN BEAR** 12-1/2in (32cm) Limited 1,500. 23-1/2 (60cm) Limited 25. 31-1/2in (80cm) Limited 5. White tag, white mohair, ceramic medallion made for Disney World Epcot Center, U.S.A. only. | $350.00 $3500.00 $6500.00 |
| 670428 | | 444 | 1999 | **EURO. LITTLE SNOWMAN BEAR** 4-1/2in (12cm) Limited 5,000, Snowman bear with a cooking pot for a hat, holding a small tree. | $145.00 |
| ——— | | 474 | 1999 | **F.A.O. SCHWARZ ANGEL BEAR** 10in (25cm) Limited 2,000, white tag, pink mohair with feather wings and flower headdress, U.S.A. only. | N.P.A. |
| 665936 | | 464 | 1999 | **GOOD BEARS "GULLIVER"** 15-3/4in (40cm) Limited 5,000, white tag, U.S.A. only. | $325.00 |
| 028403 | | 422 | 1999 | **GOODBYE DM BEAR** 11in (28cm) | $190.00 |
| 028410 670367 | | 422 423 | 1999 1999 | **HELLO EURO BEAR** 11in (28cm) **HELLO GOODBYE SET** 8-3/4in (23cm) each. Worldwide edition, open to end of the year 2000. | $190.00 $450.00 |
| 652868 | | 451 | 1999 | **HAMLEY'S JEREMY BEAR** 11in (28cm) Limited 1,500, white tag, reddish brown long mohair, U.K. only. | N.P.A. |
| ——— | | | 1999 | **HOLLAND 4TH BOER (FARMER) BEAR** 11-3/4in (30cm) Limited 1,847, white tag, boxed, certificate, blue mohair and wooden shoe design on a scarf. | $350.00 |
| 665851 | | 464 | 1999 | **HUCK FINN BEAR** 11-1/2in (28m) Limited 1,500, white tag, U.S.A. only. | $275.00 |

| Item Ear tag# EAN # | Sortiment Book Vol#1 Vol#2 | Year | Description | Value |
|---|---|---|---|---|
| 665943 | N/A | 1999 | **JACK NICHOLAS BEAR** 15-3/4in (40cm) Limited 5,000, white tag, U.S.A. only. | $398.00 |
| 408533 | 422 | 1999 | **JACKIE BEAR STUDIO** 25-1/2in (65cm) Limited 1,000, white tag. | $1,800.00 |
| 658075 | 456 | 1999 | **LAFAYETTEE 5TH BEAR** 13in (34cm) Limited 1,500, white tag, dark blue with vest, France only. | N.P.A. |
| ____ | N/A | 1999 | **LITTLE MASTRO and HUMMEL SET** 6-1/2in (17cm) and 5-1/2in (14cm) Limited 20,000, white tag. | $350.00 |
| 402166 | N/A | 1999 | **LULAC RABBIT 1952 REPLICA** 17in (43cm) Limited 1,500, white tag. | $240.00 |
| 670084 | N/A | 1999 | **MARGARET STEIFF MUSEUM BEAR** 11-3/4in (30cm) Open edition. | $180.00 |
| 670374 | 423 | 1999 | **MILLENNIUM BEAR** 15-3/4in (40cm) Worldwide edition open until the year end 2000, white tag. | $360.00 |
| 651649 | 478 | 1999 | **MINNIE MOUSE CHRISTMAS ORNAMENT** 6in (15cm) Limited 1,928, for the Walt Disney Co., U.S.A. only. | N.P.A. |
| 400933 | N/A | 1999 | **MONK KING** 7-1/4in (19cm) Limited 1,200, white tag. | $400.00 |
| 998744 | N/A | 1999 | **MORTIZ POSTMAN BEAR** 14in (36cm) Limited 2,000, white tag, dressed in a yellow and blue jacket. | $400.00 |
| 666025 | N/A | 1999 | **NOEL BEAR** 15-1/2in (40cm) Limited 1,500, white tag, wearing a dove necklace. | $250.00 |
| 665820 | 479 | 1999 | **MICHIGAN J. FROG WARNER BROS. #3** 11-3/4in (30cm) Limited 2,500, green, black top hat. | N.P.A. |
| 000379 | 489 | 1999 | **RALPH LAUREN HIGHLAND FLING GOLF BEAR** Limited 500, yellow tag, pants, sweater, jacket and hat. | $1,000.00 |
| 655487 | 444 | 1999 | **ROSEY TEDDY BABY** 11-1/4in (29cm) Limited 3,000, white tag, Teddy Baby, vivid pink mohair, Germany only. | $550.00 |
| 665967 | N/A | 1999 | **SAN DIEGO ZOO PANDA** 12in (32cm) Limited 1,500, white tag, a portion is donated to the Zoo's Center for Reproduction of Endangered Species, U.S.A. only. | $375.00 |
| 665981 | 464 | 1999 | **PEACE BEAR** 11-1/2in (28cm) Limited 3000, white tag, wearing a dove medallion necklace. | $198.00 |
| 665998 | N/A | 1999 | **SPLASH BEAR** 7in (18cm) Limited 4,000, white tag. Bear stands in a lampost vignette, U.S.A. only. | $160.00 |
| _____ | N/A | 1999/00 | **STEIFF CLUB MOURNING BEAR 1912** Limited to club members. $50.00 yearly fee. | $350.00 |
| _____ | N/A | 1999/00 | **STEIFF CLUB POLAR BEAR ON WHEELS 1910** Limited to club members. $50.00 yearly fee. | $350.00 |
| _____ | N/A | 1999/00 | **STEIFF CLUB YEAR 2000 BEAR** Limited to club members. One paw is 1999 and other 2000 in red, ceramic medallion. | N.P.A. |
| 670251 | 423 | 1999 | **TEDDY BEAR TOWN SOLDIER** 13-3/4in (35cm) Limited 2,000, white tag. | $370.00 |

(Left) Steiff. *Teddy Donald*. 1993. 12in (30cm); white mohair; short gold mohair inset face; plastic eyes; f.j.; e.s.; B.B.; white label. Limited edition 1500.
CONDITION: Mint.
**PRICE:** $850.
(Right) Steiff. *Watch Teddy Baby*. 1992. 17in (43cm); gray mohair; short beige mohair inset face; plastic eyes; f.j.; s.s.; B.B.; white label. Limited edition 4,000.
CONDITION: Mint.
**PRICE:** $575.
*Courtesy Deborah and Donald Ratliff.*

| Item Ear tag# EAN # | Sortiment Book Vol#1 | Vol#2 | Year | Description | Value |
|---|---|---|---|---|---|
| 407161 | | 421 | 1999 | **TEDDY BU 1925 BLOND** 11-3/4in (30cm) Limited 4,000, white tag. | $280.00 |
| 407185 | | 422 | 1999 | **TEDDY BU 1925 BROWN** 11-3/4in (30cm) Limited 4,000, white tag. | $280.00 |
| 407178 | | 422 | 1999 | **TEDDY BU 1925 WHITE** 11-3/4in (30cm) Limited 1,500, white tag. | $280.00 |
| 407260 | | 422 | 1999 | **TEDDY CLOWN 1926 ROSE** 11-3/4in (30cm) Limited 5,000, white tag. | $375.00 |
| 670114 | | 423 | 1999 | **TEDDYBEAR FISHERMAN** 13-1/2in (35cm) Limited 2,000, white tag, dressed in a navy blue fisherman's suit and hat. | N.P.A. |
| 030796 | | 422 | 1999 | **TEDDY LUCKY CHIMNEY SWEEP** 4in (10cm) Limited to production date 12/31/99, white tag, black jacket with HAPPY 2000 on the back. | N.P.A. |
| 675249 | | 424 | 1999 | **TEDDY PEACE** 25-1/2in (65cm) Limited 1,500, white tag, replica 1925 bear sold at 1st Steiff Festival for DM 189,550.00 | N.P.A. |
| 665974 | | 465 | 1999 | **UFDC TEDDY** 13-1/2in (35cm) Limited 1,500, blond, made for the UFDC National Convention, U.S.A. only. | $225.00 |
| 993644 | N/A | | 1999 | **UNICEF BEAR (MOHAIR)** Limited edition, white tag, light gold mohair wearing a ceramic disk, with embroidered paw Dasneue Berlin and Haptsladt Fur Kinder made for the children. | |
| 996337 | N/A | | 1999 | **UNICEF BEAR (PLUSH)** 10-1/4in (26cm) Blue gray plush. | $125.00 |
| 654749 | | 454 | 2000 | **TEDDY GEORGE BEAR** 12-1/2in (30cm) Limited 2,000, gold mohair wearing a brown tie, Teddy Bears of Witney, U.K. only. | N.P.A. |

Left:
Strunz. Bear. Circa 1908. 19in (48cm); beige mohair; shoe-button eyes; f.j.; e.s.; hexagonal button plus tag in ear.
CONDITION: Fair.
**PRICE**: $3,300 - $4,000.
*Courtesy Puppenhausmuseum, Basel.*

### Wilhelm Strunz
(Nuremberg and Allersberg, Germany)
*Important Milestones:* Founded: **1902;** produced animal figure of cloth with moveable limbs attached by wire and connected to forehead: **1904.**
*Founder:* Wilhelm Strunz.
*Trademark/Identification:* Early trademark was realistic-looking bear holding plaque with initials "W.St."; blank button in right ear (1904-5); six-cornered metal button with white pendant "Strunz Toys" in right ear (1905-6).
*Characteristics*: Remarkable similarities to Steiff products.

### Else Sturm
(Ottobeuren/Allgäu, Germany)
*Important Milestones:* Founded: **1946;** advertised "fine plush toys with shiny round eyes", featured: **1950;** specialty bottle bears, pocket teddy baby toy, play teddy and little handbags: **1958;** entire company including designs, models and stock sold to Mary Meyer: **1978.**
*Founder:* Else Sturm.
*Trademark/Identification:* Two different trademark pendants were used.
*Characteristics*: Particularly known for novelty and specialty bear and plush animal items.

Strunz. Clown. Circa 1910. 10in (26cm); beige/green mohair; shoe-button eyes; f.j.; e.s.
CONDITION: Fair.
**PRICE**: $2,700 - $3,300.
*Courtesy Puppenhausmuseum, Basel.*

Elsa Sturm. Bottle Bear. Circa 1950/1960. 11in (26cm); pale pink cotton plush; glass eyes; n.j.; arms; swivel head; tag. Original packaging; advertising plate and musical box.
CONDITION: Very good.
**PRICE**: $200 - $300.
*Courtesy Puppenhausmuseum, Basel.*

### Gebr. Süßenguth

(Neustadt near Coburg, Germany)
*Important Milestones:* Founded: **1894;** first
teddy bears: **1924;** *"Peter"* bear with moveable eyes, tongue and growling voice premiered
at Leipzig Fair: **1925.**
*Founders:* Wilhelm and Franz Süßenguth .
*Trademark/Identification:* Round cardboard
with metal rim tag sewn onto chest;.
*Characteristics:* First bear was plush, cardboard
and paper mâché; head turned, eyes moved lat-
erally and tongue moved; glass and wooden
eyes.

Right:
Gebr Süssenguth. *Peter Bear.* Circa 1925 -
1929. 12in (32cm); brown-tipped beige mohair;
glass eyes; f.j.; e.s.; with label ("Peter"
Ges.gesch. No.895257) box and catalogue.
Moves eyes and tongue from side to side.
CONDITION: Excellent.
**PRICE:** $3,300 - $4,000.
*Courtesy Puppenhausmuseum, Basel.*

### Miscellaneous German Manufactured Bears and Friends

Rudolf Haas Co. *Nickle-Nackle.* Bear. Circa 1928. 14in (36cm); varie-
gated brown/beige/gold mohair; glass eyes; f.j.; e.s. Bear nods head when
left arm is moved up and down. It turns its head from left to right when
right arm is moved.
CONDITION: Excellent.
**PRICE:** $1,600 - $2,000.
*Courtesy David Douglas.*

Rudolf Haas Co. Bear. Circa 1928. 16in (40cm); brown-tipped blonde
mohair; orange glass eyes; f.j.; e.s. Mechanism (no longer working) orig-
inally turned head via arms.
CONDITION: Fair.
**PRICE:** $600 - $800.
*Photograph courtesy Horst Poestgens Auctioneer, Germany.*

Helvetic. Musical Clown. Bear. Circa 1920s. 12in (30cm); long lilac mohair; glass eyes; f.j.; e.s.; squeeze type music box encased in tummy. CONDITION: Excellent.
**PRICE:** $2,000 - $2,500.
*Courtesy Puppenhausmuseum, Basel.*

Kersa. Bear. Circa 1930s. 15in (38cm); brown tipped beige mohair; glass eyes; f.j.; e.s.; metal label on sole. CONDITION: Fair.
**PRICE:** $800 - $1,000.
*Courtesy Puppenhausmuseum, Basel.*

Willy Weiersmüller. Baby Bear. Circa 1938. (Left to Right) 7in, 10in and 12in (18cm, 25cm, 31cm); golden beige mohair; shaved mohair snout; glass eyes; f.j.; k.s.; cardboard lined foot pads. CONDITION: Excellent.
**PRICE:** $800 - $1,000 each.
*Courtesy David Douglas*

Right:
Impex. Bear. Circa 1950s. 7in (18cm); beige mohair; hard rubber molded face; movable eyes; f.j.; e.s. Eyes and tongue move when you squeeze tummy; Impex label.
CONDITION: Good.
**PRICE:** $1,500 - $2,000.
*Courtesy Puppenhausmuseum, Basel.*

Kersa Pig. Circa 1950. 12in (31cm) tall; pink felt head and body; red felt top and boots an integral part of body; f.j. arms; stationary legs; swivel head; black button eyes; e.s.
CONDITION: Excellent.
**PRICE:** $400 - $500.
*Courtesy David Douglas.*

Right:
Kersa. Cow. Circa 1950. 4in (10cm) tall; cream felt with tan spots; glass eyes; n.j. legs; swivel head; e.s.
CONDITION: Excellent.
**PRICE:** $300 - $350.
*Courtesy David Douglas.*

# Chapter Seven
# Japanese Bears

Very few antique bears exist in Japan. Few were made and even most of those were destroyed in the Second World War. The bears that survived the early years are similar to early, less expensive American and French-style bears, possessing straight narrow bodies and limbs. Some are jointed, but are held together with wire and show exposed cardboard discs. Japanese bears of this nature usually are gold with short bristle sparse mohair, small round feet and sliced-in-ears, firmly stuffed with excelsior.

Following the war, Japanese toy makers entered the "Golden Age of the Battery-Operated Toy" and over the years "Made in Japan" evolved to become a symbol of quality. As leaders in the automated tin toy industry, they produced a variety of intriguing, electrical bear toys. These innovative toys first became evident in about 1950. Most were battery-operated with simple movements. Their unjointed, metal bodies were covered in nylon plush and sometimes clothes and accessories were glued directly onto the body.

Value and collectible desirability of Japanese mechanical toys are based on condition and amount of separate actions. A bear's value may be increased up to 10% if the original box is provided.

Unidentified Japanese manufactured bears. (Left and Center) Circa 1950. Approximately 8in (20cm); sheered rayon; sliced in ears; glass eyes; pin-jointed arms and legs; stationary head, e.s.
CONDITION: Good.
PRICE: $50-$60 each.
(Right) Circa 1940. 8in (20cm); pink rayon plush; glass eyes; pin-jointed arms and legs; stationary head; vinyl molded nose.
CONDITION: Good.
PRICE: $125 - $150.

Unidentified Japanese manufacturer. Bear. Circa 1920. 9-½in (24cm); short gold bristle-type mohair; glass eyes; f.j.; e.s. Metal bar joints arms and legs (less expensive method of jointing used by Japanese manufacturers); sliced in ears.
CONDITION: Excellent.
**PRICE:** $200-$300.
*Courtesy Bill Boyd.*

Jestia "Radio" Bear. Circa 1960. 14in (36cm) cinnamon-colored rayon plush ears and inset snout; short beige rayon plush; jointed arms and legs; stationary head; s.s.; cloth tag reads: "Jestia/Made in Japan." Radio encased in body. The nose serves as an "on" and "off" switch, the tuning knob is located on chest.
CONDITION: Excellent.
**PRICE:** $200 - $250.

Japanese Battery Operated Toys. Value and collectible desirability of these unique and fascinating toys is based on many criteria. The main ones are condition, the amount of separate actions and the bear's original box. (Left to right) Alps. "Smoking and Shoe Shining Panda Bear." Circa 1950. 10in (25cm); (Center) Y. Co., "Teddy Bear Swing." Circa 1950. 17in (43cm). (Right) Marusan Toys. *"Smokey Bear."* 9in (23cm).
CONDITION: Excellent.
**PRICE:** $400 -$600 each.

# Chapter Eight
# Advertising Bears

The value of bears as advertising symbols, "spokesmen" and logos has been acknowledged since the 19th century. Collecting these representations is not outrageously expensive and can be very fascinating. These icons reveal fads, fashions and even cultural attitudes.

Travel Lodge Bears. *Sleepy*. Circa 1980s. Sizes range 6in-14in (15-36cm); brown shades of plush; n.j.; s.s.
CONDITION: Excellent.
**PRICE:** $20-$40 each.
*Private collection..*

Ideal Toy Co. Hershey's® Bears. 1982. 11in (28cm); dark brown synthetic plush; cream plush paw pads and inner ears; plastic molded hand painted face; n.j.; s.s.; knitted sweater.
CONDITION: Excellent.
**PRICE:** $20-$30 each.
*Courtesy Emma Stephens.*

*Trudy*. Celestial Seasonings. *Sleepy Bear*. Circa. 1986. 17in (43cm) dark brown synthetic plush; black stitched eyes; black plastic nose; n.j.; s.s.; wearing white night shirt and red night cap.
CONDITION: Excellent.
**PRICE:** $25 - $35.
*Courtesy Pat Todd.*

Lever Brothers Company/Russ Berrie Co. *Snuggle*. 1986. 10in - 21in (25cm - 53cm); cream curly synthetic plush; inset beige synthetic plush snout; plastic eyes; black plastic nose; black outlines open mouth with pink tongue; n.j. s.s. Puppet *Snuggle* (Left).
CONDITION: Excellent.
**PRICE:** $35-$75 each.
*Courtesy Emma Stephens.*

Fisher Price. Quaker Oats Co. Bears. 1985. 10in (25cm); golden synthetic plush; pale cream with pink cheeks acrylic lower faces; plastic eyes with molded plastic eyelids; n.j.; s.s.; dressed in night attire. Cloth tag reads: "©Morgan Inc. 1985."
CONDITION: Excellent.
PRICE: $30 - $40 each.
*Courtesy Emma Stephens.*

Knickerbocker. *Bad News Bears*. Circa 1980. 13in (33cm) brown synthetic plush; plastic eyes; n.j.; s.s.; white cotton outfits with yellow stripes; white cotton tennis shoes; yellow cotton hat.
CONDITION: Excellent.
PRICE: $40 - $50.
*Courtesy Emma Stephens.*

Left:
Oriental Trading Co. Showbiz Pizza Place Bears. 1980s. 10in (25cm); acrylic fiber plush; hard plastic molded faces; hand painted features; hard plastic feet and paws; n.j.; s.s.
CONDITION: Excellent.
PRICE: $30 - $45 each.
*Courtesy Emma Stephens.*

Fisher Price *The Berenstain Bears*. 1962 - 1982. (Left to right) Baby. 10in (25cm); Papa 13in (33cm); Mama 12in (31cm); golden brown synthetic plush; plastic eyes; n.j.; s.s.; cotton outfits. Tag reads: "Fisher Price/A Division of the Quaker Oats Co./S and J Berenstain ©1962 – 1982". *The Berenstain Bears* have been entertaining millions of children for years with delightfully illustrated storybooks and their own television specials.
CONDITION: Good.
PRICE: $20 - $35 each.
*Courtesy Emma Stephens.*

Animal Fair. *dy-dee bear*. 1975. 11in (28cm) beige synthetic plush; white inset synthetic plush snout; large black fabric nose and red felt tongue.
CONDITION: Excellent.
PRICE: $15 - $20.
*Courtesy Emma Stephens.*

# Chapter Nine
# Artist Bears

Early antique bears are difficult to find and expensive to collect. As the worldwide demand for old bears pushes prices up and up, the independent bear artists are filling the gap with affordable, beautiful adaptations of traditional bears and individual efforts of distinctive creations. Originality, fine workmanship, flair and style set particular bear artists head and shoulders above the average hobbyist. Each talented artist puts something of him or herself into his/her work.

## Most important points to consider when buying artist bears for investment:

• How many are produced in the edition? (One-of-a-kinds are the most valuable).
• How well-known is the artist?
• How detailed is the design?
• How well-made is the creation?
• How well-designed, elaborate and well-made are the clothes?
• Are the materials used for the bear, clothes and accessories of good quality?

Janie Comito. Janie's Bears. *Little Women*. 1999. Bears. 3-½in – 4-½in (9cm - 12cm); golden mohair; glass bead eyes; f.j. s.s. Bears are authentically dressed to represent the costumes of the 1860s. Completely hand sewn. Much of the materials and trims used in the costumes are antique. The piece comes with a copy of the book *Little Women*. Created for the Teddy Bear Homecoming in the Heartland, Clarion 2000 auction.
CONDITION: Mint.
PRICE: $1,000 - $1,500 set.

Elaine Fujita-Gamble. *Halloween Treat*. 1999. Bears approximate size 2-¾ in(7cm); various colors of upholstery fabric; f.j.; onyx bead eyes; s.s. Bears dressed as a witch, devil, princess and a pumpkin. Each carries a little treat bag. A small (1-¾in [4cm]) bear is sitting in the tree. The handmade Halloween scene consists of a birch wall making a false house front, bird houses, pumpkins and fall leaves. Created for Walt Disney World Teddy Bear and Doll One-of-a-kind 1999 auction.
CONDITION: Mint.
PRICE: $3,000.

Flore Emory. Flore Bears. *Teddy For President*. (Left) Clifford Berryman Bear®. Circa 1998. 16in (41cm); brown tipped white mohair; white shaved face; "googlie"-type eyes; f.j.; s.s. Depicting Clifford Berryman's cartoon bear character. (Right) *Teddy For President*. Circa 1998. 18in (46cm); honey colored distressed mohair; glass eyes; f.j.; s.s. One-of-a-kind.
CONDITION: Mint.
PRICE: $500 - $700 pair.

Rosalie Frischmann. Mill Creek Creations. *A Treat for Toby*. 1999. Bear. 21in (53cm); dark honey German mohair; black glass eyes; f.j. (tilt head and wired arms) s.s.; dressed in green corduroy knickers with suspenders; cotton dog print shirt; ultra suede treat bag. Dog. Beige English mohair; black glass eyes; f.j.; s.s.; leather collar; engraved brass I.D. tag. Limited edition of 20.
CONDITION: Mint.
**PRICE:** $525.
*Photograph by Sutter Photography.*

Cindy Martin. Yesteryears. *Large Fat One*. 1993. 31in (79cm); extra long white mohair; glass eyes; f.j.; e.s.
CONDITION: Mint.
**PRICE:** $1,500.
*Courtesy Deborah and Donald Ratliff.*

Joanne C. Mitchell. Family Tree Bears. *Dr. Livingstone*, Purveyor of Natural Cures for a Natural World. 1999. 35in (89 cm) including hat; golden tan mohair; lead crystal with veining eyes; f.j.; s.s. Created from two different lengths of mohair. The longer one used on his head allows the artist to create the moustache, goatee and tousled hair look. His clothing designed to represent the story - discovered in a shipwrecked trunk, his tall hat with various plants, insects, mosses and ferns serves as a personal medicine cabinet for his needs. Limited edition of 30.
CONDITION: Mint.
**PRICE:** $1,150.
*Photograph by Scott Tate.*

Ann Inmann-Looms. Annemade Bears and Animals. 1990s. 8in-43in (20cm-109cm) various colors of mohair; glass eyes; armature jointed; s.s.
CONDITION: Mint.
**PRICE:** $125 - $1,500 each.

Kaylee Nilan. Beaver Valley. Bears. 1994. (Standing) *Bessie*. 36in (91cm). (Wearing pajamas) *Mathew*. 27in (69cm) (On all fours) *Rutherford*. 40in (101cm). European faux fur; glass eyes; Locline armature throughout body; swivel head. *Bessie* wears 100% cotton print dress and white pinafore. *Mathew* wears 100% cotton knit union suit.
CONDITION: Mint.
**PRICE:** *Bessie* $1,590. *Mathew* $820. *Rutherford* $1,590.

Mac Pohlen. MacAnimals. ***Mackenzie and Her Beau***. 1999. 17in (43cm); soft tan curly mohair; antique shoe-button eyes; f.j.; s.s. Girl dressed in cotton print dress; Swiss embroidered petticoat. Boy wears denim vest and abbreviated suit. Limited edition of 25 each. Created for Walt Disney World Teddy Bear and Doll Convention. 1999.
CONDITION: Mint.
**PRICE:** *Mackenzie* $350. *Beau* $295.

Steve Schutt. Bear-"S"-ence. ***Vintique*** Series. 1998-1999. 12in - 32in (seated) (31cm-81cm); various browns and neutral shades of mohair; antique shoe-button and glass eyes; f.j.; e.s. and s.s.; vintage clothes. Bears designed to fit clothes.
CONDITION: Mint.
**PRICE:** $165 - $3,250 each. *Photograph by Mueller Photography.*

Right:
Robert Raikes. Robert Raikes Collectible Bears. 1999. A representation of the wide variety of bear designs and sizes in Robert Raikes 1999 line. Sizes are from 3-½ in (9cm)-24in (62cm). Original Studio Bear. 108in (273cm). Bears have carved wooden faces and paw pads; plastic eyes; various synthetic and mohair fabrics; f.j.; s.s.; dressed and undressed.
CONDITION: Mint.
**PRICE:** 3-½in (9cm) $45-up, 5-½in (14cm) $65-up, 13in (34cm) $120-up, 16in (42cm) $180-up, 18in (47cm) $200-up, 24in (62cm) $280-up, 108in (273cm) (original) $10,000-up.
Robert Raikes Bears and Animals Secondary Market Value Report.

| Name | Original Retail Price | 2000 Price |
|---|---|---|
| *Jamie* (undressed) | $20 | $120 |
| *Sherwood* (undressed) | $35 | $160 |
| *Christopher* | $65 | $325 |
| *Tyrone* | $300 | $575 |
| *Lindy* | $100 | $625 |
| *Jester* | $110 | $225 |
| *Floyd Farmer* | $45 | $60 |
| (from "Occupational Bears Series) | | |
| *Ping Pong* (Panda) | $89 | $175 |
| *Andrew* and *Jill* 1988 | $75 each | $200 each |
| (Rabbits) | | |

*Secondary Market Value Report courtesy Raikes Review.*

Right:
Kathleen Wallace. Stier Bear. ***Dolly Bear***. 1991. 20in (51cm); white mohair; black glass eyes; f.j.; s.s. and e.s. Two-sided head, bear face on one side, felt sculpted antique doll face on the other side. Head turns to change faces. #1 of edition of three.
CONDITION: Mint.
**PRICE:** $1,800.

Jeanette Warner. Nette Bears. **Center Seam Bear**. 1998. 19in
(48cm); golden beige mohair; shoe-button type eyes; f.j.; e.s. and
s.s.
CONDITION: Mint.
**PRICE:** $275.
*Mouseé*. 1999. 5in (13cm); white mohair; jointed arms; stationary
legs; swivel head; glass eyes; s.s.
CONDITION: Mint.
**PRICE:** $85.
*Birdeé*.
1999. 3-½in (9cm); brown and beige mohair; felt wings and tail.
Wire sculpted legs.
CONDITION: Mint.
**PRICE:** $75.

Joan and Mike Woessner. Bear Elegance Exclusives. **The Show Must Go
On**. 1999. (Back left to right) **Andrew**. 28in (71cm); **Sarah**. 27 in
(69cm); (Front right) **Baby Brother**. 20in (51cm); rusty beige mohair;
large black glass eyes; f.j. (moveable flex encased in arms); polyfill and
excelsior stuffing. Dog. Mohair; glass eyes; swivel head; stationary legs.
The puppet theatre is a hand-made reproduction of a real antique theatre.
It has three backdrops to interchange scenes and is filled with toys and
puppets. One-of-a-kind. Overall size: 40in x 25in (102cm x 64cm).
Sold at Walt Disney World Teddy Bear and Doll One-of-a-Kind 1999
Auction for $2,500.

Left:
Beverly White.
Happy Tymes
Collectibles.
*Smithsonian Safari
Col. Roosevelt*.
1999. 15in (38cm);
antique gold
mohair; hand-paint-
ed blue glass eyes;
f.j.; flex-limb arma-
ture. Outfitted in
outback clothing.
Limited edition of
25.
CONDITION:
Mint.
**PRICE:** $595.

R. John
Wright Dolls
Inc. (Left)
*Christopher
Robin*.
1985. 18in
(46cm) 100%
wool felt;
painted facial
features; f.j.;
s.s.; blue cot-
ton jacket;
brown cotton
shorts; white
cotton hat;
brown
leather shoes;
paper tag attached to jacket reads: "R. John Wright Dolls/Christopher
Robin & Winnie the Pooh© Walt Disney® Productions." (Left) *Winnie-
the Pooh*. 1985. 8in (20cm); caramel colored custom-made 100% wool
"coating;" black glass eyes; f.j.; s.s.; maroon knit jacket; tag reads: "R.
John Wright Dolls Inc./Winnie the Pooh© Walt Disney® Productions."
Series #1. Sold as a set. Limited edition 1,000 each.
CONDITION: Mint.
**PRICE:** $2,800 set.

# R. John Wright

| Year | Size | Description | Value |
|------|------|-------------|-------|
| 1985/86 | 19in (48cm) & 8in (20cm) | **CHRISTOPHER ROBIN AND WINNIE the POOH SERIES #1** <br> Limited 1,000 pieces, Christopher dressed in a blue top, tan pants, white hat, with Pooh. | $2,800.00 |
| 1985/86 | 8in (20cm) | **WINNIE the POOH** <br> Limited 2,500 pieces. | $750.00 |
| 1986/87 | 20in (51cm) | **WINNIE the POOH** <br> Limited 2,500 pieces. | $1,400.00 |
| 1986/87 | 19in (48cm) | **CHRISTOPHER ROBIN WITH RAINCOAT & UMBRELLA SERIES #2** <br> Limited 500 pieces, dressed in a yellow raincoat includes an umbrella. | $2,500.00 |
| 1988 | 10-1/2in (27cm) | **WINNIE the POOH AND CHAIR DISNEYWORLD** <br> Limited 500 pieces, Pooh sitting in his chair, the Disney World Convention. | $3,000.00 |
| 1988/89 | 14in (36cm) | **WINNIE the POOH AND HONEY POT** <br> Limited 5,000 pieces. | $950.00 |
| 1985/86 | 5-1/2in (14cm) | **PIGLET** <br> Limited 1,000 pieces. | $600.00 |
| 1986/87 | 9-1/2in (24cm) | **EEYORE** <br> Limited 1,000 pieces. | $500.00 |
| 1986/87 | 10in (25cm) | **KANGA and ROO** <br> Limited 1,000 pieces. | $ 500.00 |
| 1986/87 | 10-1/2in (27cm) | **PIGLET with VIOLETS** <br> Limited 2,500 pieces. | $475.00 |
| 1986/87 | 9in (23cm) | **TIGGER** <br> Limited 1,000 pieces. | $500.00 |
| 1992 | 9in (23cm) | **FRIGHTENED DOPEY** <br> Limited 250 pieces. | $1,000.00 |
| 1993 | 9in (23cm) | **PINOCCHIO WITH EARS** <br> Limited 250 pieces, made for the Disneyana Convention Disney World Florida. | $1,000.00 |
| 1993 | 5in (13cm) | **POCKET POOH** <br> Limited 3,5000 pieces. | $650.00 |
| 1994 | 17in (43cm) & 9in (23cm) | **GEPPETTO & PINOCCHIO SERIES #2 MARIONETTE** <br> Limited 500 pieces, Pinocchio as a puppet with strings. | $2695.00 |
| 1994/95 | 17in (43cm) & 9in (23cm) | **GEPPETTO & PINOCCHIO SERIES #1** <br> Limited 250 pieces, Pinocchio as a boy with a wooden chair. | $2600.00 |
| 1994 | 2-1/2in (6cm) | **POCKET PIGLET** <br> Limited 3,500 pieces. | $425.00 |
| 1995 | 5in (13cm) & 2-1/2in (6cm) | **WINTERTIME POOH & PIGLET SET** <br> Limited 250 pieces, F.A.O. Stores only. | $1,200.00 |
| 1995 | 9in (23cm) | **POCKET EEYORE** <br> Limited 3,500 pieces. | $295.00 |
| 1995 | 11in (28cm) | **WINTERTIME EEYORE'S STICK HOUSE** <br> Limited 250 pieces, made for F.A.O. Stores only. | $ 850.00 |
| 1996 | 18in (46cm) | **GEPPETTO SEARCHING for PINOCCHIO** <br> Limited 250 pieces, Geppetto dressed in an overcoat, hat and scarf with a lantern. | $1875.00 |
| 1996/97 | | **GOLLIWOGG BOY** <br> Limited 2,500 pieces, Collectors Club members only. $35.00 membership enables you to purchase one piece. | $585.00 |
| 1996 | | **POCKET KANGA and ROO** <br> Limited 3,500 pieces. | $345.00 |
| 1996 | | **POCKET TIGGER** <br> Limited 3,500 pieces. | $345.00 |
| 1996 | | **WINTERTIME EEYORE** <br> Limited 250 pieces, made for F.A.O. Stores only. | N.P.A. |
| 1997 | | **HOLIDAY WINNIE the POOH** | N.P.A. |

| Year | Size | Description | Value |
|------|------|-------------|-------|
| 1997/98 | | **MISS GOLLI** | $525.00 |
| | | Limited, Collectors Club memberships only. | |
| 1997 | | **TEDDY BEAR** | N.P.A. |
| 1997 | | **WINNIE the POOH'S CHRISTMAS HOLIDAY** | N.P.A. |
| 1997 | | **POCKET OWL** | $310.00 |
| | | Limited 3,500 pieces. | |
| 1997/98 | 12 in (31cm) | **POCKET CHRISTOPHER ROBIN** | $895.00 |
| | | Limited 3,500 pieces. | |
| 1997/99 | 12 in (31cm) | **POCKET CHRISTOPHER ROBIN & POOH** | N.P.A. |
| | | Limited 3,500 pieces. | |
| | | **POCKET RABBIT** | $295.00 |
| | | Limited 3,500 pieces. | |
| 1997 | | **POCKET TIGGER** | $295.00 |
| | | Limited 3,500 pieces. | |
| 1998 | | **CLASSIC WINNIE the POOH** | N.P.A. |
| 1998 | | **KING CHRISTOPER ROBIN** | |
| 1999 | | **BAO-BAO BABY PANDA** | $ 595.00 |
| | | Limited 500 pieces, Baby Panda, Singapore's Precious Things Store. | |
| 1999 | | **BENJAMIN BUNNY** | $625.00 |
| | | Limited 1,500 pieces. | |
| 1999 | 17-1/2in (45cm) | **CHRISTOPHER ROBIN & POOH BEDTIME SET** | $1495.00 |
| | | Limited 500 pieces. | |
| 1999 | | **CHRISTOPHER ROBIN & POOH BEDTIME SET DISNEYWORLD** | $2250.00 |
| | | 250 pieces of the above 500 sets for Disney World Convention. Pooh has a night cap. | |
| 1999 | 12in (31cm) | **CLASSIC POOH** | $495.00 |
| | | Limited 2,500 pieces. | |
| 1999 | 15in (38cm) | **JEMIMA PUDDLE-DUCK** | $655.00 |
| | | Limited 1,500 pieces. | |
| 1999 | | **JEMIMA DUCKLINGS** | $595.00 |
| | | Limited 1,000 pieces. | |
| 1999 | 8in (20cm) | **KEWPIE** | $475.00 |
| | | Limited 1,000 pieces. | |
| 1999 | | **LITHO BACKDROP POCKET SERIES** | $185.00 |
| | | Limited 1,000 pieces. | |
| 1999 | | **POOH BEAR'S BED** | $350.00 |
| | | Limited 500 pieces. | |
| 1999 | | **PETER RABBIT** | $595.00 |
| | | Limited 2,500 pieces. | |
| 1999 | 12in (31cm) | **NIGHTTIME POOH** | $595.00 |
| | | Limited 2,500 pieces. | |
| 1999 | | **WINTERTIME POCKET CHRISTOPHER ROBIN** | $1,250.00 |
| | | Limited 2,500 pieces.F.A.O. special. Green coat & hat pulling a sled. | |
| 1999 | 2-1/2in (6cm) | **KEWPIE UFDC BOUTONNIER PIN** | N.P.A. |
| | | Limited for the August convention. | |
| 1999 | 6in (15cm) | **KEWPIE FLEUR** | $850.00 |
| | | Limited 250, for the August U.F.D.C. convention. | |
| 1999 | | **FLIT (KEWPIE BOY)** | N.P.A. |
| | | Limited 250. | |
| 1999/2000 | | **CLUB KEWPIE & BEAR** | $525.00 |
| | | Limited, Collectors Club members only. $45.00 membership enables you to purchase one piece. | |
| 2000 | | **PADDINGTON BEAR** | |
| | | Limited edition. Dressed in traditional outfit. | |

Right:
Romy Roeder. Vagabond Bears. 1999. ***Poppy and Bluebeary***. (Left)
***Poppy***. 15in (38cm); golden mohair; blue glass eyes; f.j.; s.s. (Right)
***Bluebeary***. 5in (13cm); blue sparse mohair; glass eyes; f.j.; s.s. Both bears
are entirely hand-stitched.
CONDITION: Excellent.
**PRICE:** $190 set.

Jennifer Laing. Totally Bear by Jennifer Laing. Bears. 1998-1999.
(Back) ***Roger***. 12in (31cm); (Front) ***Billie***. 5in (13cm); (Left and Right)
***Bertie***. 4in (10cm). Made of various types and colors of German mohair.
Entirely hand-stitched with either hand-painted paw pads or dimensional
toes; waxed noses, softly stuffed with poly/pellets. ***Roger*** has antique
shoe-button eyes. Small bears have onyx glass eyes. One-of-one.
CONDITION: Mint.
**PRICE:** $175 - $275 each.

Right:
Helga Torfs. Humpty Dumpty Bears. ***Dwarfbear Pardoes***. 1999. 20in
(51cm); rust sparse mohair; mohair beard and paw pads are airbrushed;
black glass eyes; f.j.; pellet and polyester fiberfill stuffing; handmade
clothes. Limited edition of 8.
CONDITION: Mint.
**PRICE:** $450.

Maude Blackburn. Canterbury Bears. *The Countess*. 1994. 21in (53cm); white mohair head; pure ivory silk covered with pearls and sequins body; silk paw pads; glass eyes; f.j.; s.s.; diamante tiara; seated on a purple suede cushion. Sold at Walt Disney World Teddy Bear One-of-a-Kind 1994 auction for $2,500.
*Courtesy Mark Allen.*

Jo Greeno. (Left) *Amber*. Bear. 1999. 23in (58cm); gold mohair; large black glass eyes; f.j. Wearing yellow fur coat, gold mohair handbag decorated with a bear's head. Peeking out of the handbag is a 4-½in (11cm) gold mohair jointed bear and a 2-½in (6cm) off-white mohair dog. One-of-a-kind. (Right) *Valentine*. Bear. 1999. 24in (61cm); pale beige mohair; large black glass eyes; f.j. Wearing a cotton print dress carrying a 5in (13cm) red velvet teddy bear purse. One-of-a-kind.
CONDITION: Mint.
PRICE: *Amber* $950 - $1,200. *Valentine* $850 - $1,100.

Gregory Gyllenship. Gregory Bear. (Left to Right) *Humbug, Jason, Arnold* and *James*. 1999. 14in-16in (36cm-41cm); various colors of mohair; old shoe-button eyes; f.j.; s.s. and e.s. Mostly one-of-a-kind or small editions.
CONDITION: Mint.
PRICE: $500 - $850 each.

Elaine Lonsdale. Companion Bears. Fairyland Series. 1999. 7in - 4in (18cm - 10cm); various hand-tinted English mohairs; black glass and onyx bead eyes; f.j.; s.s.; decorated with vintage flowers, beads and ribbons. Hand-painted antique metallic lace, silk and organza wings.
CONDITION: Mint.
PRICE: 7in (18cm) $495 each. 6in (15cm) $395 each. 4in (10cm) $330 each.

Paula and Simon Strethill-Smith. Schultz Teddy Bears and Characters. *Mr. Punch*. 1999. 4in (10cm); hand-dyed dark gold antique plush; matte glass eyes; f.j.; s.s.; leather paw pads; leather collar with rusty bells.
CONDITION: Mint.
**PRICE:** $240.

Sue Quinn. Doormouse Designs. *Finlay Junior*. Puppet Bear. 1999. 15in (38cm); pale gold distressed mohair; glass eyes; f.j. arms and legs; stationary head; s.s.; body lined with mohair. Opening in back allows moveable mouth to be activated in puppet motion.
CONDITION: Mint.
**PRICE:** $325.

Carolyn Willis. *Primrose*. 1997. 2-¼in (6cm); distressed ivory miniature plush; glass eyes; f.j.; s.s. *Primrose* sits in a cluster of vintage flowers.
CONDITION: Mint.
**PRICE:** $245.

Left:
Marie Robischon. Robin Der Bär. ***Elvis***. 1999. 20in (51cm); gold wavy English mohair; black glass eyes; f.j.; wood-wool and pellet stuffing; voice box. One-of-a-kind. Custom-made outfit from owner's old blue jeans.
CONDITION: Mint.
**PRICE:** $980.

Dagmar Strunk. Bärenhöhle. ***The Golden One***. 1999. 19in (48cm); golden mohair; glass eyes (artist designed); open mouth with two glass teeth; f.j.; s.s.; posable fingers, glass finger and toenails. One-of-a-Kind.
CONDITION: Mint.
**PRICE:** $1,500.

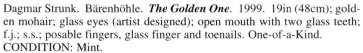

Left:
Claudia Wagner. Weini-Bären. ***Small Colar Bear***. 2000. 16in (41cm); German mohair; glass eyes; open mouth; trapanto quilted ultra suede paw pads. Limited edition of 25.
CONDITION: Mint.
**PRICE:** $380.

Kazuko Ichikawa. *Flower Hat*. 1999. 10in (25cm); (left) brown mohair; blue glass eyes. (Right) ivory mohair; black glass eyes; f.j.; s.s.
CONDITION: Mint.
**PRICE:** $210 each.

Ikuyo Kasuya. Bruin. *Ellcy and Fairy*. 1999. *Ellcy*. 12in (31cm); golden tan mohair; black glass eyes; f.j.; s.s.; dressed in Liberty print dress decorated with silk lace. *Fairy*. 3in (8cm); pink fabric; black bead eyes; f.j.; s.s.; tulle lace wings. Inspired by the movie "Fairy Tale."
CONDITION: Mint.
**PRICE:** $350 set.

Right:
Mari and Akemi Koto. Koto Bears. *Celebrating the Century - Love and Peace*. 1999. (Left) *Love*. 3in (8cm); white upholstery fabric; black glass eyes; f.j.; s.s. Dressed in Japanese children's formal silk kimono. (Right) *Peace*. 4in (10cm); golden brown upholstery fabric; black glass eyes; f.j.; s.s. Dressed in polyester dress printed with the Star Spangled Banner; mounted on a heart-shaped wooden base. Created for Walt Disney World 1999 Teddy Bear and Doll Convention. Limited edition of 25.
CONDITION: Mint.
**PRICE:** $180 set. *Courtesy Mari and Akemi Koto.*

Terumi Yoshikawa. Terumi Bear/Rose Bear. ***St. Francisco Javier Landing in Japan***. 1998. (Right) Bear. 20in (50cm); white mohair; glass eyes; f.j.; e.s. Costume is made from Japanese wedding Kimono. One-of-a-kind.
CONDITION: Mint.
**PRICE:** Approximately $1,500 set.

Michi Takahashi. Fairy Chuckle®. ***Chizuru®***. 1997. 22in (56cm); light beige distressed mohair; black glass eyes; f.j. (jointed with nuts, bolts, disks and washers) armatured arms; s.s. Outerwear. The "Yuzen" process silk kimono. Undergarment. The "Rinzu" weave silk kimono. Sash. The "Kinran" (gold brocade) silk, handmade traditional wooden clogs "Pokkri." Completely hand-stitched. ***Chizuru*** means Peace Forever. Created for a special project for Huis Ten Bosch, Teddy Bear Kingdom, Nagasaki, Japan.
CONDITION: Mint.
**PRICE:** $4,000.

Mayumi Watanabee. Mammie Bear. ***The Family in Japanese Woods***. 1998. Bear. 17in (42cm); golden mohair; brown suede pads; antique shoe-button eyes; s.s. One-of-a-Kind.
CONDITION: Mint.
**PRICE:** $2,200.

Annemieke Koetse. Boefje Bears. The Netherlands. *Nokkie*. 1996. (Prototype) 11in (28cm); blonde mohair; black glass eyes; f.j.; s.s. *Nokkie* is the name of the Dutch Olympic games mascot. Dressed with tulip hat, a green grass colored top with #1, cow-design trousers and wooden clogs.
CONDITION: Mint.
**PRICE:** $200.

Monique Kooman. Nikke Bear. *Pierre*. 1999. 3in (8cm); red mohair; cream upholstery fabric inset snout; black bead eyes; red stitched nose; f.j.; s.s. Limited edition of 25.
CONDITION: Mint.
**PRICE:** $150.

Lyda Rijs - Gertenbach. Lyda's Bear. (Left) *Winston*. 1998. 8in (20cm); cinnamon mohair; black glass eyes; f.j.; s.s. Limited edition 10. (Right) *Wynona*. 1998. 8in (20cm); medium brown mohair; black glass eyes; f.j.; s.s. Limited edition 5.
CONDITION: Mint.
**PRICE:** $200 each.

Audie F. Sison. A Bear by Audie. *Sabrina*. 1999. 20in (51cm); German distressed gold mohair; shoe-button eyes; f.j.; e.s. Wearing antique lace dress and vintage hat.
CONDITION: Mint.
**PRICE:** $1,500.

# Chapter Ten
# Teddy Roosevelt Memorabilia

Bear lovers everywhere owe a debt of gratitude to one of the greatest statesmen in the history of the United States, President Theodore Roosevelt. In addition to our beloved teddy bear, there are hundreds of Teddy Roosevelt related items to collect. Roosevelt collectibles range from buttons, post cards, books, tins and advertising examples to figurines and dolls. He is present in numerous books, toys and games. The subject of an early Edison motion picture, *The Teddy Bears,* and with the same name as the children's book heroes *The Roosevelt Bears*, Theodore Roosevelt was internationally celebrated in conjunction with the Teddy Bear. The Republican Party adopted Clifford Berryman's well-known cartoon symbol for the President's political campaigns showing him on political cartoons, postcards, pins and mementos of all descriptions. For more information about this important man and his impact on our beloved teddy bear, please refer to my book, *"The Teddy Bear Men"* (Hobby House Press, 1987).

An interesting and attractive display of Teddy Roosevelt memorabilia from 1907-1979.
CONDITION: Excellent.
PRICE: $100-$300 each.

Teddy's Rough Rider's Hat. Circa 1898.
CONDITION: Good.
**PRICE:** $250-$300.
Theodore Roosevelt Campaign Pins. Circa 1904.
CONDITION: Excellent.
**PRICE:** $25-$250 each.
*Courtesy Martha and Jim Hession.*

Teddy and the Bear Toothpick Holders. German china. Circa 1907. 3-½in (9cm); several similar versions produced.
CONDITION: Good.
**PRICE:** $175-$225 each.

Roosevelt Rough Rider Bandana. Circa 1900. Cloth with portraits around edge and Teddy Roosevelt's initials in center.
CONDITION: Excellent.
PRICE: $200-$275.
***Teddy B and Teddy G*** Bandana Clip. Circa 1907. 2in (5cm) high; ***Teddy B and Teddy G*** embossed in brass.
CONDITION: Excellent.
**PRICE:** $200-$300.

(Left) Chalk painted Theodore Roosevelt Bust. Circa 1910. Marked on front "Roosevelt in Africa". Marked in back "Copyright 1910 By Boston P. Plastic Art Co., Boston, Mass".
**CONDITION:** Fair.
**PRICE:** $150-$200.
(Right) "Teddy and the Bear" Mechanical Bank. Circa 1910. 7-½in (19cm) tall x 10in (25cm) long.
**CONDITION:** Excellent.
**PRICE:** $2,500-up.

*A True American Rough Rider.* Center pages from *Judge* magazine 1902.
**CONDITION:** Mint.
**PRICE:** $100-$150.
*Courtesy Martha and Jim Hession.*

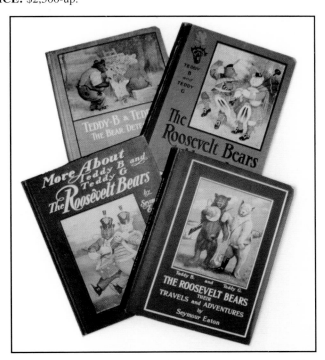

Roosevelt Bear Books created by Paul Piper under the pen name Seymour Eaton. The first book, *The Roosevelt Bears, Their Travels and Adventures*, was published in 1905. Three more books in this series followed: *More About the Roosevelt Bears* (1906), *The Roosevelt Bears Abroad* (1907), and *The Bear Detectives* (1907) published by Edward Stern & Company, Inc., Philadelphia. Hardback cover is 8in (22cm) by 11in (29cm).
**CONDITION:** Excellent.
**PRICE:** $300-$400 each.
Not pictured. The follow-up series to the first four volumes of the *Roosevelt Bears* book by Seymour Eaton were small editions with fewer colored plates.
**CONDITION:** Excellent.
**PRICE:** $175-$200 each.

Roosevelt Bears Cloth Picture. Copyright 1907 Bernhard Ulmann. 24in x 24in (61cm x 61cm).
**CONDITION:** Excellent.
**PRICE:** $500-$650.
*Courtesy Martha and Jim Hession.*

# About the Author

Linda and Wally Mullins with their pet poodle Nikki, and some of their favorite early 1900s Steiff bears from their collection.

She and her husband Wally are currently building a new residence for themselves and their bears in their hometown of Carlsbad, California. The Victorian-style manor will incorporate a private museum to house Linda's extensive bear and toy collection along with Wally's sizeable assembly of music box and band organs. The new home is scheduled for completion in 2001.

She currently works with Little Gem Teddy Bears and the Teddy-Hermann GmbH Co. (Germany) in exciting projects to reproduce some of her rare early bears and her own designs.

After an all-out effort coordinating an auction of international artist's bears designed to raise funds for Kobe, Japan's earthquake victims. Linda Mullins became instrumental in shaping that country's Huis Ten Bosch's Teddy Bear Kingdom in Nagasaki, Japan. She is a supervisor and honorary director of the museum.

As the year 2002 marks the 100th anniversary of the teddy bear, Linda is at work with various organizations, institutions and private collectors the world over to celebrate this historical landmark.

It is Linda's lifelong goal to continue on her mission to make the teddy bear an ambassador of world love and peace.

Linda Mullins was born and raised in England. She emigrated to America in 1969. Her present collection of more than 2000 bears began in earnest when her husband, Wally, gave her an antique teddy bear as a gift. That hobby escalated to a full-time profession and today Linda Mullins' knowledge and expertise are in demand throughout the United States, Europe and Pacific Rim.

A Southern California resident, she produces the region's most popular two-day show: Linda's San Diego Teddy Bear, Doll & Antique Toy Show and Sale. It is held twice a year. The January show of 2000 is the 42nd of these events which continue to draw international attention because of the excellent antique, collectible and artist Teddy Bears, Dolls and Toys on exhibit and available for purchase.

In addition to collecting, speaking, educating and traveling, Linda has written 14 books and countless articles on the past, present and future of teddy bears.

**Teddy Bear Books by Linda Mullins:**

*Teddy Bears Past & Present, Volume 1* (Fifth Printing)
*The Teddy Bear Men* (Second Printing)
*Raikes Bear and Doll Story* (Two Editions)
*Teddy Bears Past &Present, Volume II*
***Teddy Bear & Friends Price Guide***
*A Tribute to Teddy Bear Artists*
*American Teddy Bear Encyclopedia*
*Creating Heirloom Teddy Bears*
*A Tribute to Teddy Bear Artists—(Series 2)*
*Teddy's Bears*
*American Artist Teddy Bears — Patterns and Tips* (Second Printing))
*A Tribute to Teddy Bear Artists — (Series 3))*
*Creating Heirloom Teddy Bears Pattern Book (Series 2)*
*Linda Mullins' Teddy Bears & Friends Identification and Price Guide*
*Creating Miniature Teddy Bears* (To be released 2000)
{All books published by Hobby House Press, Grantsville, Maryland}

---

**Front Cover:**
Steiff. Bear. Circa 1905. 28in (71cm); golden wavy mohair; large black button eyes; f.j.; e.s.; <u>FF</u> button.
CONDITION: Excellent.
**PRICE:** $16,000-up.
Steiff. Tulla. Geese. Circa 1960. Blonde mohair; orange felt beaks and feet; glass eyes; n.j.; e.s.
CONDITION: Excellent.
**PRICE:** (Left to Right) 10in (25cm) $250-$300. 5-½in (14cm) $125-$150. 5in (13cm) $85-$100.

**Back Cover:**
Steiff. ***Teddy B and Teddy G Bears***. Circa 1907. 14in (36cm); (Left) white mohair. (Right) honey colored mohair. Both bears have shoe-button eyes; f.j.; e.s.; <u>FF</u> button. Wearing stocking-knit sweaters, pale blue overalls with white embroidered names. Purchased as a pair by original owners from Marshall Fields of Chicago. The costumes are based on Seymour Eaton's ***Roosevelt Bears***.
CONDITION: Excellent.
**PRICE:** $20,000-up pair.

**Title Page:**
Steiff. Bears. All are made of mohair, have shoe-button eyes; are fully jointed with excelsior stuffing and the <u>FF</u> Button. (Top Left) Circa 1907. 10in (25cm); white mohair.
CONDITION: Excellent.
**PRICE:** $3,500-up.
(Center) Circa 1905. 24in (61cm); apricot mohair; center seam in head.
CONDITION: Excellent.
**PRICE:** $14,000-up.
(Bottom Left) Circa 1910. 7in (18cm); gold mohair; no paw pads.
CONDITION: Excellent.
**PRICE:** $1,000-up.
(Bottom Right) Rattle. Circa 1910. 6in (15cm); white mohair; glass eyes; no paw pads; rattle encased in tummy.
CONDITION: Excellent.
**PRICE:** $1,500-up.
Steiff. Bully Dog. Circa 1927. 8in (20cm); ginger and white mohair; glass eyes; wire framed ears; swivel head; n.j. legs; horsehair collar ruff; <u>FF</u> button.
CONDITION: Excellent.
**PRICE:** $600-up.